—Architecture
in Scotland
2006—2008
—Building
Biographies

—Contents

—06　Foreword
　　　Nick Barley
—08　Introduction
　　　Morag Bain
—10　An Architecture of Elsewhere
　　　Oliver Lowenstein
—26　The Buildings — An Overview
　　　Oliver Lowenstein

— The Projects Scotland
—36　Lotte Glob Studio
　　　Gokay Deveci
—44　Housing Telford Drive
　　　Gordon Murray +
　　　Alan Dunlop Architects
—52　Swinton Affordable Housing
　　　Oliver Chapman
—60　Strathnairn Community
　　　Forest Shelter
　　　Neil Sutherland Architects
—68　The Pier Arts Centre
　　　Reiach & Hall Architects
—76　Culloden Battlefield
　　　Visitor Centre
　　　Gareth Hoskins Architects
—84　Taigh Chearsabhagh Arts
　　　Studio Extension
　　　Locate Architects
—90　Talla Choinneachaidh
　　　Dualchas Building Design

— The Projects Europe
—100　Extension Winery
　　　 Gantenbein, Switzerland
　　　 Bearth & Deplazes
　　　 Architekten
—108　Terrihütte, Switzerland
　　　 Gion A. Caminada
—116　Mountain Chapel, Austria
　　　 Cukrowicz Nachbaur
　　　 Architekten zt Gmbh
—122　Frühling — Spring, Austria
　　　 architekturwerk THE EDGE
—130　Svartlamoen Nursery, Norway
　　　 Brendeland & Kristoffersen
　　　 arkitekter AS
—136　Juvet Landscape Hotel,
　　　 Norway
　　　 Jensen & Skodvin Architects

—Essays
—146　re-Emerging Architecture
　　　 Neil Gillespie
—152　Highlanders Have Long
　　　 Travelled
　　　 Mary Arnold-Forster
—158　Designing a Future Forest
　　　 Bernard Planterose
—166　Narratives of Place in
　　　 the Scottish Landscape
　　　 Johnny Cadell
—172　Placing the Region:
　　　 A New Highlands Architecture
　　　 Oliver Lowenstein
—178　The Significance of
　　　 Building Culture —
　　　 Building as Discourse
　　　 Robert Fabach
—188　The Contexts of Graubunden
　　　 Steven Spier

—Credits
—206

P. 4

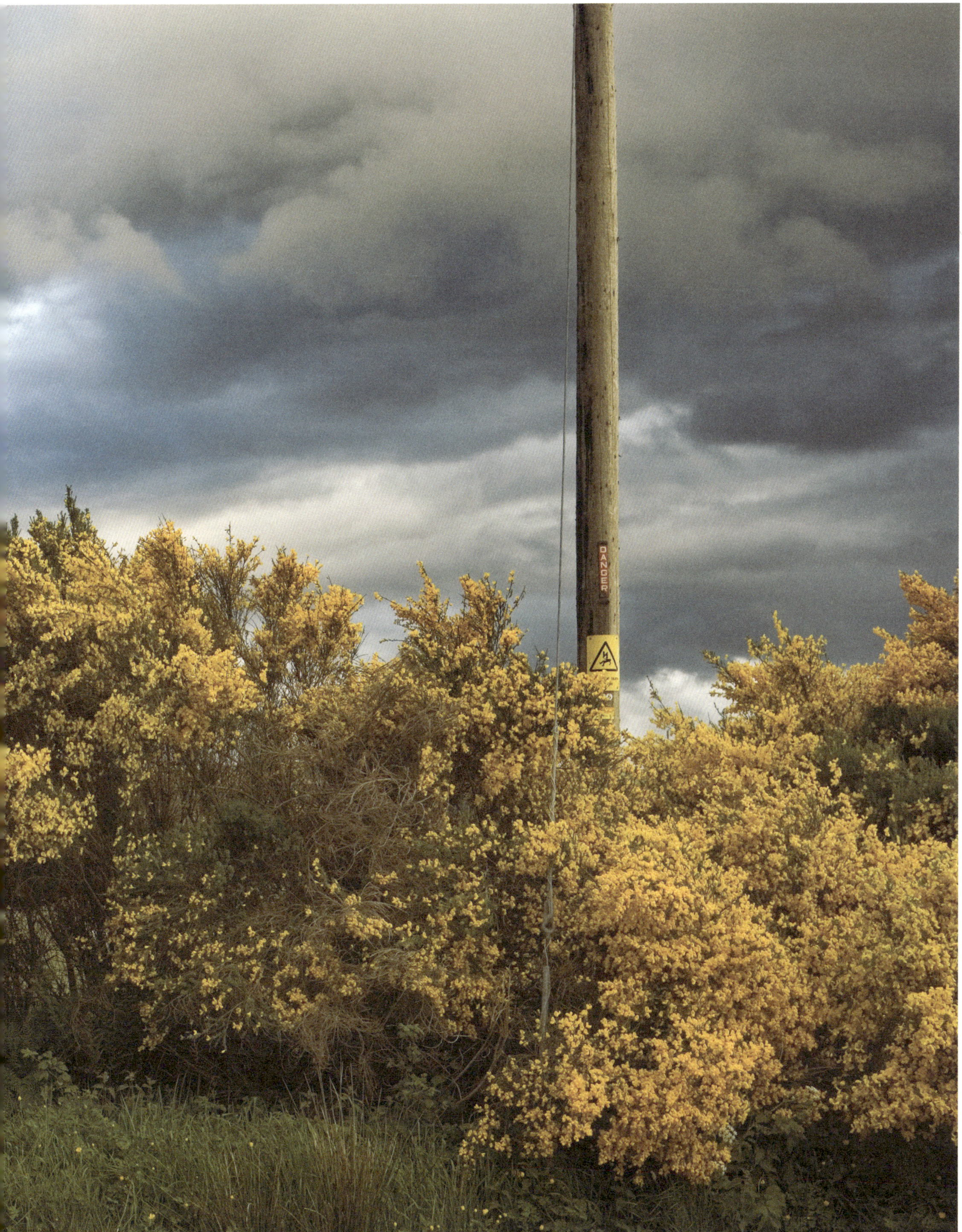
DANGER

— Foreword
— Nick Barley

Every building has its own story to tell. The journey from a client's dreams and an architect's ideas to the three-dimensional reality of a building involves an inordinate number of decisions, negotiations, setbacks and snags. Factors that influence how a building will look and feel — how it exists in the world — will include landscape and topography; available building materials; the scale of ambition of the client; the talent and creativity of the architect; and a cocktail of cultural, aesthetic and political forces. Every building will in turn influence the biographies of the people who occupy it.

For this book, and the exhibition which accompanies it, the point of departure was to ask to what extent today's new buildings are a reflection of the region in which they are produced. In effect, we wanted to find out whether there is such a thing we can describe as a 'new Scottish architecture', or a 'new European architecture', or even a 'new regionalism' and if so, what exactly these phrases might mean. But as the project has progressed, its scope has become more refined, and at the same time possibly more fundamental. By asking 'what are the factors which make a building the way it is?', we have ended up searching for answers to the question of what architecture might stand for in a post-industrial, post-fossil fuel, post-Modern age.

In order to tackle this question, the co-curators, Morag Bain and Oliver Lowenstein, have surveyed a selection of buildings recently completed in four European regions which enjoy some topographical similarities: namely, the Vorarlberg region of Austria; the hilly terrain of Norway; the Scottish Highlands; and the mountainous Graubunden region of Switzerland. The similarities between these areas go beyond their hilly or even mountainous landscapes: each also contains significant rural areas which were not sites for intensive industrial activity during the past 200 years. As a result, they are not renowned for having spawned modernist architecture characteristic of the machine age. Nor are they the new locations for voracious growth fuelled by soaring land values or stock market bonanzas. By contrast with cities such as London or Tokyo, or countries such as the United Arab Emirates or China, the locations selected by the curators are relatively sparsely populated and have not played host to the kind of supercharged architecture that emerges from the culture of high-risk, high-return capitalism. In other words, they have not witnessed an explosion of steel-framed, glass clad commercial developments whose detractors contend that parts of Dubai are becoming indistinguishable from Guangzhou or Dallas, and nor are they generally home to signature buildings by architects whose 'style' is a more dominant factor than the location of their work. Instead, the areas selected for this exhibition have each witnessed the steady indigenous growth of an approach to designing buildings which aims to be deeply in tune with its local context.

The comparison of recent buildings in these areas is more than an attempt to spot the emergence of new rural vernacular styles. For a start, some of the approaches — described as 'building cultures' by Robert Fabach in his essay in this book — have been consistently developing since as long ago as the 1950s, and they can not therefore be characterised as new styles. More importantly, the term 'vernacular' may seem pejorative, deriving as it does from the Latin 'verna', or home-born slave, and implying in this context a blinkered local approach to building, whereas the architects selected for this exhibition are without exception keenly aware of international issues, both architectural and political. As Fabach points out in his essay, several of the pioneer craftsmen in the Vorarlberg region of Austria had either studied in Ulm with the likes of Otl Aicher or were heavily influenced by Scandinavian modernism. Moreover, many of the architects featured in this exhibition are working in conscious response to international political issues. The so-called 'second generation' of architects working in the Vorarlberg region in the 1970s developed a concept of 'Simple Building' as a direct response to the oil crisis of 1973. Meanwhile, as Mary Arnold-Forster of Skye-based practice Dualchas points out in her essay, many of the Scotland-based architects featured in this exhibition are as influenced by architects like Glen Murcutt in Australia, Brian Mackay-Lyons in Canada and Peter Zumthor in Switzerland, as they are by the Scottish cultural contexts of the Highland Clearances and several centuries of devastating deforestation.

What emerges from this survey of architecture from four different countries is an interest in the power of the local to act in intelligent opposition to pernicious standardising forces of globalisation. As Oliver Lowenstein argues in his essay, the architects featured here seem to be uniting in opposition to three clear tendencies: the rise of the 'starchitect'; the rise of anonymous corporate architecture; and the rise of what Lowenstein describes as 'the ostentation and overkill of postmodernism'. There are other things that architects have the urge to fight against, such as a deeply troubled planning system, as problematic in Norway and Austria as it is in Scotland.

Just as important as these causes to fight against, is a set of 'attractors' towards ways of practising a form of architecture that feels appropriate to the twenty-first century. Perhaps most dominant among these is the drive for sustainability — a much-debated word, but one that nonetheless represents a legitimate desire to create buildings which use resources appropriately. Sustainability is a subject fraught with complexity, as Mary Arnold-Forster points out when she reveals that it is cheaper to buy Chinese or Indian slates in Inverness than it is to purchase slates which have been mined locally in Ballachulish or Caithness.

Less immediate than sustainability, but just as important for many of the architects featured in this exhibition, is a desire to embrace a more haptic understanding of architecture: that is, a design of buildings which is responsive to all of the senses, and not simply the visual. Ever since Le Corbusier, architects have been quick to appreciate that photographs are an important means of influencing critical reaction to their buildings. Architectural magazines and books have served to emphasise the visual over every other sensory reaction to buildings, and yet for the people who are actually using Frank Gehry's Guggenheim Bilbao or Herzog & de Meuron's Olympic Stadium in Beijing (to take two random examples), how the buildings feel, how they smell, and how their environments work acoustically, will be just as important as the visual images beamed across the world on TV screens and in magazines and newspapers.

The third key motivating force is the desire among architects in these countries to forge a way of making buildings which is at the same time comfortable in its regional context, and conscious of global realities. This balance is what Robert Fabach describes as 'a productive relationship between the local and the universal'. In Vorarlberg, Fabach argues, 'a deep-rooted mix of curiosity and scepticism has emerged. Only what is proved in practice will slowly be accepted and recognised'. The same could be argued for all of the regions featured in this book.

On top of these 'attractors' are a variety of concurrent and sometimes conflicting forces: there is the urge to continue embracing the modernist passion for sunlight, allowing as much light as possible into buildings even if that means exposing them to the vagaries of harsh weather at the same time; and the desire to celebrate crafts skills in construction. At the same time, there is a consensus that unnecessary architectural showboating is to be avoided.

All of these disparate factors — and many more described in the essays in this book — are helping to build an emerging consensus, across four European regions, that the forces of globalisation can productively be balanced with an architecture which speaks the language of local community.

Since the Canadian theorist Kenneth Frampton popularised the term 'critical regionalism' in the 1980s as a response to the postmodernist language of facadism, and the Norwegian writer Christian Norberg-Schulz described the 'phenomenology of place' in the 1970s, there has been an increasing focus on the question of how we can make good places. With around 20 million separate buildings in the UK today, and the vast majority less than a century old, the role of architecture remains of vital importance to the framing of social and national identity. And yet the brutal reality is that most of the buildings we create are deeply uninspiring, formulaic constructions that make little meaningful contribution to our environment, and still less to our sense of place. Our planning system remains locked in a managerial approach that does not insist on quality and celebrates a mythical stylistic status quo, while regulations for roads and amenities departments mitigate against the creation of places designed primarily for people.

Can a regionalist sensibility provide a framework for encouraging a higher general quality of construction? Probably not on its own. But if we can better understand the forces which make a building the way it is, perhaps we can more easily identify and control what is needed to pave the way for significant improvements in the future.

Nick Barley is the Director of The Lighthouse.

—Introduction
—Morag Bain

Building Biographies is the latest biennial review of a diverse range of Scottish architecture. Within the exhibition and this accompanying book recent Scottish projects are presented with European examples from Norway, the region of Vorarlberg in Austria and the region of Graubunden in Switzerland, placing the buildings of Scotland and their biographies within an international perspective. By looking at issues such as the culture of place, regional identity and globalisation, the exhibition asks the buildings to tell their stories and begins to answer the question that was the initial concept and approach for the exhibition — Why is it like this?

To understand the ethos of each project, the decision making process, how the building was made and the culture in which these projects arose, the architects were asked to not only present a project description but also to respond to themes and influences, present an historical image and submit a story by themselves or the buildings users.

In simple terms, the idea of why decisions are made could be looked at under two headings — the human and the non-human. The human is the culture in which it is conceived and made i.e. the political, client, social, communal, ideas, senses. The non-human is the physical world in which it is conceived and made i.e. place, geography, climate, costs, materiality, local/global. These two themes interconnect (a choice of material can certainly affect the senses) and of course both of these themes also contain economic, sustainable and environmental issues.

It is worth while listing the themes and suggestions – if only to let others consider some, but not all the issues, that may affect the design process and also that some of these areas are vital and present within good architecture whether unconsciously or consciously considered.

The architects were asked to submit two images under each theme:

1— Where is it and why?
i.e.
Geography
Soil/rock formation
Built surroundings
Population
Client decision

2— Why choose these materials?
i.e.
Senses
What it feels like emotionally
Resources – Near to hand / far away – building miles – proximity principle
Natural/man made
Durability
Cost

3— Why make it like this?
i.e.
Procurement process
Craft/skill
Mass production/ease of or speed of construction
Junctions/connections
Experimentation
New media (computer design or build)

4— What affects it?
i.e.
Weather (and protection from)
Time
Eco systems
Adaptability
Geography
Site

5— What does it feel like (rationally or emotionally)?
i.e.
Rooted/floating
Sheltered/exposed
Poetic/rational
Permanent/temporary
Of the moment/timeless

6— What were the influences?
i.e.
Past /present/future
Local/global
Lifestyle
School studied at
Other architects
History of the region
A piece of text/poem
A desire

Architects were also asked to submit an historical image. We also wanted to know a story behind each building. A story of a relevant factor that had influenced the building. It could be the dream of a client, a conversation, a passage from a book, a planning process, music...

Along with a project description, three images relating to these themes and the story are presented within each project in this book. The films shown at the exhibition dealt with the themes more fully and added a fantastic richness to the presentation. I would like to thank all concerned as this was no easy task in terms of both time and thought. The reaction was interesting – a few architects were initially resistant but most came on board fully.

The book is in three distinct parts. It begins with Oliver Lowenstein, co-curator and co-editor in his opening essay An Architecture of the Elsewhere. This sets the scene wonderfully by discussing many aspects including critical regionalism, culture, the global and the local, materiality, sense of place, sustainability, the reaction to modernism etc. In part two, The Practice of the Wild, he extends into a discussion on bioregionalism and geopoetics and expands further by bringing phenomenology, the physicality of place and cultural landscapes into the foum. He follows these introductions with a text which sums up each of the fourteen projects together and draws each into these contexts.

Thereafter, follow the projects – eight from Scotland and two each from Norway, Vorarlberg and Graubunden. The projects are in a format that allows a project description, the story and three of the themes to work alongside images of the buildings, giving as much of a flavour as possible to the reader. The book finishes with a series of essays, five on aspects of Scotland and one each on the European regions. These essays vary greatly in approach from hard hitting sustainable issues, to analytical thought on ideas and place, to historical and political backgrounds. All are supported by strong visual presentations.

For myself, whilst co-curating the exhibition and co-editing this book, three aspects of the initial question – Why is it like this? – came to the fore, not only through researching the projects but also reading the essays: the culture they are built in (and here there is a vast difference between Scotland and our European neighbours); the context they respond to, not only the programme and the immediate surrounding but also the extended landscape and this extremely powerful feeling that these buildings belong, whether urban or rural, to that landscape; and finally a great sense of materiality – you can't help but be extremely conscious, of how they look and feel, of what they are made from and how they are crafted – whether by a robot or a stone mason.

Morag Bain is the co-curator and co-editor of Architecture in Scotland 2006–2008: Building Biographies. She is the ACCESS to Architecture Project Director at The Lighthouse.

—An Architecture of Elsewhere
—Oliver Lowenstein

Part I

Many years ago, travelling in the lowlands of Scotland, I found myself watching a flock of geese, heading west. Spread out across the grey winter's sky, their great v-formation arced over what must have been at least a half-mile of land below. Later, perhaps months later, my mind rolled back to the vivid imagery of that afternoon; the geese, semi-independently, yet seemingly all part of some kind of avian group-mind, each and all heading towards the same horizon. At the time and to this day, migrating geese continue to conjure this metaphor in the mind's eye; of journey's separate yet joined, apparently in part unconscious, and in part animal consciousness, all heading in what is roughly the same direction.

If the metaphor is old and hardly original its imagery does, in these post-fractal days, luminously evoke complexity, collective intelligence, and the nascent awareness of the human group-mind. Indeed, the emergence of the complexity sciences was one of the many transformations wrought by the arrival of computers throughout the 1990s. The digital revolution also reconfigured architectural practice in ways that are continuing to play themselves out, including a whole wave of architectural aesthetics and emerging theory devoted to complexity. At the time, closely associated with post modernisms moment, that wave of architectural complexity is gone; while the period's fractal 'chaos' sciences have become part and parcel of the current cultural landscape.

Emergence is ongoing however, and there is a sense that a new architectural mood is evolving in which elements of complexity may be attributed, as well as – and more poetically and naturalistically – the semi-independent phenomena of birds all heading towards the same horizon. If this image is credible, the landscapes over which this putative architectural wave is moving, contains a mix of attractions and reactions. Three contested and often overlapping fields of response and reaction spring immediately to mind. The ostentation and overkill of post modernism; the rise to planetary dominance of a few hundred star architects selling particular brands of iconic signature buildings around the planet; and the big, corporate, yet terrifyingly soulless architecture which pervades the building culture dimension of Globalisation. Considerably more interesting, is what is perceived as being on the horizon. For instance the attempts

— The grid and the pathway: Foster & Partners Swiss Re building in the city district of London and a detail of strickbau Swiss joinery.

to once again uncover the human element contained within architecture's modernist tradition; a thread which begins with Frank Lloyd Wright and in Europe, the Finnish architect, Alvar Aalto and continues as a half-hidden line running through the last century up to the present day. Perhaps the most identifiable characteristic of this counter-modernist tradition, is its relative suspicion of the supremacy of the rational and, to a degree, technological, finding expression both in regional and local cultural difference. Both continue to animate current day heirs to this contemporary tradition, be it in the work of Glen Murcott, Brian MacKay-Lyons, or Peter Zumthor.

A second thread might be identified in the renewed interest in the vernacular amongst architects, and also the wider public, stemming arguably from the opening up of the planet to mass travel. Intertwined with each has been the arrival of a definable ecological architecture into the mainstream over the course of the last twenty years. The vernacular speaks as much to environmental yearnings of self-sufficiency, as it does increasingly – in modern eco-speak – to the 'proximity principle'; each guided to greater or lesser extent by alarm, which among some environmental communities can reach almost apocalyptic proportions: including certain convictions which dovetail with building culture, such as radically severe resource limits and an intuitive, if naïve, belief that building with materials closest to hand always makes the best ecological sense. Although definitions differ, if you look to wherever ecological architecture has rooted itself across the developed world, the emphasis time and again begins with community oriented perspectives; lo-tech and hands-on approaches to building, along with an abiding, and often thoroughly unfashionable respect for 'making', and the craft of building. Workmanship preceding showmanship. If some of the original eco-architectural community has moved towards the mainstream in recent years, there remains a world of difference between these lower tech eco-architects and the hi-tech school of Rogers, Grimshaw and Foster et al, however much hi-tech is 'redressed' in eco-garb. Closer to the green scene, and comprising a third strand, are those architects who have rediscovered a consuming passion for materials and materiality, often identified with continental rather than the dominant Anglo-American thinking. These various European instances have not pursued architecture's rush to globalisation, rather the overlap is with regionalist variants of modernism, and with the relations of the senses to architectural culture. Here, perhaps, is the last in the nexus of influences pulled into this loose, yet coherent field. If post-modern, corporate and iconic architecture all speak to the sensation of visual experience, 'eye-candy' as we have grown to know and call it, the turn to the materiality is searching for an experience with 'our kinds' – human beings – complete sense system, not only the sense of our eyes. How far these interrelated strands can be woven into a single coherent grouping, converging at some shared vanishing point, is open to interpretation and inevitably, in architectural circumstances, argument. Still, to return to the migrational metaphor, I'd suggest that this particular flight-path turns out to be a set of interrelated connections and relationships.

The impulse is hardly specific to architecture. Rather it is part of wider social and cultural currents. Indeed, that comparable regional architectures both in Europe and across different parts of the planet are quite easily identifiable, suggests a broader cultural zeitgeist at play. The dialects may be different yet a shared language is spoken. And although this exhibition's architectural focus is primarily on Scotland, if a net is cast further afield, one finds comparable, and in various ways more developed scenes across parts of Europe, and many areas and regions of the developed world. The countries and regions within them, represented in the exhibition and which this catalogue accompanies, all provide examples of how place, local communities and local and regional culture continue to provide a vital wellspring from which contemporary architecture can, has and does emerge. How similar or different these architectural cultures are is a matter of social and sociological factors as much as cultural and anthropological consideration; although I would suggest that an argument may increasingly be made that the ecological imagination adds an additional layer of influence. At least in the Scottish context, there is a degree of overlap in mindset between elements from some representative architecture with what animates a range of ecologically-hued types. In this I would include the activism of rural-provocateur Alistair McIntosh and Edinburgh's Centre of Human Ecology, through the Reforesting Scotland network, to the poetic language of Kenneth White and the Institute of Geopoetics.

Perhaps cultures of place and of region are now most fully bound by the accelerating dynamic of Globalisation as it has developed out of the 'industrial take-off' of the last hundred traumatic years. So much architecture and building culture is implicated in Globalisation's restless culture of continuous upheaval, while the prospect of this McLuhanite global village getting ever smaller seems almost inevitable given how the speed and exponential growth of our non-place of virtual meeting – cyberspace, remains in its early days. In such a context regionally inflected architectures stand out. They can also be seen as either paralleling, or part of, other social and cultural waves all involving comparable turns to regional, or more personalised understandings of living our lives. For instance the rise of 'World Music', while primarily a marketing term, can be translated as the emergence of numerous, if hitherto invisible, regional voices within a broadly Western musical hegemony; cultural difference as seen through the lens of multiple musical forms rooted in place and the physical, tacit world. Another example might be the burgeoning popularity in the West of regional foods from all over the world, what in effect could be called 'world cuisine' or 'world food'. Here, again are overlaps with regional issues, which in this latter instance has also energised significant parts of the green grassroots and the development of 'slow food' as part of the, albeit often symbolic, movement to counter the march of Globalisation.

"Progress is destruction with a compass" Richard Powers, Plowing the Dark

"Ours has undoubtedly been," Jonathan Porritt recently wrote, "the Age of the Global."[1] If power centres, whether Brussels, New York or Shanghai, pursue policies which admit no alternative to the ongoing globalising model, this has not been for the lack of attempts to bring alternative options to the table, not least by the patchwork of constituencies usually identified as the greens, with their decentralising, regionalist agendas tugging at their hearts. From the perspective of the built environment, there has been an unambiguous relational dynamic between the global internationalisation of industrialization and the disappearance of many elements that comprise the older anchoring co-ordinates of place, identity and meaning. Not only this, the increasing homogenisation of culture is reflected in architectural culture and the built environment as much as any other field, which retrospectively may come to define how the modern industrial world has emerged through the twentieth century. Still, it may be hard to discern these issues up close to the slipstream of Globalisation, with its jet-setting iconic building culture emerging across the competing cities of West and East alike. For those in the higher echelons of architectural culture, meaning bounded by place and region is no longer relevant. Frank Gehry has stated that he 'doesn't do context', while Jacques Herzog of the Swiss super-starchitects Herzog & de Meuron has suggested that to speak of any regional architectural perspective in today's globalised economy is an irrelevance.[2] Aspects of architectural modernism's universalist claims, Herzog seems to imply, foreshadowed its part in globalisation. This chimes readily with how the internationalisation of its architectural aesthetics have become the bedrock of the aesthetics of choice for the majority of the planet's elites, be they national governments, the transnational corporate sector or buildings, museums, gallerys, culture halls, which serve and present a country's cultural dimension. While this quick broad-brush overview oversimplifies, the international construction sector operates on a global scale, with regions and the connection to place that grounds much of the regional perspective insignificant or wholly absent. Although extreme examples, the steel hi-rise towers of twenty first century Dubai could just as well be in Chicago, Canary Wharf or Eastern Europe; and the weekly production lines of new Chinese cities discussed in the broadsheet media, are but high profile instances of the seemingly ineluctable turbo-charged thrust of the engines of modernity. At the smaller, domestic end of building scales, the arrival of the suburbs, of high volume housing, where towns and districts rise up from ground level across the world, reproducing blandscapes of identikit environments are further expressions of the 'anyplace' principle.

It is true that this argument concentrates on the downside of the consequences of industrialisation with its logic of mass production and economies of scale. The social, health and economic well-being and security significantly advanced are part of the other side of the equation. However, signs that such consequences have reached certain thresholds are becoming increasingly apparent across both the built and un-built environments. One linguistic clue to this is how we talk of man-made environments, where the interchangability of one environment for another has spawned a new descriptive language of spatial anonymity: to add to 'anyplace', there is 'sprawl' and 'nowheresville' and in somewhat dated language, 'urban wasteland'.

Looming over these linguistic novelties, and becoming only too pressingly evident and visible, is that the consequences of aspects of industrial modernity are accelerating the most urgent crisis of these times – the planetary environmental crisis. So much so, that many environmentalists, as well as other cultural commentators, believe that we may well be on the verge of much vaster change than is generally acknowledged. For the likes of Jonathan Porritt we have been living through an age of globalisation, but this is on the verge of coming to an end. Porritt is certain that the next decades, with continued oil shocks and escalating energy and food risk issues, mean globalisation is past its high water mark. This will, and is already triggering renewed momentum for the regional, decentralised modes of social organisation long advocated by the greens. It will

— One World, One Dream: Beijing's Olympic finale, with Herzog & de Meuron's Bird's Nest taking centre stage. 2008.

— Wild avian consciousness and man-made office design. Still from Raptor, a video by Dalziel + Scullion.

include, Porritt interestingly suggests, a renewed interest in ecological philosophies such as bioregionalism, which attempts to work 'in partnership' with, rather than imposing an industrial edifice upon natural systems. Porritt describes such a future to regionalism as a form of civic globalisation, in contrast to the corporate model; envisaging it as contributing to a 'breakthrough' process within what he believes is the inevitable traumatic 'breakdown' that lies ahead.

The question to ask, if the cracks in the official future which Porritt's analysis uncovers are credible, and even if it isn't as catastrophically full-on as the undertow of his language somewhat ruefully suggests, is where to search for architecture and building cultures that represent and reflect such a return to the regional.

From Aalto to Zumthor (and back again)

The emergence of an identifiably modern regionalism is usually traced to the response and reaction to modernism's early guiding principles in the early middle decades of the twentieth century. If one looks to architecture's modernist project it quickly becomes clear that its earliest identity-defining commitment to the rationalist, future and technology focus, began to splinter within a few short decades. Corbusier's 'Machine for Living' aesthetic may have thrilled architectural and design futurists in the very early twentieth century, but by the interwar period a small number of architects were already beginning to question the sources of modernism's rationale. In Europe, the Finnish architect, Alvar Aalto moved further and further towards a more humanist perspective; one that acknowledged the influence of the past as much as the present on contemporary architecture, as well as the use of materials specific to the culture that it was part of, for which Aalto meant his homeland Finnish culture. His Paimo Tuberculosis Sanitorium is seen symbolically, as a 'watershed' Aalto project demonstrating the 'extended rationalism' and human dimension of warmth and compassion finding expression within the building and design ethos that the architect was increasingly being drawn to[3]. This turn to the regional was acknowledged by modernism's primary literary theoretician, Siegfried Gideon, with Aalto as pre-eminent regional example. Ever since Aalto, this regionalist turn has been a crucial root to the counter-modernist currents both in

Early regional modernism's master:
Alvar Aalto's mid-period Villa Mairea,
Noormarkku, Finland 1938.

theory and architectural practice up to present times. In the United States the other primary influence on a regionalist aesthetic framed within modernist practice, has been that of Frank Lloyd Wright. Age and career-wise Lloyd-Wright predated Aalto (he was a significant supporter of the Finn when he came to the USA in the 1950s). Lloyd Wright's influence on subsequent generations of, particularly if not surprisingly, North American architects was vast. This is particularly evident around Taliesin, the independent school, which Lloyd Wright initiated. Lloyd Wright is again a key contributor to modernism's regionalist undercurrent, as well as part of the related and interlinked organic architectural tradition.

This sets the scene for the turbulent 1960s and the awakening to vernacular architecture, often sourced to the 1965 New York MOMA exhibition, Architecture without Architects, also the title of curator Bernard Rudofsky's influential book. The book's popularity amongst architects and public alike, echoes a new pessimism about industrial modernism in the developed world in the aftermath of World War II, and exposure to the otherness of the world tradition of vernacular culture. Far from its rhetoric of liberation, architectural modernity with its vast rebuilding programmes, the emergence of high-rise, as well as the corporate takeover of modernist architectural language, began to be identified with the aura of oppression. By contrast, vernacular architecture spoke the language of community as much as it did the local. Interest in vernacular architecture also benefited from the emergence of mass global travel, and the exposure for the first time of relatively large numbers of recent generations to the sheer diversity of world architectures; an increased sensitisation to both buildings and wider cultures disappearing across the developing world. The vernacular has maintained this appeal to greater or lesser extent ever since.

The notion of a rehumanised modernism also began to take serious root, and with the once avant-garde modernist language appropriated by the corporate world and technosphere by the 1960s and '70s, architecture could be construed — whether by architects or others — as a gesture of defiance and critique of what was by now, the commercial mainstream. This prefaced the arrival of Critical Regionalism, identified, if not coined by the Canadian theorist, Kenneth Frampton[4]. Critical Regionalism gained a cultural cachet

— Regional Modernism today:
Nova Scotia's MacKay-Lyons Sweetapple's Ghost Lab buildings: Ghost 6's tower and (background) the unfinished Ghost 8 research studio.

— Peter Zumthor's atmospherics:
The Kunsthaus Bregenz, 1997.

during the 1980s as a rejoinder to the emergence of post-modernism, and a bulwark of authenticity in an age where style, irony and political detachment became a prevailing architectural orthodoxy. Although Critical Regionalism faded from view during the 1990s and into the present decade, the credence of an architecture which speaks as much from a grounding in regionality and the differing human, and non-human contexts that such grounding infers, is today reinvigorated. Two identifiable and partially intertwined strands of architectural energy, in part characterise renewed and updated regionalism, and have already been referred to above. First, an emerging wave of sustainably-hued architects in the UK, in Europe and in the rest of the developed world, North America, etc. Second, the appearance of a generation of mainly continental architects influenced by the aforementioned concern for materiality – often underpinned by appeals to phenomenology, not least the work of the German philosopher, Martin Heidegger, who inhabits the philosophical terrain of this new regionalist consciousness, as well as being core to Frampton's argument. In the latter instance, materiality mixed with the 'ding an sich', 'the thing in itself' has ushered in an architecture of presence, of atmosphere and of the tacit. While liking materials does not necessarily imply any overt regional or local agenda, although quite often the two go hand-in-hand and materials being used by interested architects may well be sourced from the locale and context they work in even if they have not allied themselves directly to a sustainability ethos.

Today, popularity with such embodied approaches to architecture continues to get the architectural heart beating that much faster, its best-known and most enigmatic practitioner being the Swiss

— Material matters: Stonework detail at the Lotte Glob studio.

— Gion Caminada's Vrin: Foreground, one of the village's farm cattle barns, using strickbau timber jointing and 'lesesteine' ('harvested stones') and mid-distance a Caminada chalet.

Architect, Peter Zumthor. Zumthor, if pushed to consider the basis of his architecture, invokes the phenomenological when speaking of the atmospheres of place.[5] This is also the case with the Swiss mountain architect Gion Caminada. As Heinz Wirz points out in his introduction to the recent English version Caminada monograph, Cul zuffel e l'aura dado, Caminada's architecture is intimately connected to a society's way of being. He quotes from the Heideggerian architectural text. "The way that you are and I am, the way that we as human beings are on this earth, that is architecture, is dwelling. Both types of architecture – architecture as a caring act and architecture as the construction of buildings – are inherent in that which is truly architecture, truly the act of dwelling."[6] Caminada's way of being, of working as the village architect, is clearly interpretable as an act of caring. In similar vein, the other examples speak of this act of care; from the topographical work of Jensen and Skodvin in Norway to the social housing issues of the young Vorarlberg and Trondheim architects, Christoph Kalb and Brendeland & Kristoffersen respectively. In Scotland materiality is most fully and immediately apparent in Reiach and Hall's Pier Stromness Art Gallery. This building can also be interpreted as an act of care. Yet it is also present in the smaller, less attention bringing works of the highlands and islands architects. If these are a more workmanlike architecture for the everyday, they also derive from the conditions of care, that is care for the planet and for our current ecological predicament, as well as for community and the meaning of community.

The issue of materiality surfaces repeatedly in relation to the buildings of the exhibition. Yet, despite Heidegger's emphasis on the life-world, on 'dwelling' and on 'being', the European phenomenological tradition has not in the main provided sustained ways into thinking and being ecological. If, as I've been suggesting there are affinities of sensibility between those for whom materiality matters – the maturing sustainable architectural community – and those architects and indeed, members of the general public engaged with continuing architecture without architects – uncovering the roots of this shared sensibility may enable a new wholly embodied and ecologically sensitive architecture to find more permanent roots. While one form of sustainable architecture, well formed and ready for building action, has indeed emerged over the last decade, it is not, perhaps, an ecological architecture. Nor is it an architecture necessarily embedded in materiality. A vividly relevant question in this transitional early twenty first century moment, is how might such embeddedness be reconciled with a much more fully ecological relationship to our environment? And how might this express itself through architecture? A first step is to engage with ecological philosophies, to see if these may act as pathways into just such a possible reconciliation.

Part 2
The practice of the wild

What soil series are you standing on?

What are the major geological events that shaped your watersheds (faults, uplifts, doorwarps, volcanics, sea floods etc)?

Does your community give them special attention?

How did the original inhabitants eat, clothe, and shelter themselves?

How did they celebrate the seasonal changes in times before you?

Name the major plant/animal associations that thrive in your bioregion?

Name five resident and migratory birds; five grasses; five trees; five mammals and reptiles or amphibians. Which are native?

Name the plant or animal that is the "barometer" of environmental health for your bioregion. How's it doing? Endangered? Thriving?

When I originally read this series of questions, my immediate response was both threat and challenge, as I knew that I could answer very few of these simple and direct questions. Reprinted in the Millennium Whole Earth Catalogue[7], and based on a famous bioregional issue of Co-Evolution Quarterly from the early eighties, implicit in the questions is that people at a very 'roots' level are out of touch with not only the environment at our feet but also the larger environment surrounding us. Whether you agree or not, ask yourself if you can answer these questions.

Bioregionalism began as a way in which our kind (the human species) might be a part of, rather than apart from, the wider natural world. Look not, bioregionalism suggests, to man-made maps and lines for knowing where one region ends and another begins, but to which plants grow where; to the food chains plants, mosses and insects support; and to river watersheds, to apprehend the boundaries of a place.

Primarily North American in its sources, the bioregionalist ethos flourished in the 1980s and into the '90s, providing an empathic way for working, and prospectively, in the case of architects, designing with — rather than against — ecological systems. Its flowering was part of a broad group of contemporary science-savvy ecological philosophies of the time,

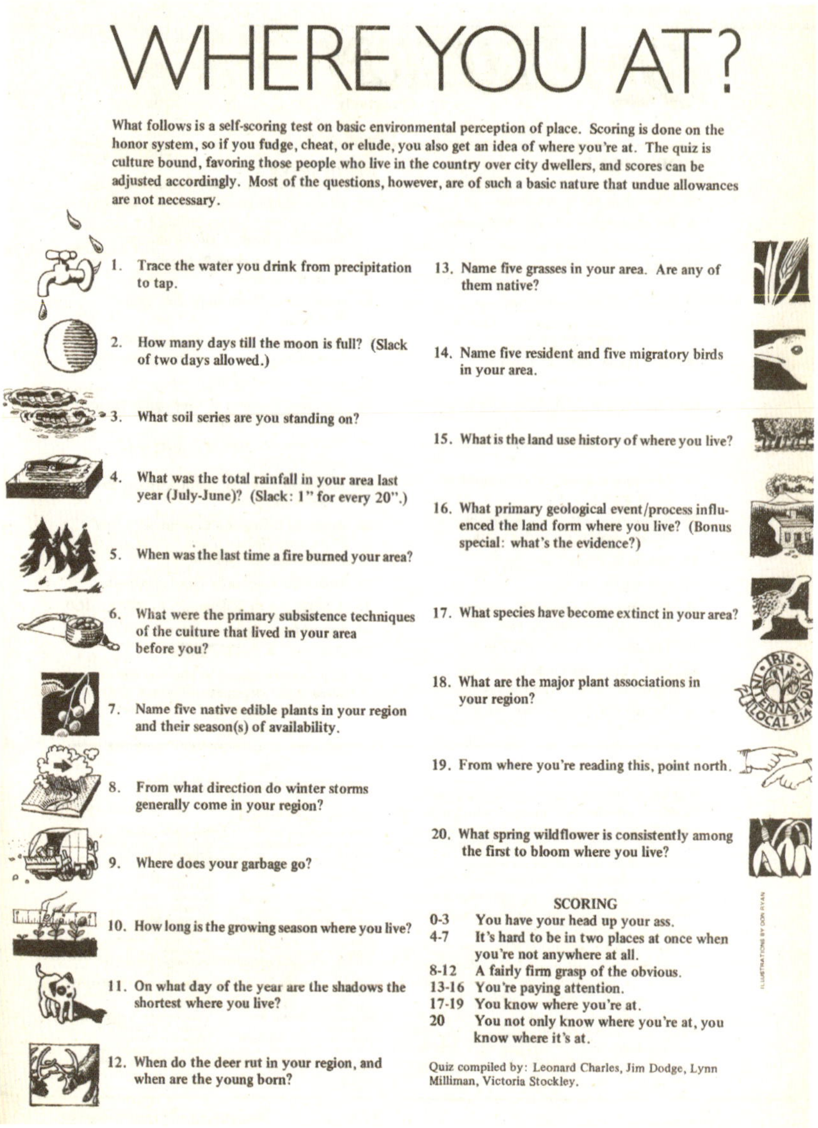

WHERE YOU AT?

What follows is a self-scoring test on basic environmental perception of place. Scoring is done on the honor system, so if you fudge, cheat, or elude, you also get an idea of where you're at. The quiz is culture bound, favoring those people who live in the country over city dwellers, and scores can be adjusted accordingly. Most of the questions, however, are of such a basic nature that undue allowances are not necessary.

1. Trace the water you drink from precipitation to tap.
2. How many days till the moon is full? (Slack of two days allowed.)
3. What soil series are you standing on?
4. What was the total rainfall in your area last year (July-June)? (Slack: 1" for every 20".)
5. When was the last time a fire burned your area?
6. What were the primary subsistence techniques of the culture that lived in your area before you?
7. Name five native edible plants in your region and their season(s) of availability.
8. From what direction do winter storms generally come in your region?
9. Where does your garbage go?
10. How long is the growing season where you live?
11. On what day of the year are the shadows the shortest where you live?
12. When do the deer rut in your region, and when are the young born?
13. Name five grasses in your area. Are any of them native?
14. Name five resident and five migratory birds in your area.
15. What is the land use history of where you live?
16. What primary geological event/process influenced the land form where you live? (Bonus special: what's the evidence?)
17. What species have become extinct in your area?
18. What are the major plant associations in your region?
19. From where you're reading this, point north.
20. What spring wildflower is consistently among the first to bloom where you live?

SCORING
- 0-3   You have your head up your ass.
- 4-7   It's hard to be in two places at once when you're not anywhere at all.
- 8-12 A fairly firm grasp of the obvious.
- 13-16 You're paying attention.
- 17-19 You know where you're at.
- 20   You not only know where you're at, you know where it's at.

Quiz compiled by: Leonard Charles, Jim Dodge, Lynn Milliman, Victoria Stockley.

— 'Where You At?': The famous questionnaire from the Bioregional issue of Co-Evolution Quarterly, no 32. How did you do?

— An Architecture of Elsewhere
— P.18

all with eloquent and passionate advocates. In the bioregionalist instance the Californian poet Gary Snyder brought to bioregional awareness a particularly eloquent understanding, informed by ecology and anthropology as much as native American knowledge. Climate, soil and elevation, Snyder wrote in an essay on the bioregional, are the substrate for understanding the bounds of a region, determining what does and doesn't grow. Fold into this dynamic how places pass through time, with different forms of growth developing. These forms — including grasses and forests and, in Scotland as in other mountainous areas, glaciers — are witness to time's, as much as places, influence on a region. Snyder notes, "regions seen according to natural criteria are sometimes called bioregions," and how "the landforms between natural regions are never simple and clear, but vary according to biota, watersheds, landforms, elevation"[8]. Most strikingly Snyder draws place and interspecies consciousness into dialectical class awareness. "Bioregionalism is the entry of place into the dialect of history," he announces, before adding, "...also we might say that there are 'classes' which have so far been overlooked — the animals, rivers, rocks, and grasses — now entering history."[9] While an immediate understanding is through locality, the watershed, for instance, something of bioregionalism's original power comes from its capacity to scale from the very local to the very large, macro geographical regions of the world in a series of concentric nested, boxes, in such a way that avoids the artificial boundaries of man-made borders and divisions.

Snyder's bioregional ethos contains similar commitments to that of Deep Ecology, not least in that of biospheric egalitarianism. First expressed by Arne Naess[10], the Norwegian mountaineer and also the country's leading philosopher, Deep Ecology has since been developed by others[11]. At the heart of Deep Ecology is self-realisation for all beings, which include all life forms, whether species or ecosystems. Through such realisation, an opening into the larger ecological whole becomes clear, as does the realisation that the individual and the human species is only a part of this greater whole. Although less anthropological, as with the bioregional approach Deep Ecology contains both challenges and provocation for many, including architects.

Both Bioregional thinking and Deep Ecology are not unrelated to the work of exile Scottish poet Kenneth White — (at times White has been referred to as Scotland's Gary Snyder). White dislikes the word 'region', preferring 'territory' for his oeuvre of geopoetics; the word, White says, evinces aura and connection to the totality of the cosmos. Yet both he and Snyder are poets, and both articulate a mindscape connected to, rather than alienated from, land and landscape; cultural topographies which are at once local and global. For White, Geopoetics is a form of mental mapping which can hold the line against cultural reduction, through what he describes as moving beyond the oppositional dyad of local-global into an 'Open World'. "By being large-mindedly, wide-eyedely local," White said a few years back, "you are naturally global." The Open World begins "with where one stands," and rather than a neglect of the local "this world", White writes, "begins with knowledge of place". Thoroughly known, every place is open. From the smallest rivulet, via a network of rivers, one arrives at the ocean. A little geology allows one to know that not all the stones on the local beach are necessarily of local origin, that glaciers may have brought them in from elsewhere. Likewise, from one layer of local rock, one can move across nations and continents. An informed look at the sky will see not only wind-driven cloud, but the tracks of migratory birds. To all of this must be added the movements of population and language.[12]

"The region is the elsewhere of civilisation" Max Cafard[13]

Are the turns of phrase of the bioregional, geopoetic and deep ecological, dialects of too distant a language to speak in any meaningful way to the modern architectural professional? As a writer who publishes regularly on British and European sustainable architectural communities I have yet to meet an architect who has referred to any of these, or any other, deep ecologically-hued philosophies. Occasionally architects profess interest in permaculture, particularly its adaptation into sustainable design strategies.[14] Yet, for the most part the deeper ecological philosophies appear to be an unknown world for the architectural community. Indeed, bioregionalism, Deep Ecology and geopoetics may be the far reaches of the ecological spectrum, requiring a complete re-orientation of mindset. For most, including many sustainable architects, a resource, data and fundamentally 'technique' driven understanding of the natural world pre-dominates. My experience of those who look to philosophy, do so from within scientifically credible vantage points. This isn't surprising given that both the architect's training and subsequent working environment is as much about physics, engineering, technology and technocracy, as it is design and form. There is also both a fault-line and implicit unease between the deep greens rejection (perceived and real) of industrial modernity, on which so much of building culture is premised, a divide only rarely reflected on within the profession. Not for nothing are architects modern, after all. Given this, what chance two poets and a mountaineer? Recording architects levels of credulity to such poetic thought, could well show where along the non-industrial/industrial continuum a participating architect might be positioned.

Architectural susceptibility to technique is of course well-known. A micro example of such susceptibility might be CABE's recently published report underlining how very few English low to zero energy projects addressed sustainable design issues from a holistic perspective.[15] Time and again, the report confirmed, there was the ever-present fixation with kit. Particularly susceptible to the modern myth of progress, the mainly urban architectural, technology-fascinated sensibility, has imbued a well-developed discomfort towards the rural. Citing pragmatism and the 'real world' the architectural community has shown a continuous disinclination to consider deep green futures as either interesting or credible.

A further oft-made rejoinder to deep green philosophies, is to associate it with reaction and romanticised notions of the countryside and of land. This is in the main anachronistic, confusing deep green philosophy with both conservative and nationalist energies. Snyder reminds those who confuse the bioregional with the "exercise with 'nationalism', the imposter,

— Earth First? Jenson & Skodvin's Juvet Landscape Hotel in Geiranger Trollstigen, central Norway 2008.

the puppet of the State, the grinning ghost of the lost community", how far off the mark they are. Those in the bioregional community have been adamant that theirs was not only about a rural programme, but also the greening of cities, and the re-making of community in living urban environments. Snyder writes of seeking, "the balance between cosmopolitan pluralism and deep local consciousness"; that is an elegant version of localism.[16] As Joel Russ states in his essay introduction to the bioregionalist approach, "Bioregionalists don't want to go back to the past but forward to a more ecologically sophisticated future that enfolds our accumulated scientific and technical knowledge."[19] Professional skepticism towards the rural also doesn't help considering the shape of a possible future architecture rooted in the bed-rock of deep green philosophy. This doesn't necessarily imply the inferred rejection of all the fruits of industrial culture, but rather new apprehensions of how we, the human species, might connect to technology while also being alive to our speciesness and connectedness within 'biospheric egalitarianism'. For Naess this is part of the age-old and wider goal of self-realisation. For Heidegger, it is "an act of care". Others express related sentiments in different language; those advocating 're-wilding', or the writer Jay Griffith's,[17] call for another modernity, one that is able to encompass the wild in us as much as that outside us.

Nevertheless, so far within the architectural and design profession interest is muted. Where meeting points occur, these turn out to be instrumental in their purpose. For instance, many in the architectural world know the term Bioregional, but only because it has been semi-colonised as a developers brand in the service of the nascent eco-district developments. In terms of its adaptation by the social developer Bioregional, while this organisation carries out valuable work in developing local, and often naturally sourced, materials infrastructure, such as charcoal and lavender within its patch of South London, Bioregional has next to nothing to say about re-energising a rural agenda. For the architectural fraternity then, such philosophical entreaties to embed architectural practice within a more thorough 'deeper' ecological ground, appears way beyond the community's comfort zones. There is however a renewed receptivity to another, if somewhat different regional apprehension: that of the already mentioned Critical Regionalism.

"Regionalism is a form of cultural empathy that you develop, that you can transport to other places. It's a discipline, it's a way of looking at the world, looking for authenticity." Brian MacKay-Lyons[19]

Where theory, whose time is apparently passed, may be expected to gradually disappear, with Critical Regionalism this hasn't fully happened. Rather than a story of terminal decline the cultural and political conditions, which feed regional cultures, continue to surface and remake such cultures critical and resistant to the centre. Architecture which speaks with a regional voice has been continuing to renew itself decade on decade. This may be because of regionalism's outsider status, but also because it is inextricably linked to issues of meaning, which is re-asserted time and again. Why is it that a Peter Zumthor or a Gion Caminada is so respected in the architectural ether? Why do new generations of architects such as Brian MacKay-Lyons in Nova Scotia, the Australian regional voices of Murcott, Richard LePlaistre and Peter Stutchbury, or so much closer to home and to the point, the new Highlands and Islands regional architecture discussed elsewhere in this catalogue, keep on appearing and working far from the perceived centres of their countries. Despite such choices of working far from where economic power, contracts and contacts lie, these – hardly the easiest of, paths – pulls a minority of architects in again and again. Frampton, influenced by Paul Ricouer, saw Critical Regionalism as an expression of the negotiation between universal civilisation and national cultures. Such an interpretation understands the regional as a local 'minority culture's' responses to the centralising energies at both national and global levels. This makes sense with both the Rhaeto-Romanic Caminada and

Dualchas's Gaelic culture identification. But it doesn't completely satisfy sustainable architecture's more generalised identification with the region, which, while partially drawing from the specifics of such minority cultures, does not do so exclusively. Both Caminada and the Nova Scotian architect, Brian McKay-Lyons speak of being entirely open to working beyond the borders of their home terrain, transporting their regionalist way of looking at the world to other contexts and circumstances. Cultural empathy, McKay-Lyons calls it. And in relation to the pull of the region for elements within sustainable architecture, I'd suggest this is linked, in Max Cafard's words, to the pull of 'the elsewhere of the region'.

If regionalism with a critical edge is returning into architectural currency, there is also a continuing admiration for the Finnish architectural theorist, Juhani Pallasmaa, known for his advocacy of an architecture of tactility. The human experience of tactility and its relation to architecture is most effectively explored in Pallasmaa's influential if short polemical essay, The Eyes of the Skin.[20] The book is an argument for an architecture of all the senses – what Pallasmaa calls the sense-system – rather than that of an ocular architecture, that is, of the eye. This contrasts markedly with an architecture dominated by its relation to the eye, generally where the façade presents the building for visual sensation, and which has reached its apogee in the iconic building sector. Brush your hand against the warm oak staircase in the Stromness Pier, sit deep in the interiors of a Caminada chalet or stand back-turned against the stone masonry of the Lotte Glob studio, and you are released into the felt world of materials, a palpably different experience to that of seeing through – 'the great monopolists of the senses' – the eyes, or more likely indirectly, images brought to you through television, internet or print media of sensational Dubai high-rises, and this summer, the trophy 'wows' of the Chinese Olympics. In the main the materiality elements of these European and Scottish examples re-connect our experience to the wider range of the senses. The foregrounding of materiality, of touch and of feeling, whether in wood, stone, steel, brick or other materials remakes the sensuality of the experience. It may also remake our relation to landscape and to place, partially when the materials originate from the locality, though also by opening up a new experience of places. Common perhaps to bioregionalists and geopoeticians alike, is their quest for a deepening of our connection to the ground we stand on. While tactility in architecture may draw us into the built, and natural, environment's materiality, it also returns people to the physicality of place.

Such acknowledgement of the tactile also infers a defence of craft, of skill and of making, and a critique of the accelerating electronic world and ever-increasing dominance of computer-mediated eye-centric design. An embodied architecture, so this interpretation goes, originates out of making rather than through design. For those interested in the merits of the maker, some small holding action of "the triumph of description over the thing," in American novelist Richard Power's words[21], may have been achieved. If this is common, converging ground between the darker greens and the various strands of architectural phenomenology, neither party engage in whether the

Cattlefeed huts on the way to Vrin. The village in the mountainous Lumnezia part of Graubunden, has been able to maintain it's agricultural base despite migration to urban Switzerland.

An Architecture of Elsewhere
P.22

technologies of the post-industrial world might work for, rather than against, architectures of tactility and a re-sensitising to place and ecosystems. Beyond the industrial fault-line that divides architects from the deeper green communities, the question of whether a different kind of modernity might still use the assemblage of, for instance, new media technologies for, say, bioregional ends is there to be asked. There are not that many examples of a world beyond the binary divisions between materiality and virtuality, but the craft robotics on display at the Flasch winery is just such an intriguing hybrid. Where, it seems to demand, does digital materiality feature in the spectrum of materialities? The knee-jerk reaction is to envisage the Flasch robotics as symbolising all things industrial and post-industrial, and yes, this is its likely partial endgame. New technologies, however, are often at their most interesting during their earliest R&D stages and before their applications are clearly defined; they still embody possibilities. The use of robotics at the Flasch winery could be seen as an instance of a post-industrial technology being applied to an agricultural context, and one where the vernacular has been remade by its architectural treatment. Flasch enables one to at least imagine robotics working in a rural or agricultural context. And there is nothing as such to definitively state that robotics might not work in a decentralised, bioregional future, even if this may feel unlikely. While some darker greens cannot wait to throw out the entire assemblage of industrial society, the use of technologies allows the imagination to at least consider such an example as that at Flasch embedded within very different futures of other modernities.[22]

Combining bioregionalism with robotics is probably too far a cry for many, including architects who, as predominantly urban 'modern' creatures, are uneasy with ecological philosophies that envision non-industrial agricultural futures, let alone hybridising these with a cutting edge technology. By contrast one might be more hopeful in envisaging converging lines and something of an emerging common ground between the phenomenologically rooted architectural theorising, and the deeper eco-philosophies. There are occasional moves towards such discussion. In a special issue of Rassegna, an Italian architectural review, the question of critical regionalism still being relevant was raised. Amidst other contributions, Franco La Cecla's

— The Gantenbein winery by Bearth & Deplazes, Fläsch, 2008. Through mixing a traditional building form with robotics, the Gantenbein winery rewrites the regionalist rule-book.

essay 'Towards a New 'Science of Living' concluded with the call for architecture to move from regionalism to bioregionalism[23]. If Cecla's take on the bioregionalist turn is principally anthropological it does suggest that such issues are at least there on the radar. The difficulties begin with ontology; how the different philosophical perspectives know the world. How do you resolve what seems initially irreconcilable, that of an anthropocentric with an evolutionary or biologically-informed ontology? One next step might be reconciling the bio with the critical under the shared preface of the regional.

Architecture routinely professes its receptivity to interdependence and interconnectivity, yet in the main it speaks its modernist category without appeal to any wider apprehension of the broader conditions across the cultural landscape; selectively ensuring that it is fully fire-walled from any leakage of these wider influences into its domain. A version of this mindset is found within the growing numbers who today comprise the sustainable architecture community, apparently incurious to many of the roots of ecological thinking. The first and obvious strategy advanced for indifference is the need for professional 'realistic' pragmatism. Yet, in the next moment, tactility is celebrated, and inspired by an architect such as Zumthor's ability to create atmosphere. Yet atmosphere is continuous, and rooted in the wider biospheric 'more than human' experience as much as the man-made world. Atmospheres convey the capacity to feel, and this in turn brings us back to what it means to feel, and the Heideggerian meaning of care. If we extend this to the 'more than human' world of ecology and of earth-knowledge, we arrive, perhaps, at the felt and atmospheric world of the sensuous. Here, from the geopoetic perspective, the human creature is both aware, part of and can read the territory s/he finds her/himself standing on. At his 2005 Ullapool high North talk Kennneth White, reminded the audience of how, geologically, the east coast Scottish rivers flow into the North sea, and are a continuation of the Rhine delta system which also flows into the North sea, comprising together an underwater continuation of the Northern European plain.[24] Peter Zumthor's Haldenstein studio stands a few hundred metres from the Rhine, and meltwater from the Caminada alpine village hillside flows into the upper Rhine much of the year. While not so far along its seabound journey, the river flows into the Bodensee or Lake Constanz, running alongside the edge of Vorarlberg.

Looked at this way, while remaining sensitive to earth-time, connections made from the geological, as much as the hydrological and linguistic abound. Accept such intimate geological connection between Scotland and central Europe, and it is an easy step into awareness of a connection to the country's long geological Dalradian and Cambrian timeframes. Not dissimilarly, Gary Snyder's simple exercise in bioregional awareness grounds the participant in place. If you are alert, Snyder observes, to how the presence of a certain species of tree (his example

Two rivers flowing into the North Sea: (Above) the Telford bridge over the river Tay at Little Dunkeld, Perthshire and (Right) upper Rhine as seen from the 'first' bridge at Ilaz, Graubunden in the earliest stages of the river's journey north.

An Architecture of Elsewhere

is Californian Douglas fir), will indicate both rainfall levels and temperature range, this provides the necessary information for the steepness of the pitch of your roof as well as, when, "raincoats are needed".

How similar, how different are the strands and threads of thinking of this regional diaspora? Where might an architecture, which is as fully attuned to the layers of ecological awareness, as it is to the embodied realm of tactility come from? I'd like to think that in a way the examples highlighted in the exhibition provide some markers towards this 'elsewhere of the region'. This isn't to begin to say this is any true kind of ecological architecture, far from it – rather only one path among a plurality of possibilities. Yet, in terms of possible futures it may point us towards new vistas, spaces to open up talking of possible Caledonias as much as possible Vorarlbergs. Were it to be uncovered such an architecture could yet contribute to a very different kind of modernity, that is to say, to steps towards a civilisation of the wild.

Biography

Oliver Lowenstein runs the cultural review, Fourth Door Review www.fourthdoor.co.uk, which integrates an architectural focus into a wider inter-disciplinary, ecological and relational approach. He has written on architecture, contemporary art, new media, craft and new music for, amongst others, the Independent, the Financial Times, AJ, Building for A Future, Blueprint, Metropolis, The Wire, and Resurgence. He also created and co-ordinates the Cycle-Stations Project, www.cyclestations.org, and will be launching a new timberbuild and wood culture website alongside the next Fourth Door Review, Annular, www.annular.org. He has lectured both within the higher education sector and at conferences on many of these subjects.

To be published soon the new Fourth Door Review, no 8 will feature a complimentary section to the Building Biographies exhibition. The River Runs Regionally features extensive interviews and articles on Graubunden and Vorarlberg. Including, from Graubunden: Peter Zumthor; Jurg Conzett; Bearth & Deplazes; Gramozio & Kohler; and Corinna Menn. And from Vorarlberg: Dietmar Eberle; Hermann Kauffmann; Marte.Marte; Vorarlberg's eco-scene – Passivehaus and the Dornbirn Energy Institute; and Christoph Kalb. For further information www.fourthdoor.co.uk

Footnotes

1 — p38 The first sentence from a chapter entitled 'Rediscovering the Regions' from Globalism and Regionalism, Jonathan Porritt, one of a series of polemics from The Edge Futures, Black Dog Publishing, 2008

2 — As Hugh Perman wrote a while back "Herzog is a firm believer in internationalism." "I don't believe in 'genius loci' (spirit of place)," he says. "The exchange of information is so rapid today. You cannot not be influenced by what's happening elsewhere." Hugh Pearman interview with Jacques Herzog, Surprise, Surprise, 15.05.2003 Sunday Times. While fellow Swiss Peter Schmid quotes Herzog as stating, "We perceive rural areas in which towns exist. In fact the situation is quite the reverse. We live in an urbanised network that includes leftover landscape". From p36, Vrin, by Peter Schmid, in Cul zuffel e l'aura dado Gion Caminda, Quart Verlag, Eng edition, 2008

3 — The Other Tradition of Modern Architecture: The Uncompleted Project 3 Colin St John Wilson's 1995, revised 2007 Black Dog Publishing. This is generally seen as the most authoritive exposition of the alternative modernist tradition.

4 — The term Critical Regionalism was originally coined by Liane Lefaivre and Alexander Tzonis in an essay 'The Grid and the Pathway', first published in 'Architecture in Greece; the Work of D. and S. Antonakakis', 15, in 1981. This influenced Kenneth Frampton who used and popularised the term in his own well-known essay, Towards a Critical Regionalism: Six points of an architecture of resistance, which first appeared in Hal Fosters, The Anti-Aesthetic, Essays on Post Modern Culture 1983, Bay Press. In 2004 Le Faivre and Tzonzis revisited the debate with their Critical Regionalism: Architecture and Identity in a Globalizing World, Prestel, 2004

5 — See both Atmospheres and Thinking Architecture, Peter Zumthor, Birkhauser, 2006

6 — Quoted by Heinz Wirz in the preface to Cul zuffel e l'aura dado, Gion C Caminada p7 Eng Edition 2008, quoting from Heidegger Martin, Builang, Dwelling, Thinking, originally published Bauen, Wohnen, Denken, 1952

7 — Co-Evolution Quarterly, the Bioregional issue, no 32, 1981, questionnaire composed by Jim Dodge, re-compiled for the Millennium Whole Earth Catalogue, 1990, Harper San Francisco.

8 — From Snyder's The Place, the Region, and the Commons essay, in The Practise of the Wild, Gary Snyder, p25 – 47, North Point Press, 1990

9 — ibid 8

10 — An up to the minute compendium of Naess's philosophical exposition can be found in The Ecology of Wisdom: Writings by Arne Naess, ed Alan Drengson, and Bill Devall Counterpoint, 2008, In the last decade Naess has developed Ecosophy T, the T referring to the plenitude of ecosophies that all beings could develop. See Ecology, Community and Lifestyle: Outline of an Ecosophy by Arne Naess and David Rothenberg, 1993, MIT Press

11 — Bill Devall and George Sessions are the best known. See their Deep Ecology; Living as if Nature Mattered, Gibbs Smith 1985. The reader Deep Ecology, ed Michael Tobias, Avant Books, 1985, also covers the territory well. See also the work of Ray Dasmann and Peter Berg. See also issue 12 of Reforesting Scotland, in which Doug Aberley discusses Bioregionalism in the Scottish context, suggesting the ecological ethos may have been Born in Scotland.

12 — Geopoetics: Place, Culture, World, p20, Alba Editions, 2003

13 — From Max Cafard beautiful quixotic The Surre(gion)alist Manifesto1990, which can be found at www.raforum.info/maxcafard/spip.php?rubrique12

14 — I am mainly thinking here of the English sustainable practice Architype. Also Devon practice Gale & Snowdon have worked with permaculture principles.

15 — Sustainable design, climate change and the built environment, CABE, 2007, see www.cabe.org.uk/defaultaspx?contentitemid=2077

16 — Ibid Snyder

17 — This is part of the contention of Wild, Jay Griffiths, Bloomsbury 2007

18 — Brian McKay-Lyons, by Oliver Lowenstein, in Blueprint December 2006.

20 — The Eyes of the Skin, Architecture and the Senses, Juhani Pallasmaa, Academy Editions, 1996

21 — From Richard Powers remarkable Virtual Reality novel, Plowing the Dark, Farrar, Strauss & Giroux, 2000

22 — For further exploration of the Flasch example of robotics, craft and digital materiality, see my contribution, Craft after Virtuality in Luminous Green, forthcoming from Fo.am, Brussels. Also for an interview with Gramazio & Kohler see Fourth Door Review 8, also forthcoming.

23 — For Towards a New Science of Living by Franco La Cecla's see Rassegna, issue 83, p122-127

24 — Kenneth White, North Atlantic Investigations, talk in Ullapool 29th October, 2005, see www.hi-arts.co.uk/geopoetics_project.html

—The Buildings —
An Overview
—Oliver Lowenstein

Step beyond the various beltways dividing insiders from outsiders across the hubs of metropolitan Europe, and it doesn't take long to realise that thought provoking architecture and building cultures don't necessarily stop at the city gates. What the collective examples represented within the Building Biographies exhibition show is how alive and vital this outsider architectural culture is and continues to be. Connecting in with these four outsider architectural communities is very much at the heart of this exhibition, as is making the connections between the communities. The sampling of Scottish projects comes almost entirely from outside the country's central belt, and in similar respect the other countries and regions chosen fall outside the usual pull of architectural attention; in the case of the other whole country represented, Norway, as much as the two central European regions, Vorarlberg in Austria, and Graubunden in Switzerland. All four regions share a degree of geographic overlap, in parts they are all mountainous, two are bordered by long stretches of coastal shoreline, while two present a degree of Alpine similarity in their middle European settings. But there are also of course significant differences, both in geography and in building culture; Scotland is usually considered a stone country, Norway one of the core timber culture strongholds. A social project such as Vorarlberg's Christoph Kalb's Wolfort housing seems as unlikely in Graubunden as Bearth & Deplazes' Flasch wine yard experiment in digital materiality would in Vorarlberg. So Building Biographies attempts to work with the common ground in these regional cultures as much as their differences, a point which becomes engagingly evident the more familiar you become with the range of showcased projects.

This said, the Scottish examples presented extend across a broad range of architectural projects from the last two years. A majority, though not all, are from the high north, providing an evocative illustration of a diversity of styles currently emerging across the Highlands and Islands, while at the same time offering evidence of an emerging Highlands and Islands regional architectural culture and community. Dualchas, who are based on Sleat, Skye, have over the last ten years developed a quickly identifiable architectural language relating back to the Hebridean longhouse tradition. During this decade Dualchas have refined this language, transposing the tradition and vernacular with contemporary materials and abstracting elements of the longhouse with clear modernist intent, cleanly proportioned lines which give their projects a distinctive identity and appeal. In recent years as the sustainable agenda has moved to the fore, Dualchas increasingly working with wood, have been specifying locally-sourced timber, a move which appears to have done nothing to dim their popularity with new and old clients. Talla Choinneachaidh, the specific house project shown is from the Outer Hebrides, the Breanish holiday home on the north east edge of Lewis, with a second adjacent building which serves as a mission house (there was a chapel on the original site.) Talla Choinneachaidh again shows how land, climate and weather continue to conspire in determining many aspects of a building's genesis, and its relation to how Western Isles (and other parts of the high North) homes and other buildings are still mainly built on the outcrops of rocky Lewisian Gneiss, in effect the only surfaces that a permanent building could, amidst the peaty bogs, hope to be sited. For some the feeling is of buildings as semi-sculptural extensions of the rock, pushing out of the ground. How much this was a conscious piece of pragmatism is intriguing. For as Dualchas's Mary Arnold-Foster notes in her catalogue contribution, across the water, on Skye the situation is reversed, with buildings being dug deep into the sides of their hillside sites, a certain self-consciousness at breaking the line of the land. What is common to both the island and mainland west coast is a continuing relation to weather; the small windowed long houses, facing away from the ocean and prevailing wind — the best strategy to contend with the elements. This is a clear change brought by contemporary architects, the scale of windows and a new relation to weather, which while still not directly visible, is experienced and arguably, faced in a completely different way. Dualchas, along with other architects and builders, have introduced this modernist derivation, sizeable windows which enable a new relation to geography, topography and to land; the world outside can be seen without necessarily having to contest the conditions. Such acceptance of windows is perhaps as much a cultural evolution as it is acceptance of technological change.

This is also the case with Locate Architects extension to the Taigh Chearsabhagh Arts Centre at Lochmaddy in North Uist. Using its beautiful waterfront position to make the most of the sea vista, this straightforward piece of work adds a new dimension to the arts centre. In a sense this is a double extension in that the arts centre was initiated by two architects, Donald and Helen MacDonald, who after renovating the original shoreside house, designed and built the first gallery extension, consisting of cafe and gallery space, adjoining the old house, in 2000. Seven years on the extra two roomed education spaces draws the building out into the harbour quay. While the extension from an immediate visual sense doesn't shake the world, a quiet white space, demarcates the fissures in how buildings evolve, both working from and adding to the earlier extension and the original shoreline house in which Taigh Chearsabhagh was conceived.

Neil Sutherland is based in the more central Scottish Highlands not far from oil city, Inverness. Since leaving Glasgow over a decade ago Sutherland's emphasis is partially encapsulated in his slogan-like commitment to "putting architecture back on the rural agenda". In the intervening years Sutherland has sought to make good on this with a whole system design and build service, encouraging and helping those who want to build their own homes (mostly) as well as offering architectural guidance where it is needed. The Straithnairn community woodland centre is a representative sampling of Sutherland's work, highlighting the significant community dimension underlying Sutherland's work as much as it does his local wood philosophy. The educational centre is made from Douglas fir sourced from the community's own wood, and then milled near to the site. From conventional architectural perspectives, perhaps, this isn't the sexiest of buildings, but for others looking to Sutherland's manifesto, the engagement with rural communities, working with low budgets, and without the sort of resources that are often assumed available in large metropolitan centres,

— **Taigh Chearsabhagh Arts Studio Extension**
Locate Architects

— **Talla Choinneachaidh**
Dualchas Building Design

— **Strathnairn Community Forest Shelter**
Neil Sutherland Architects

such aspects of Sutherland's determination are to be admired.

Compared to these examples the Aberdeen based architect Gokay Devici, emphasises the contemporary application of stone in far more detailed and sustained forms. His ceramics studio for the Danish potter Lotte Glob, is a case in point, providing an evocative counterpoint to his first building for the potter, the Lotte Glob House, which looks out over Loch Eriboll up on Sutherland's far northern shoreline. The result of patient collaboration between Glob and Devici, the studio is a simple yet beguiling piece of work which had to wait until the pair finally found Alan and Anne Warwick, the husband and wife stonemason team who carried out the main work. The re-used studio walls stones are from the original croft, or the crofting land Glob lives on. Symmetrical along its back façade, with four narrow light slits, the patio courtyard is surrounded by a continuation of an open wall, while the actual studio entrance comprises sliding glass doors, with timber cladding for its façade and a corrugated iron roof sitting on simple block work. The studio's stone masonry compliments the reason the building is there; Glob's ceramics, each part of a larger statement regarding tactility, craft and the felt world in the early twenty first century. Lean up against or run your hand across the stone surface of the wall, and then lift one of Glob's ceramic pieces and your body will feel and sense the differences as much as your eye will pick out information about their contrasting textural and visual qualities. These are as much about touch; the world both beyond the eye, and of eye and hand in concert, in the careful, understated work of craft.

In comparison with this quartet of high Northern examples, first contact with either the affordable housing of Oliver Chapman Architects (OCA) in the small Borders town of Swinton, or Murray Dunlop's Telford Drive, within Edinburgh respectively, suggests these two housing projects exist in a different category order. Look again at OCA's semi-detached house, sitting both as part of and apart from the small housing estate and again there is a sensitivity to what can be achieved through a careful attention to form and detailing. Using the volumes of the neighbouring semi's what may have felt like less than promising sources has been turned around into the still simple house, that is noticeably thought-provoking, providing a basis for how affordable housing budgets can achieve interesting aesthetic results, in this case Swinton's clear, clean aesthetic. Designed for the Berwickshire Housing Association, Chapman's Swinton house applies a range of sustainable strategies, including whole house ventilation, glazed sunspaces and rain water harvesting to ensure lower energy requirements. A timber post and frame, its immediate visual appeal relates the careful mix of stained Baltic larch across its lower half and cement fibre slates on both the upper walls and pitched roof, a strategy more recently repeated on the practice's Todlaw housing for disabled, completed earlier this year. There again is a reserve and modesty to the building, with both volume and farm edge site a reminder

— **Lotte Glob Studio**
Gokay Deveci

— **Swinton Affordable Housing**
Oliver Chapman

— **Housing, Telford Drive**
Gordon Murray + Alan Dunlop Architects

of the central place of agriculture to its lowland border country, and its cement-slate roofs drawing on Scottish architectural sobriety while also offering a way to frame such references in a lighter future. A similar resourcefulness can be found at Telford Drive, where tight budgetary constraints has been put to imaginative use by Murray Dunlop with just a few gestural touches. The slight contrast in the palette of bricks, along with the first floor cantilevering, and the soft pitching of the roofline all break the conventions of a low rise housing block. As Morten Sjaadtad infers in his Authenticity Reconsidered essay for this catalogue, "the scope for authenticity appears to be narrower in the city" as, when it is sought, sources for authentic precedents relating to place as much as the natural world are all but absent. At the same time, as Gordon Murray suggests, the fault-line between an architecture of attention-grabbing iconoclasm and one of reserve and restraint divides the profession. To what extent can one frame such self-effacing appeals within the language of authenticity? If, as I believe it is, the answer is yes, such housing projects as these, both at Telford Drive and Swinton sit alongside the rural exemplars framed within the same category.

The two cultural centres, one arts, the other visitor, represent different paradigms and emphases, bringing to both the Highlands and the northern Isles the world of cultural regeneration. If Gareth Hoskins Architects new Culloden battleground visitor building represents expressive drama lying low along a highland horizon, the Reiach & Hall Pier Arts Centre is a study in restraint. Culloden plays with its grid of hard rectilinear planes cutting into and extending across the open battlefield ridge. Two sharply contrasting right angled lines cross each other – one, the finely finished slate wall runs along the centre's external facade, the other, the building's timber ramp running up from the edge of the battlefield onto the buildings green roof – do much to relate the building, material-wise, to its place. Overtly modernist in form, these volumes play with the canon, even as the chosen materials make something of a localist link.

The long slate wall adds another layer of craftsmanship to that introduced by the stone masons at Lotte Glob's studio, while the timber stair berm shows how locally sourced Scottish larch can add to simple, functional decoration as well as to its primary requirement of external cladding. The building applies much of the latest low-energy technological kit to draw down its energy footprint, and shows a way of marrying contemporary modernist form with sustainability. This said Culloden is very much in the mould of cultural destination, and as a National Trust of Scotland site finds itself positioned oddly in any debates regarding the relation between cultural building type and historical context, even as it does so outside the conversation of vernacular and history.

A concern for the care implicit in craft practice is a clearer bridge between Glob's Sutherland studio and Reiach & Hall's Stromness Pier Arts Centre, the highly praised Stirling Prize contender in the Orkney Island town of Stromness. The Pier may have seemed out of character for Reiach & Hall, a firm known for office, commercial and infrastructure projects. Yet those visiting the Pier will immediately observe the extensions restraint, the quietness of its statement in its waterside context, the care with which both detailing and the craftsmanship have been carried out. Built onto an original Hudson Trading Company's building, the waterfront extension faces out to sea just as it would in Trondheim or any Norwegian Atlantic fishing port, to which the Orkneys as much

— **Culloden Battlefield Visitor Centre**
Gareth Hoskins Architects

— **Pier Arts Centre**
Reiach & Hall Architects

as the Shetlands, is still so signiifcantly bound. Wrapped in a skin of dark grey zinc, the use of such a contemporary material for the extension's façade is its most striking gesture, generating a texturally rich dialogue between old and new with both the Gallery's adjoining original stone premises and the red fishing shed clapperboard on its southern side. With the harbour-front windows used to deepen this compositional effect, and the long circulatory corridors of the internal exhibition space, the cut of the windows overlooking the harbour echoes the tilt of the original stone building's gable. Inside, the detailing, for instance the careful finish to the oak staircase, underlines the care with which the building approaches its use of materials. As an essay in materiality, the Pier is unusual in both the Scottish and British context.

Indeed, by making material its central qualitative and architectural gesture, Reiach & Hall are yoking this Orkney Island building to the materialities thread which is so much more pronounced across European, than in the Anglo-Saxon, architectural communities. This is perhaps only half the connection, but if we now move to Scotland's immediate northern neighbouring mainland, Norway, these concerns become quite as exquisitely evident in the work of the Oslo practice Jensen & Skodvin, as it is in each of the other regional European examples, Vorarlberg and Graubunden. So much so in fact, that Jensen & Skodvin are architects who engage with the natural material within the site as much as the manmade material that is brought for the building process. With several of their works they have worked topography; the contours of the natural world, be it in rock faces or the trunks of trees are integrated in Jenson & Skodvin's work into the heart of buildings and structures. Admittedly Norway is a country with some of the most dramatic and compelling natural environments in Europe, and in their strikingly poetic compositions the practice are surely responding to the experience of their mountainous land. At both their Mortensrud church and the Ropied ferry terminal the bedrock which the buildings have been built upon push through the man-made walls and floors. This is not the case with the Gudbransjuvet Hotel, a series of one or two bedroom huts deep in the woody gorges of Geiranger Trollstigen, near Alesund in central Norway, part of the partners latest contribution to the country's De-tour programme. Here a mix of wood and glass have been dropped into the wooded valley, by turns wild and dramatic, to make up the small collection of modern huts. Providing guests with an unusual closeness to the environment, while maintaining a degree of creature comforts that would not be possible sleeping out under the stars, the sensuality of Jensen & Skodvin's work is evident in how nature is generously and evocatively mirrored in the hut-hotels large scaled windows. Even if the partnership demote conventional interpretations of sustainability in favour of their sensuous topographical and material sensibility, Jensen & Skodvin have developed a language which speaks to and of the Norwegian land and landscape. The challenge may be how to reconcile this within the constraints of zero carbon footprints.

By contrast Brendeland & Kristoffersen's Svartlamoen nursery, within the Atlantic shoreline city of Trondheim is an exercise in urban, social and ecological thinking. Brendeland & Kristoffersen came to notice after completing their low energy, three-storey, massive wood residential social housing in the same street. Three years later, as part of a more extensive master planning of the rundown district, one of the adjacent buildings, a onetime car salesroom, has been converted into a nursery based on the post-war pedagogical principles of the Italian town Reggio Emilia. This anonymous industrial unit can be construed as part of the vernacular urban fabric; a building which would have otherwise disappeared unlamented. While the external façade remains in place, the architects have divided up the internal space, radically re-orienting the building into a series of uniquely resolved timber divided rooms. Both in terms of social and sustainable agendas Brendeland & Kristoffersen show how remaking the old can be as exciting as making the new.

If Norway is close to Scotland, and the two countries geographical proximity demonstrates how differently two cultural landscapes evolve, by comparison Vorarlberg and Graubunden are in the next metaphorical, and almost literal, valley to each other. Yet each has developed different and singular identities. That said there are many similarities and overlaps. They are in each regions in Alpine countries, Austria and Switzerland respectively. They also share, as with Scotland and Norway, a mountainous terrain.

The two Vorarlberg exhibition examples demonstrate the longevity of this dynamic European architectural region. Cucrowicz Nachbaur Bureau are part of the third generation of the Vorarlberg scene, while Christoph Kalb arguably represents an emerging fourth generation. Kalb's social housing was for seven families who banded together to commission a set of buildings which met their needs and desires, is an update of the strong housing emphasis of the Vorarlbergers. This social housing project in the small town of Wolfort recalls something of the early days of what is called the Vorarlberg Baukunstler, from which the second, most influential generation of architects emerged. At the time in the late seventies (as Robert Fabach relates in his essay contribution) these Vorarlberg architects designed their first work for friends and professional colleagues, as ongoing conflict with the then current planning bureaucracies made it otherwise almost impossible to build. It is from these social and ecological beginnings that housing, rather than cultural showcases, has become the influential lynch-pin to Vorarlberg's architectural identity. Kalb's small-scale co-operative venture, which replaced a developer's three storey proposal the residents found wanting, echoes those earlier times even if it is hardly on the scale of the work of the leading Vorarlberg practice, Baumschlager-Eberle's thirty year mission to raise the bar across the housing typology, from social, cultural through to sustainable. Vorarlberg's message, as others have noted, may well be this social dimension, a message which has gone out far and wide, making this small county or 'land' internationally known.

One can frame aspects of the social housing at Telford Drive and Swinton, as well as Svartlamoen in Trondheim within the same comprehensive trajectory found in Vorarlberg. This contrasts to Graubunden, which cannot be said to be so unambivalently identified with the questions attending social housing. This is what Vorarlberg arguably represents, an exemplar — where, incidentally all new domestic housing will be required by law to meet passive standards from the beginning of 2009 — for new standards in the often overlooked though critical building typology, house and home, that is, where so many of the planet's population actually live.

CucrowiczNachbaur's contribution highlights another critical aspect of the Vorarlberg scene. How the outlying reaches of Vorarlberg, particularly the farming and forested Bregenzerwald, has been a central, active part of the emergence of this local architectural and building culture. With poor soil, wood, as Dietmar Eberle has repeatedly pointed out, was the only

— **Juvet Landscape Hotel**
Jensen & Skodvin Architects

— **Frühling — Spring**
architekturwerk THE EDGE

— **Svartlamoen Nursery**
Brendeland & Kristoffersen arkitekter

resource which the region contained on any scale. When fused with the long carpentry and joinery tradition this became a key to the growth of Vorarlberg's architectural culture; in effect a natural building material co-joined with the skills to deliver the buildings. Today, far from being a backwater, the Bregenzerwald is one of the most dynamic wood industry centres across the entire Southern German speaking part of central Europe. Cucrowicz Nachbaur's small Bregenzerwald chapel reflects the continuing agricultural dimension of Vorarlberg life; the chapel is for a farmer's family sitting within view of the farm and at rest on Alpine meadows. Designed and built from the farmer's immediate stands, the timber chapel harks back to the traditional chapels of earlier eras. Cucrowicz Nachbaur having taken the age-old Alpine Strickbau form and designed a simple stopping place of shelter and reflection. Those who rest within its wooden walls, whether visitor or farming family, are held within the timber shell, separated and reassured by the warm materiality of the small building's living material. Small devotional chapels go back almost literally thousands of years in the Allegmanic Alpine cultures, and this is a poignant example of just how alive religious devotion remains in central Europe. Such a point may or may not hold our attention for a moment or two, but what is equally striking about the chapel, one of the newest of the buildings exhibited, is the active involvement of the farming clients. It was they who organised a competition for local Vorarlberg architects to participate in, and then played a full and significant part in much of the resulting decision making for site and building; a graphic reminder of how the umbilical link between local materials, culture, crafts people, client and architect continues in Vorarlberg, unbroken to this day.

The local is also a key into the Graubunden canton, although distinctively different to that of Vorarlberg. Less than 90 minutes drive or train journey Graubunden is far more mountainous than its Austrian valley-rich neighbour. The small villages, as with all these regional exemplars, face the challenge of how to hold onto their diminishing populations drawn to the opportunities urban towns and cities offer. If there is an embeddedness in place common to both these regional cultures, there has also been a similar return to vernacular, to craft and to place. In Vorarlberg, however, there is no-one comparable to Gion Caminada, the Rhaeto-Romansch architect who has made his base his home village of Vrin high in the Sulveda mountains of Western Graubunden. Caminada is a self-described village architect who has been building houses, farm buildings, a school and other buildings and structures required by the community he lives in and is part of, since the 1990s. It has made him known around the world and provides a singular way of working, wholly at odds with Globalisation and the architects who pursue its model. Much of Caminada's work has explored the potential for developing contemporary languages out of what for many is the closed book of local vernacular building

— **Mountain Chapel**
Cukrowicz Nachbaur Architekten

— **Terrihütte**
Gion A. Caminada Architect

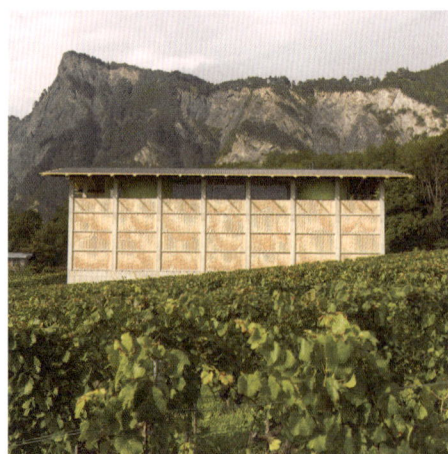

— **Extension Winery Gantenbein**
Bearth & Deplazes Architekten

form, notably in this part of Graubunden, the timber 'Strickbau' knitting of timbers into strong, long-lasting structures, resilient to the strictures of Alpine winter. At the same time the considerable design element is absolutely contemporary and unsentimental. The Caminada Bureau's most recent building, the Greina mountain lodge, further up in the mountains above Vrin, is only accessible by two hours walking or by helicopter. Basic in services, Alpine mountain lodges are a long held Swiss tradition, continuing to this day. The Greina lodge reiterates Caminada's repeated exploration of the Swiss chalet form, although instead of timber cladding, Greina's Swiss mountain association's three storeys are constructed from stone as much as wood. Inside fresh timber makes up the internal finishes, the detailing revealing a simple minimal aesthetic. It is noteworthy that Caminada, (and also Peter Zumthor) began his working life as a cabinet-maker. This is directly comparable to a number of the original Vorarlberger Baukunstlers, who began their working lives as carpenters before becoming architects. Although Caminada also holds a post teaching at the Zurich ETHZ, his work remains firmly rooted in the small village community from which he came. In this he has become a hero of sorts for his commitment to a way of working, which many believe to be dead and buried across so much of the developed world. The question that an encounter with Caminada's work poses refers to the meaning of architecture; who and what building buildings is for?

The other example from Graubunden pushes the envelope in a completely different, albeit related, direction. Bearth & Deplazes are among the best known of the established Graubunden practices, their bureau has been partially determined by an attention to form and a willingness to experiment with the everyday materials palette of concrete and timber. Through a number of individual houses, along with various well-considered public building commissions, the bureau have become respected throughout Switzerland and the regions beyond the country's borders. With one of their most recent commissions the bureau have completed a showcase which may well draw a new generation of architects to this eastern Swiss canton. The dimensions and form of the Gantenbein winery in the village of Flasch, relate and observe the original self-built wine yard barn. And yet the building's materials – or rather, what has been done with them – is pretty much completely unique. Using a robotic arm the wine yard barn's external façade brickworks have been individually placed to micro-millimetre managed detail so that their precise angling and positioning create an optical illusion effect. The precision required is to the level of detail that would be impossible to achieve through human eye-to-hand co-ordination. One consequence is the reversal of the usual skills assumed to be the privilege of skill and of craft. Here robotics, what its new media architectural designers, Gramazio & Kohler, describe as digital materiality, is completing a process which is too refined for the human hand to accomplish. The effect, in terms of its perforated facade, is remarkable, and as such the use of this technology brings a whole new layer to the identity of the Graubunden architectural region. It seems to be outside the writ of being considered in pragmatic and protestant Vorarlberg. Just as digital materiality introduces additional dimensions to our understanding of materiality, to skill and to craft, so also it, perhaps, re-maps the meanings of the vernacular.

If the Bearth & Deplazes wine yard is the most singular and radical appropriation of vernacular building form, all these projects provide an evocative canvas to gauge the diverse currents currently running through the resurgent wave of regionalist architectures. If some ground themselves in readily recognisable interpretations of this architectural slipstream, all seem in different and/or overlapping ways, to be facing, rather than denying, elements of the new conditions building culture finds itself in the early twenty-first century.

— The Projects
Scotland

P.35

—P.36
—Project Name
Lotte Glob Studio

6mm

Projects
P.36

Lotte Glob

Architect
Gokay Deveci

Location
Laid Croft, Loch Eriboll, Durness, Sutherland, Scotland

Client
Lotte Glob

Budget
£60,000

Completion Date
June 2007

Build Time
6 Months

Building use
Ceramic Studio

Lotte Glob is a Danish ceramic artist whose practice is closely identified with the wilderness landscape in North-West Scotland. Initially she commissioned a house (completed in 2004) that would enable her to integrate her practice, business and lifestyle. She stipulated that the design should be affordable and context-sensitive, as well as complementing her aesthetic vision and reflecting her passion for the light across the hills of Sutherland.

On completion of the house, Lotte Glob commissioned a studio that would adhere to the same principles. Embedded within the contours of the landscape, the studio reflects the local vernacular architecture in Sutherland. The 60m^2 studio space comprises a double-height internal working and exhibition space with a large south orientated terrace, and a compact service space. Roofed with rust-coloured corrugated iron and finished internally with local pine boarding, the external construction is blockwork faced with reclaimed stone. The internal structure is insulated timber framing, finished with plywood. Large sliding glazed doors allow the studio space to spill out onto the terrace and give views of Ben Hope and Loch Eriboll. Two wing walls at west and east create a frame for an evolving sculpture garden.

In five years, inspired by her creativity and determination, Lotte Glob has transformed an area of barren windblown rocks into a landmark where people can visit and be inspired both by the monumental nature of the landscape and by her own sculptural artworks created in response to it.

Set in a remote and dramatic landscape, the innovative design proposes new planning strategies, typologies, site response and building construction detailing in rural architecture. The main objective was to have as low an impact on its setting as possible whilst applying the affordable construction and low energy principles.

Materials were chosen that would weather in colour and texture, ageing gracefully in harmony with changes in the seasons. The design incorporates local materials wrought by the local workforce.

View showing the house in the foreground and the studio behind.

Projects
P.38

Lotte Glob

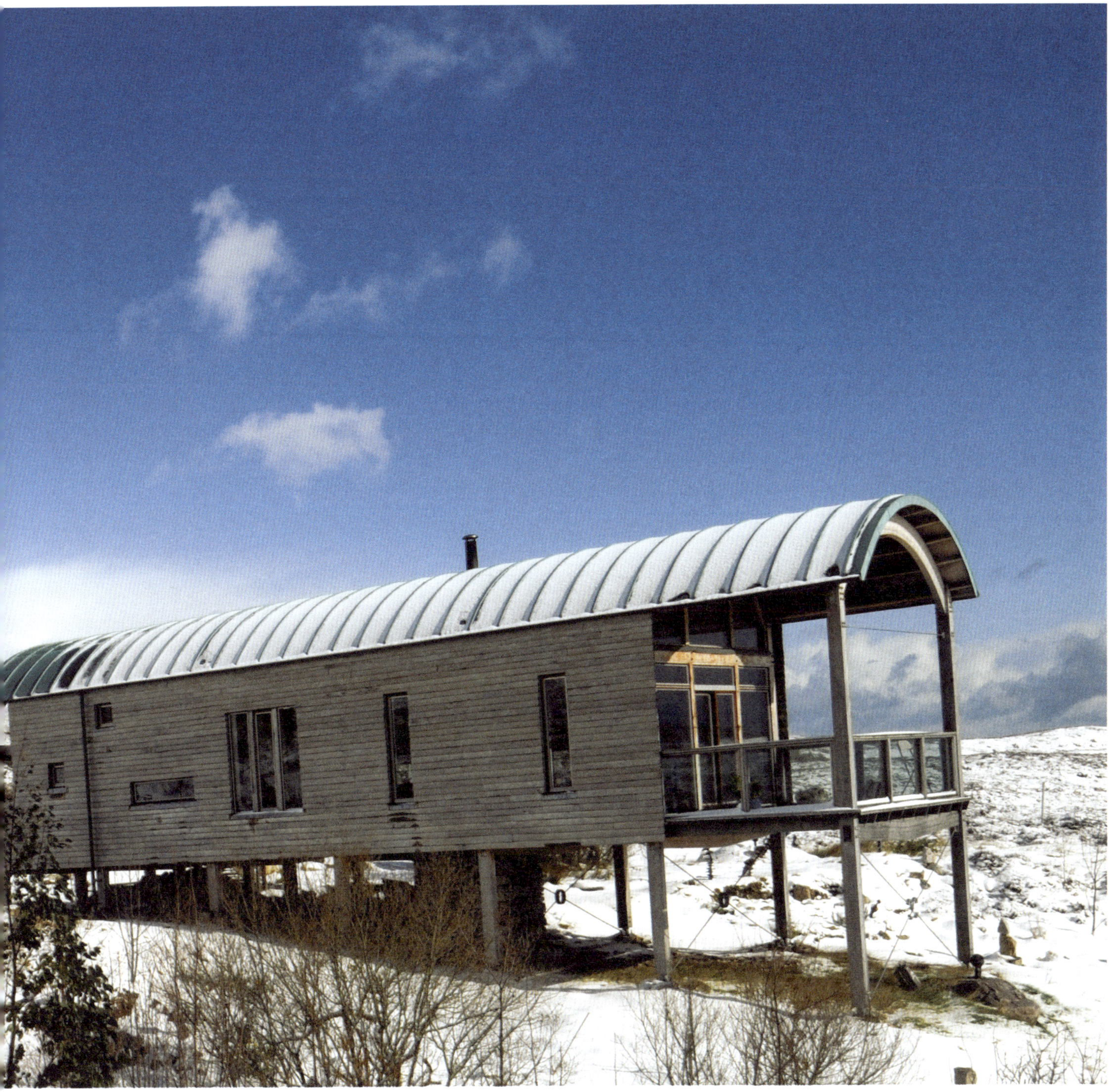

Projects
P.40

Lotte Glob

P.41

The Story
Lotte Glob

My dream place: from a young age I always wanted to live and work by water, rocks and wood with wide open distances, spaces and mountains – with land to create a sculpture croft – remote yet near to a small community.

At Loch Eriboll I am surrounded by rocks and stones – small ruined crofts from the clearance time, a 2000 year old wheel house on the hill, endless stone dykes marking the boundary of the crofts, the glacial slabs of rocks on the hillside, the shore line of rocks at Loch Eriboll of mostly quart site and pipe rock, beautifully built old lime kilns of rocks. In my wood fired kiln, partly build with rocks, I re-fire the rocks into my sculptures. It came naturally to me that my studio should also be build out of the Loch Eriboll rock and rocks from the old ruin – like a hill fort. All the rocks and stones from the old ruin at my croft were reused for the studio.

As well as the solid feeling of rocks I wanted wood and light to be included in the build – the smell and the sound of wood and large glass doors and windows to let the light in. In this, my Loch Eriboll new age 'fort', the outside can come in. I feel secure with the surround of the heavy stone walls with their long elegant slit windows at the back facing north – the light and openness facing the Loch and Hope.

I am protected from the weather and road above and I can let the weather into the studio when it is kind. I am cosy with my wood stove in the winter – easy to light, smelling and sounding good. In the dark days of winter when the gales are raging I am warm and happy watching the storm, listening to music with a blazing fire in the wood stove – happy working. When the sun comes out, doors are open. I move out in the sun with work.

What affects it?
Time – as a ruin the old warehouse is still part of the landscape.

— Interior of studio.

— Where is it and why?
Inspired by the monumental nature of landscape and artist's artwork created in response to it.

— Why choose these materials?
Minimum palette of recycled materials were chosen that would weather in colour and texture ageing gracefully.

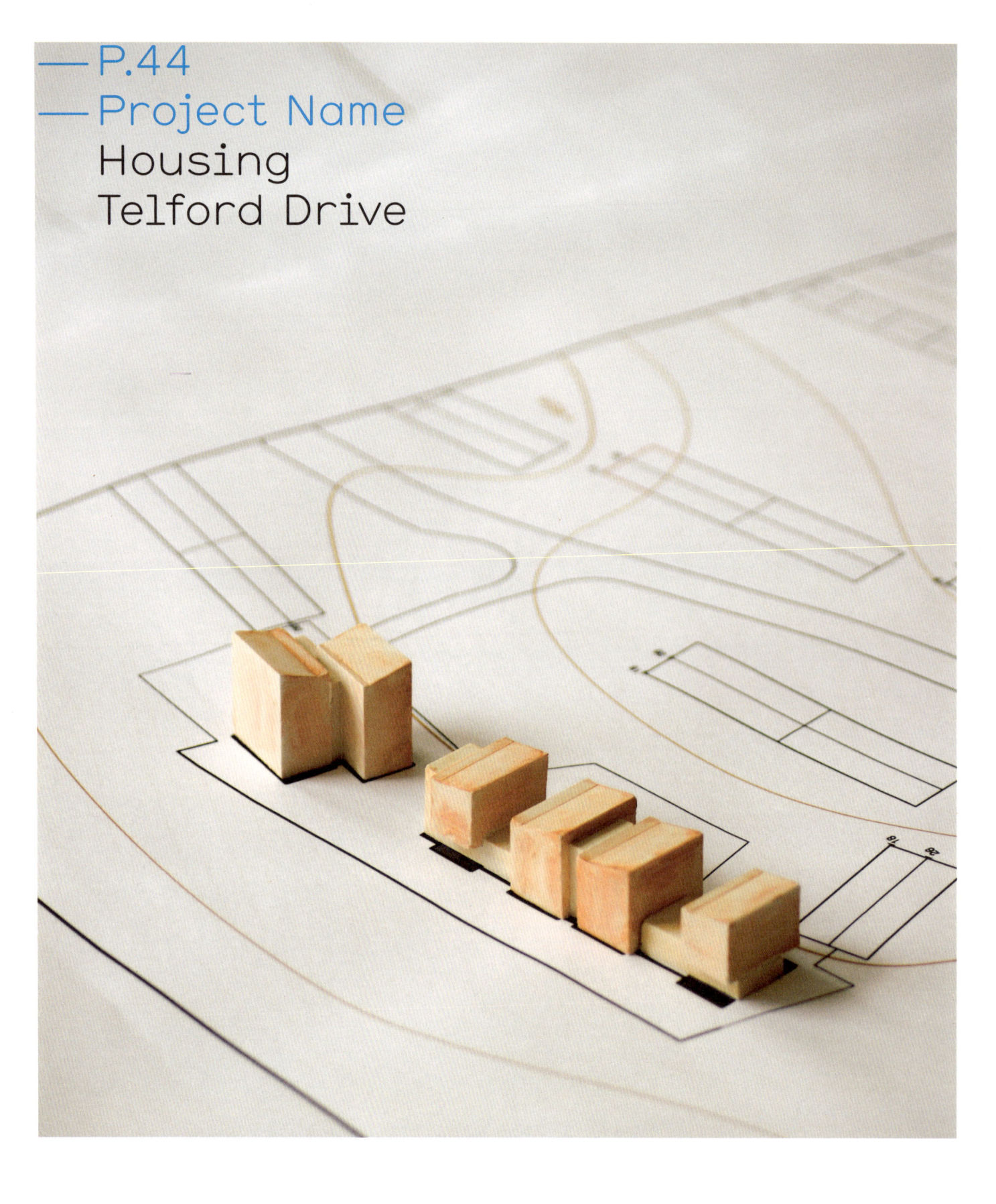

— P.44
— Project Name
Housing
Telford Drive

- **Architect**
Gordon Murray + Alan Dunlop Architects
- **Location**
Telford Drive, Edinburgh
- **Client**
Manor Estates Housing Association
- **User**
As above
- **Budget**
£1.7million
- **Completion Date**
June 2006
- **Build Time**
14 months
- **Building use**
Residential (social housing)

Telford Drive is a housing development for Manor Estates Housing Association comprising 20 units, 4 of which are for tenants of 'varying needs'.

The terrace and tower that have been built were developed as phase one of a larger 'masterplan' but were designed to act as a stand-alone development. A temporary landscaped strip replaces the 'landscaped street' until completion of the future phases, and provides a shared space for all residents.

The client, whilst ambitious for a progressive design, had a very specific and prescriptive briefing document. The buildings have been designed to adapt to the varying needs of the residents over their lifetime with the integration of several fully accessible flats on the ground floors, as well as flexible and easily changeable layouts above, which allow for various family groups, providing flexibility and choices in the way people live.

The design creates shared terraced gardens for residents at first floor level maximising amenity for the residents. Projecting 'winter gardens' maximise the south-west aspect of the blocks and allow a visual connection to the 'landscaped street'. Sustainable principles were adopted throughout, emphasising social interaction, personalisation of spaces whilst maintaining levels of privacy and encouraging a feeling of ownership.

The main block (a) of phase one is made up of four brick 'towers' which cantilever off the first floor podium. These form shared terraced spaces, and begin to define external spaces below. The stair cores are generous with extended glazed landings, which begin to encourage the residents to use them as conservatory spaces and allow for individual expression.

The 'tower' block' (b) comprises eight flats in a tenemental arrangement, articulated as two shifting blocks. The projecting windows are all south facing.

The design has a northern European feel and warm, simply detailed brickwork is complimented with western red cedar boarding and timber windows.

Their proposals form part of a larger masterplan currently being undertaken by gm+ad for EDI.

Projects
P.46

Housing
Telford Drive

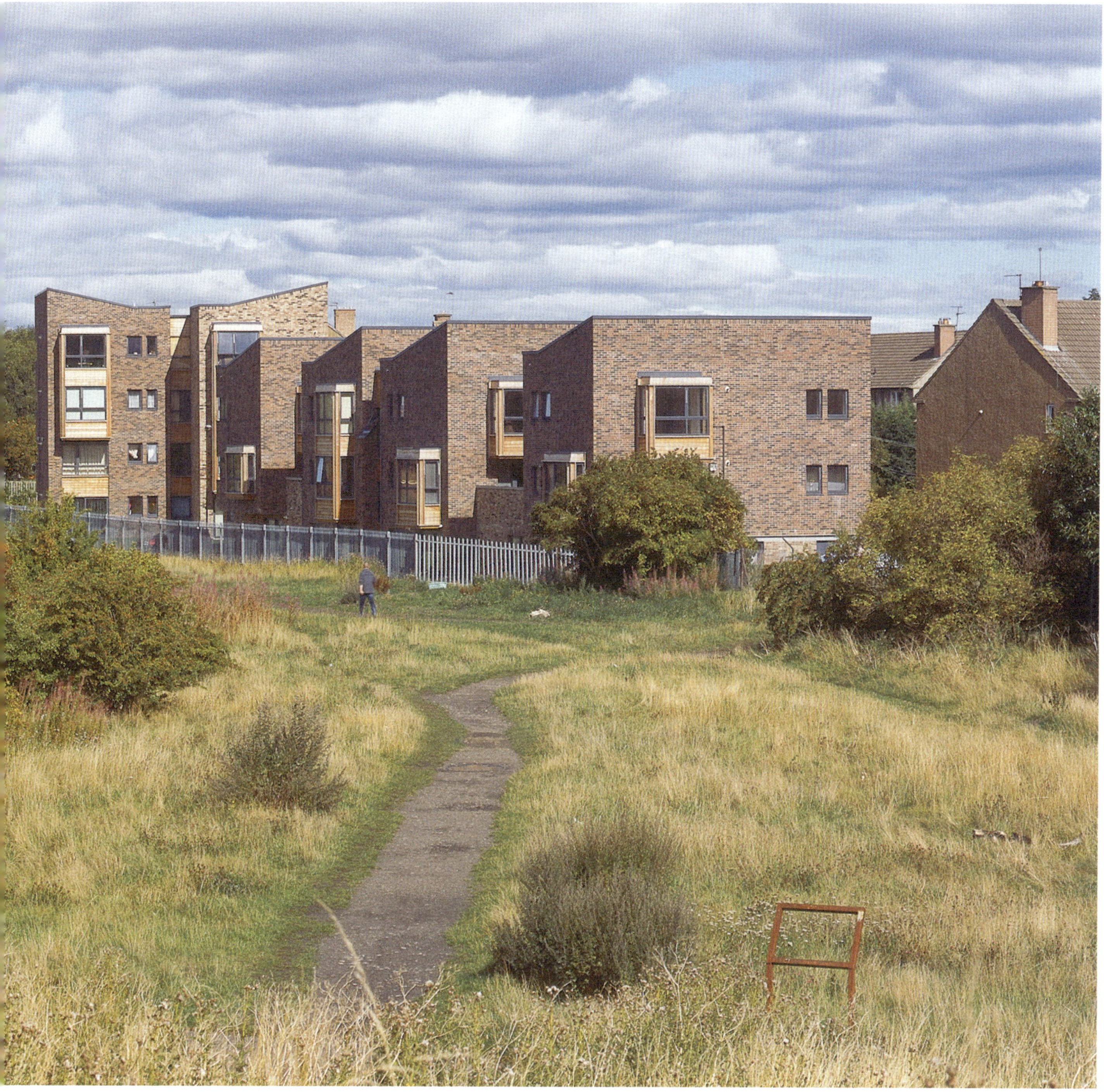

The Story
Stacey Philips

In many ways Telford Drive was an absolute dream of a project, a change in scale for the office and our first new build affordable housing project. It represented a real opportunity to design housing with a real social conscience, which not only established a new community but also had to regenerate and encourage an existing one.

The ambition of the client, at Manor Estates Housing Association, to initiate improvements to the local environment provided us with the scope to explore the notion of community: could architectural moves, on a small scale, encourage interaction and involvement?

One of the critical aspects was the belief that architects have a responsibility to provide 'homes' — or at least the basis for them.

"A house is a home when it shelters the body and comforts the soul…" Phillip Moffitt.

This demanded the exploration of fundamental principles — how do we create a defined and shared set of ground rules. Themes such as interaction, individualism, privacy, openness, belonging, ownership, pride, and threshold — all influenced the design of the scheme.

The design concept looked at creating a focus — a shared central space open to all residents. Spaces then filter from entirely public to semi public / semi private to private gardens at the building edges, almost allocated as small allotments to encourage the residents to take ownership of these areas.

"Public housing is more than just a place to live, public housing projects should provide opportunities to residents and their families…" Carolyn McCarthy.

Ownership of space is fundamental to its success. Establishing an opportunity for residents to express themselves was considered in several ways and defining opportunities for personalisation became a priority of the scheme.

Telford Drive was a really rewarding experience and a great relationship with a client, who completely understood the issues facing their residents, significantly encouraged our design philosophy.

Projects
P.48

Housing
Telford Drive

— **Where is it and why?**
Client's ambition to improve the locale, to provide a sense of place and belonging for new and existing residents.

— **What affects it?**
Habitation… the importance of expression in the personalisation of spaces and a sense of ownership…here is where my world makes sense — no sign of man's indifference.

— **What were the influences?**
Salk Institute, Louis Khan
"reduced to the maximum…"
Gordon Cameron Murray
"no unnecessary applied aesthetics…"
Ruth Morro, Duncan of Jordanstone

Projects
P.50

Housing
Telford Drive

P.51

— P.52
— Project Name
Swinton
Affordable
Housing

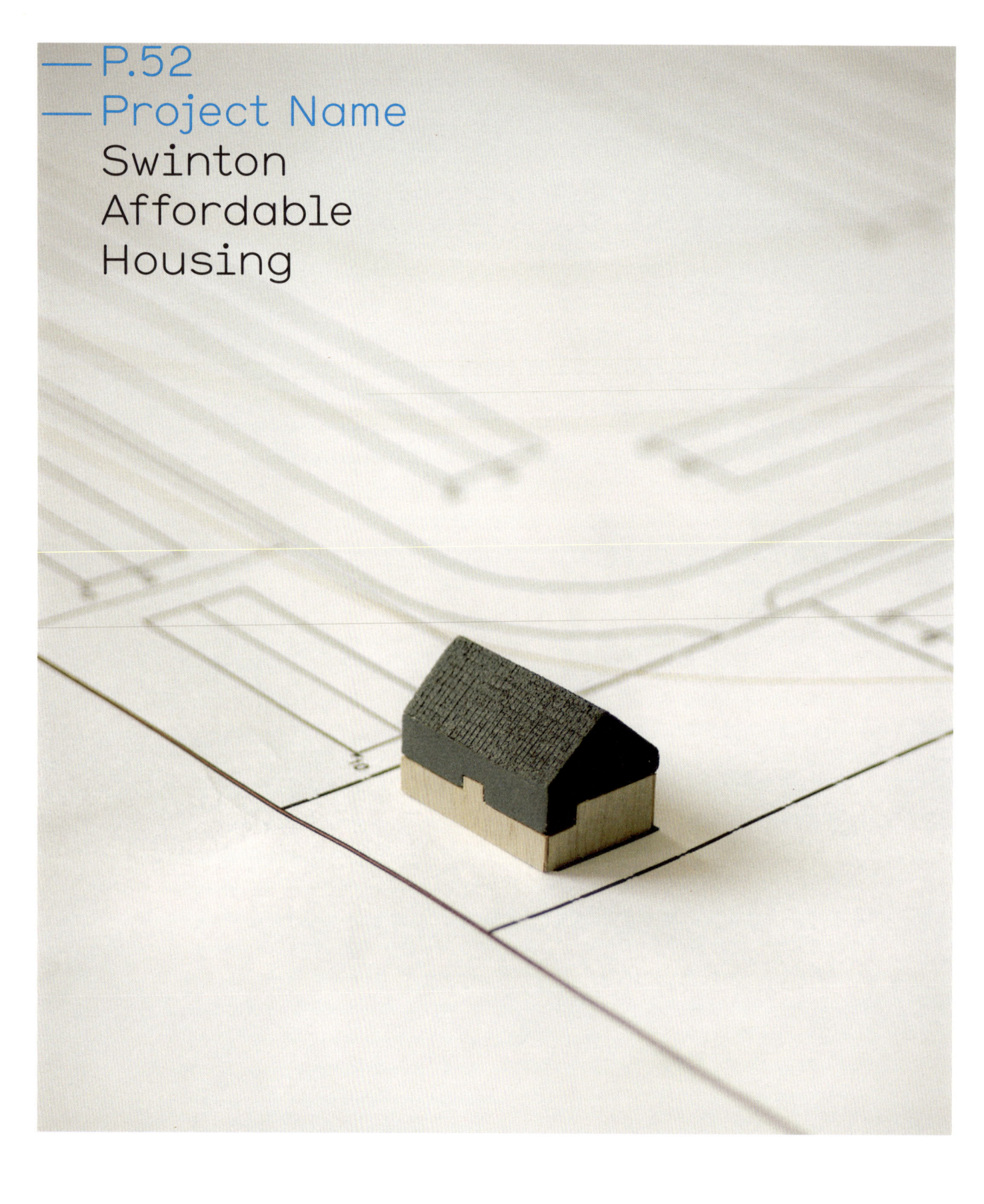

- **Architect**
  Oliver Chapman
- **Location**
  Wellfield, Swinton, Berwickshire
- **Client**
  Berwickshire Housing Association
- **User**
  Client and tenants
- **Budget**
  £80,000 per house
- **Completion Date**
  December 2006
- **Build Time**
  6 months
- **Building use**
  Affordable Housing

Designed and built for Berwickshire Housing Association for rent at an affordable price, this prototypical pair of three bedroom, semi-detached houses set out to raise the standards of sustainable design in residential developments. Energy conservation methods employed include the collection of solar energy through a whole house ventilation and water heating system, glazed sunspaces and rain water harvesting.

The appearance of a simple form of a house has been achieved by detailing flush junctions between walls and roof pitches, recessed rainwater downpipes and discreet details to conceal cavity barriers. The built form reflects the commonly understood archetype of a house – a duo pitched roof with gables and no additional protruding secondary forms. Seen from the street the form contextually responds to the building line and ridge heights of its neighbours. Seen across fields on approach to the village it reads as a silhouette on the slight ridge of a hill, much as an agricultural building's form is seen across a landscape.

The construction is lightweight and quick to erect. Well insulated breathable timber frame walls are clad in cement fibre slates and timber boarding. Rather than use external materials to identify conventional elements like wall and roof planes and windows, the rainscreen cladding appears to wrap the exterior with little obvious visual articulation of the eaves and verge details – emphasising the 'form' rather the planar 'walls' and 'roofs' elements. Dressed and stained Baltic larch is used board on board on the lower half of the building.

Energy conservation strategies for the project include both renewable and passive systems. An integrated solar system allows solar thermal energy to produce hot water, hot air, air cooling and ventilation. This system can reduce the running costs by 50%. The roof mounted solar air collectors are fitted on the south facing roof. Heated water is provided by the hot water cylinder which is connected into the system. A rainwater harvesting system is also installed.

Projects
P.54

Swinton Affordable
Housing

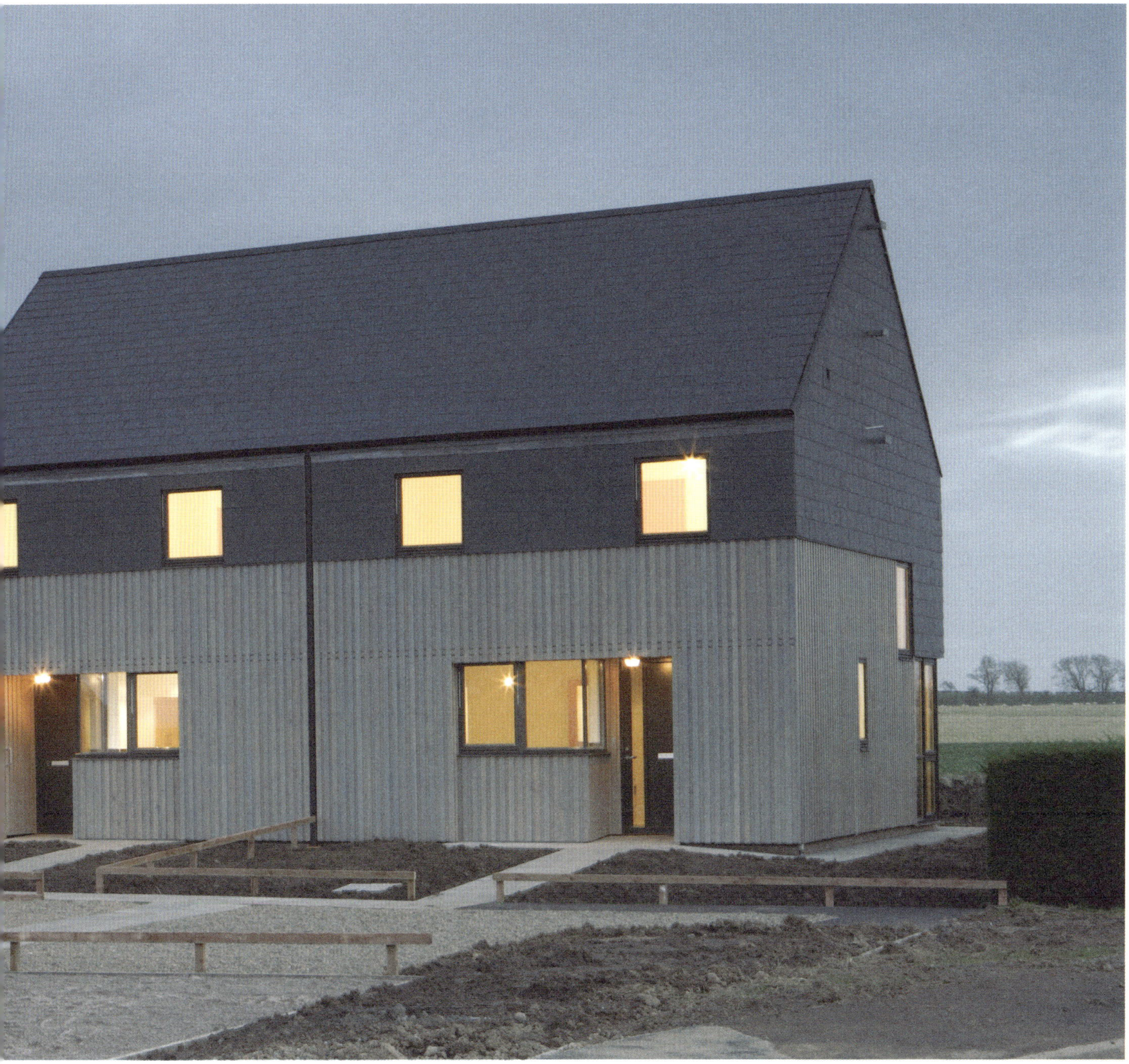

The Story
Oliver Chapman

Architects are trained to challenge conventions, not to just repeat solutions without questioning first principles. But do we all agree on what those conventions are when it comes to housing? Bedrooms upstairs, must have a chimney, door at the front? Ill-considered assumptions and generalisations about house owners, or in this case tenants' expectations lead to patronising decisions on how a house should look. Adding dormers and porches and using render on walls and concrete tiles on the roof dilutes the final product into a watery version of its neighbours.

What can one safely assume are conventions worth working with? Is it the outer covering of materials or the form?

We accepted what we understood to be the conventional form – a pitched roofed gable ended form. In the terms of the surrounding houses and the Scottish house building industry this form is prevalent and cost efficient. The planning of the rooms was tightly constrained to avoid the need for dormers, or projecting porches or projecting sun spaces. Instead porches and sun spaces are recessed, with the added benefit that the storey above limits excessive solar gain in the summer when the sun is high in the sky.

Challenging conventions was more appropriate when choosing the outer covering. The skin is deliberately lightweight and supported directly off the timber frame panels, relieving us of the need for the usual concrete block outer level (often rendered) and wider supporting foundations. This reduces the cost but also the embodied energy of more masonry and concrete. The materials and detailing of the fibre cement tiles and the timber is intended to have the quality of a dressmaker; an 'empire line' seam separates timber from tile below the first floor window, a stitch line marks the mundane line of the horizontal cavity barrier, and the tiles wrap over the eaves and verge without creases.

Why make it like this?
Archetypal, universally recognised form of a home.

What were the influences?
Dressmaker's details affect the appearance of the outer skin of materials; an 'empire line' seam separates timber from tile below the first floor window.

Projects
Swinton Affordable Housing

— **What does it feel like?**
It has two identities; one similar to most modern agricultural buildings whose geometric form contrasts with a rolling landscape setting.

— P.57

Projects
P.58

Swinton Affordable
Housing

P.59

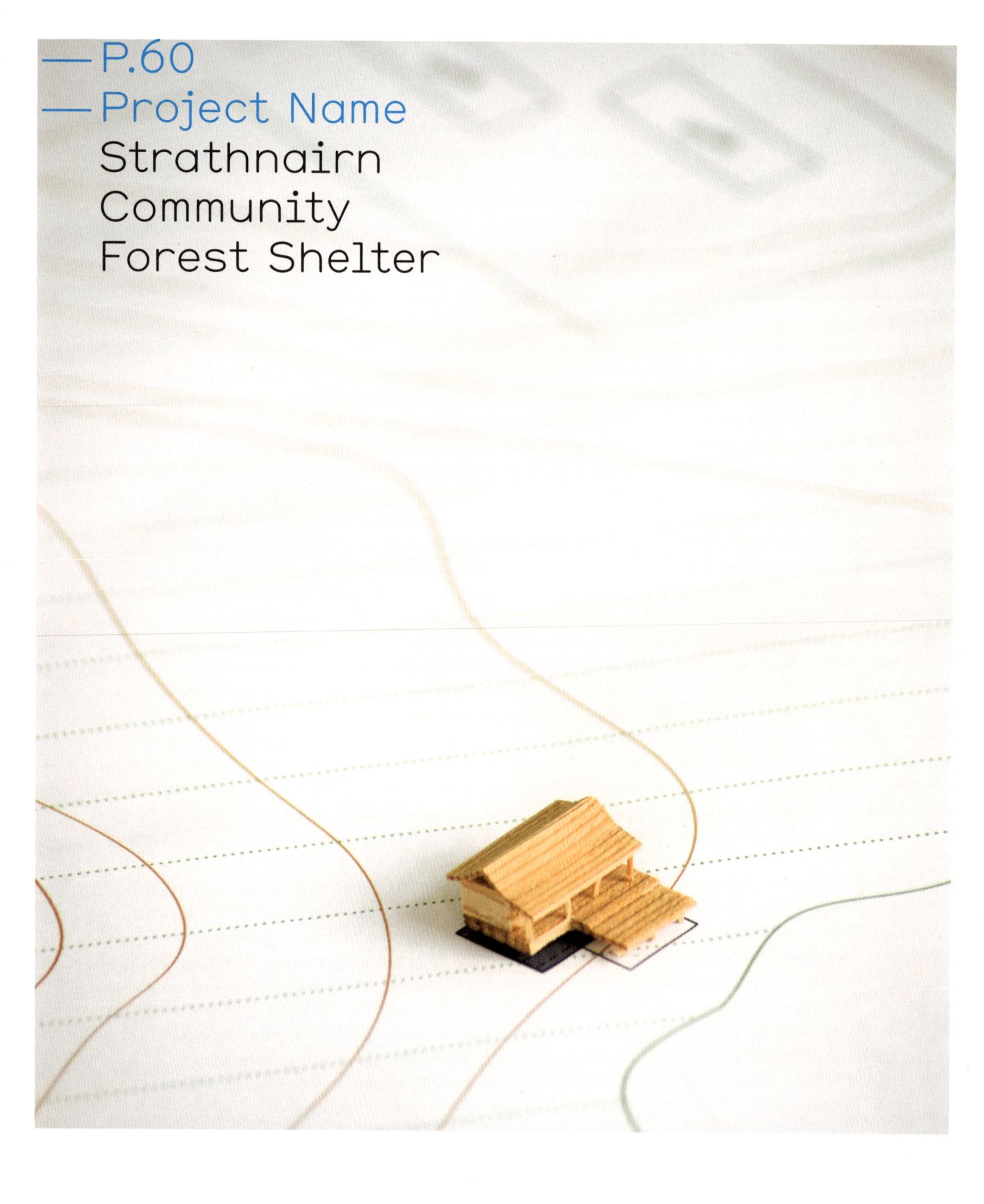

— P.60
— Project Name
Strathnairn
Community
Forest Shelter

Projects
P.60

Strathnairn Community
Forest Shelter

- Architect
Neil Sutherland Architects LLP
- Location
School Wood, Farr, Inverness
- Client
Strathnairn Community Woodland Group
- User
Strathnairn Community Woodland Group, local school and community
- Budget
£40,000
- Completion Date
Spring 2006
- Build Time
3 months
- Building use
Outdoor classroom

The new structure promotes increased use of the woodland by the community – providing a gathering point and focus for activities. It is also used by the local primary school located 200 metres away.

The structure was conceived as a flexible space anticipating a wide variety of uses and functions. It is made up of three elements; a large deck, sheltering roof and forty square metres of enclosable space – which fully opens up to the deck through vertical opening doors. The structure sits tight within its forest context, so tight that one tree grows through the decking which steps to follow the natural slope of the site.

The timber construction is from selected trees, felled and transported five miles, returned once pre-finished for rapid construction. The two timber species used are European Larch and Douglas Fir. They have different properties; strength, workability, season-ability, durability. The nature of each material allowed them to be complimentary within a construction context.

An innovative design-build arrangement was used where the architect's sister construction company carried out the construction for an agreed fixed price. With the designers then working for the contractor their combined experience ensured the project was delivered on budget, on time and as originally conceived.

In recent times communities and individuals have woken up to the potential for real benefit offered by forestry and woodlands. This project acknowledges and aims to make a contribution to the rediscovery of a timber culture currently gaining pace in areas such as the Highlands. To perceive an elegant and functional structure formed by trees that have been grown locally is a fresh and dramatic experience for many. Value connections are rapidly made between the multiple benefits of forest land-use and cultural worth leading to associations of health, creativity, local materials, a sense of place and the interconnection of people and the built and natural environment.

Projects — P.62 — Strathnairn Community Forest Shelter

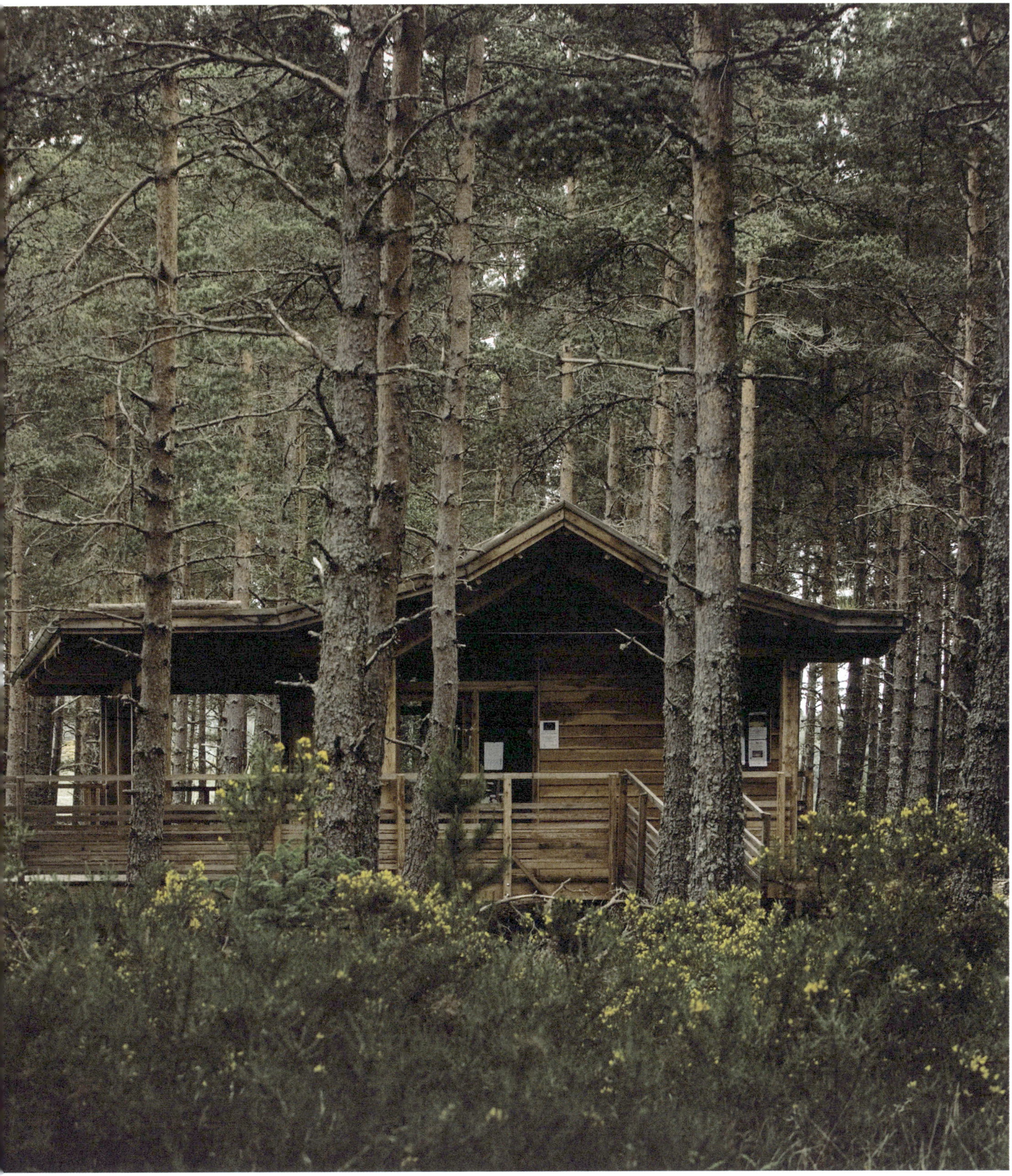

Projects
P.64

Strathnairn Community
Forest Shelter

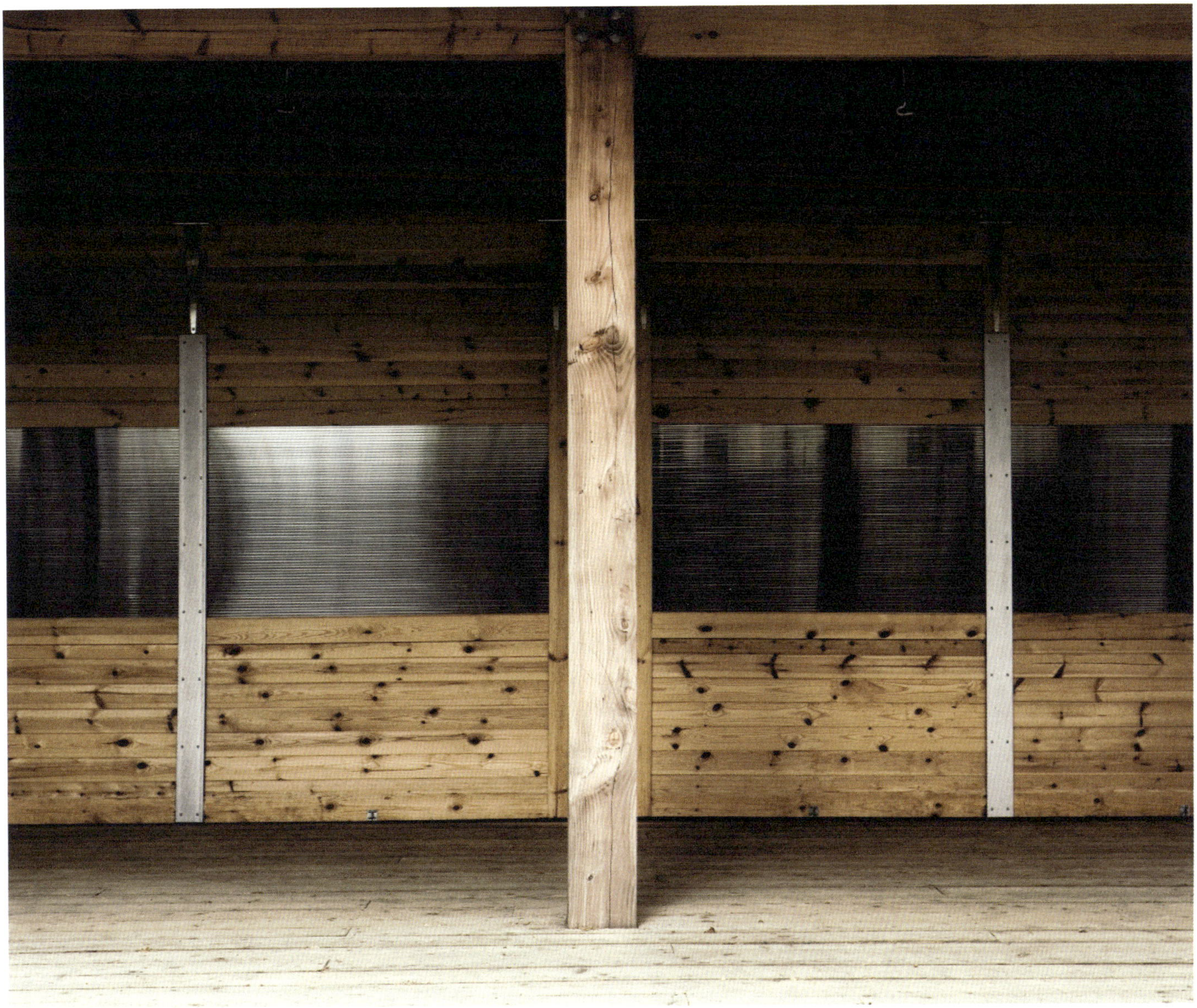

What does it feel like?
The shelter is structurally rational and spacially fluid. It combines warmth — something familiar; pitched roof / depth of timber colour, with a cool directness — something unfamiliar; contemporary form, echos of other cultures distant in time and place.

Projects
P.66

Strathnairn Community
Forest Shelter

— The Story
— Neil Sutherland

A representative of Strathnairn Community Woodland invited us to deliver a timber building for forty thousand pounds within an eight month period. The programme and budget were finite and how we got this done was down to us. The brief was not defined and we had a free hand to define this also.

The general site was identified close to the primary school. It quickly transpired that the school hoped to make use of the building in an informal way. We approached the school and I was invited to give a presentation on architecture to a mixed age class of fifteen or so and to lead a discussion. I sought out images from across the world which told the story of our collective search for suitable building forms; expressive, beautiful and engaging. Black-houses, Igloo's, Japanese Temples, African huts, brick, timber and stone houses. I talked about the snowflake structure and how and why a building's own expression is defined by its structure and construction. The only memorable question was whether a building could be built from cheese.

As ever, once the programme was defined the design concept came quickly – a day of drawing and a late afternoon meeting at the school and we had our building – on paper. Trees were identified, budget derived and agreed, contract written, health & safety consultant consulted, we were building. Trees and cut logs were moved to our yard and converted into sections, pre formed into structure and erected. Almost everything was pre-formed and made from materials derived from the locality, metal fixings, doors, windows, decking etc.

The woodland shelter was opened to 100+ locals and a puppet show in June 2006. Characteristically the community were quietly appreciative of the proceeding construction process. What had changed however was the connection with their trees.

— Why choose these materials?
Scottish sourced timber is generally regarded as inferior in quality to timber sourced from outwith the country. This irrational position is rooted in our abstract/confused connection with land-resource-use and our collective history of colonial plunder and international trade.

— What affects it?
Pine needles, snow, wind and rain – sometimes light sometimes torrential. Sunlight filtered through straight pines. Human feet, laughter, serious discussion, children combining learning and fun. Insects, birds and animals of all colours and sizes.

—P.68
—Project Name
The Pier
Arts Centre

Architect
Reiach & Hall Architects

Location
Victoria Street,
Stromness, Orkney

Client
Pier Arts Centre

Budget
£2.8 million

Completion Date
November 2006

Build Time
19 months

Building use
Arts venue

The Pier Arts Centre originates from the internationally important Margaret Gardiner Collection of St.Ives artists. The Pier holds this collection, which is constantly being extended and added to, and temporary gallery spaces for local and international artists.

It sits within a conservation area of outstanding merit on the water's edge in the harbour of Stromness. The detailed design development and execution of the three architectural 'houses' forming the new Pier Arts Centre presented different challenges of conservation, renovation and substantial alterations to three separate, distinct buildings with a fourth, new building, plus marine civil engineering works.

It has been designed to be strikingly modern, yet complement the surrounding architecture – the stone houses and boat sheds that give Stromness its unique appeal. The practice were interested in a building which is at once part of the town's topography, yet signals its occupier as an important and cultural organisation. To achieve this they chose to use a form that is inherently traditional, yet stands out through exploration of contemporary materials and details.

The original venue comprised two separate buildings on two and three levels.

The new wing sits parallel to the Pier building but while the original building is stone and solid, the new is glazed and standing seam zinc cladding. The cladding satisfied design considerations (long product design life within marine environment) with excellent sustainability credentials.

Barrier free access throughout the new Pier Arts Centre venue was one of the major catalysts setting the redevelopment in motion – the other being care for the Collection.

Accessibility was considered in all aspects – taking into account the needs of visitors with impaired movement, hearing, sight and other less common conditions, e.g. spatial awareness.

Projects
P.70

The Pier Arts Centre

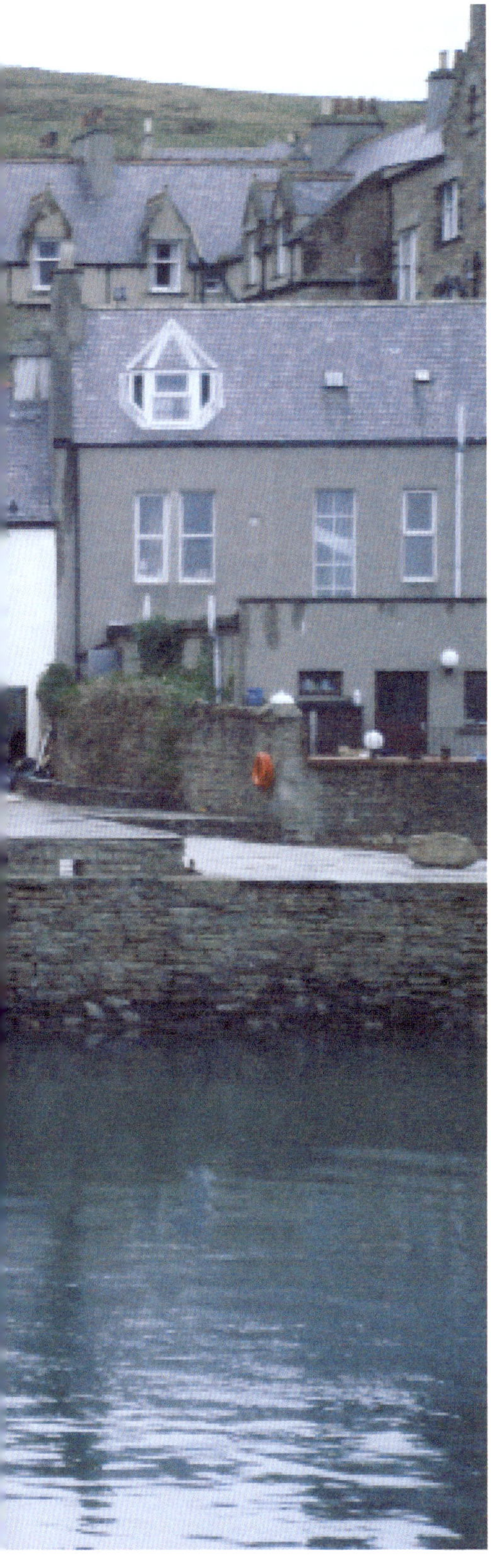

The Story
Neil Gillespie

To a lowland Scot, The Pier Arts Centre is located in the far north, a place more Scandinavian than Scots. To an Orcadian, Orkney lies on the southern threshold of a more vivid, imaginative North, a line where hyperborean thoughts of Thule begin. While mainland Scots look south for cultural confirmation, we have a natural inclination towards an idea of north.

We enjoy buildings and places that promote reflection. Thomas A Clark, wrote that "reticence is a kind of shade". As fair skinned northerners it is wise to seek out the shadows, to work from the margins.

Freud in his essay, The Uncanny 1919, says "it may be true that the uncanny is something which is secretly familiar which has undergone repression and then returned from it and that everything that is uncanny fulfils this condition".

The form of the new building is familiar yet it wears the black vestment of a dignified and valued elder. While signalling that this is a cultural building it also has a quality that is ambivalent and melancholic. The softness of the blackened zinc has an air of absence, a sense of Neil Gunn's horror vacui, or fear of vacant spaces.

The existing building onto Victoria Street is the antithesis of the black house, all is white. The whitewashing of vernacular buildings is common practice yet it too evokes a sense of the uncanny. The whiteness of the refurbished building has a hint of the spectre, in contrast to its stone and render neighbours. Internally the spaces are a backdrop to the art, surfaces are bleached or translucent. Within these muted spaces there are moments of clarity with views out to the Hamnavoe, a connection to the land.

The culture we experience in the North is suited to our need to work quietly, to understand a situation, to create buildings that are not only useful but also poetic.

— **Why make it like this?**
Ragna Robertsdottir Lava Rock Wall, Form Moves From the Transparent to the Translucent to the Obscured.

Projects
P.72
The Pier Arts Centre

— The entrance from the street.

— **Where is it and why?**
Pier Wall.

— **What does it feel like?**
Night Shot, The New Spectre.

P.73

— (Top) One of the gallery spaces

— (Bottom) View from a gallery space.

Projects
P.74   The Pier Arts Centre

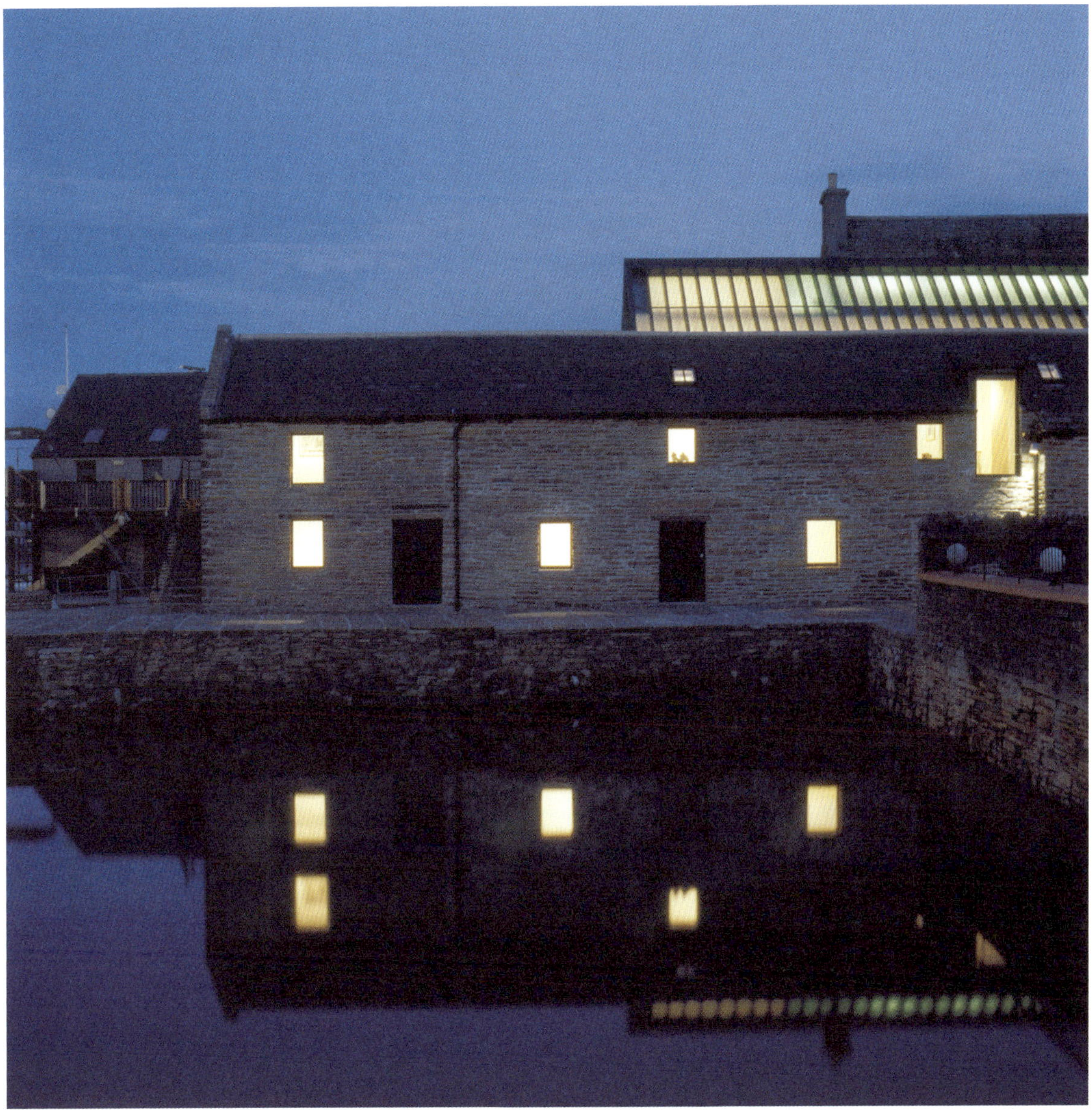

—P.76
—Project Name
Culloden
Battlefield
Visitor
Centre

Projects
P.76

Culloden Battlefield
Visitor Centre

- Architect
Gareth Hoskins Architects
- Location
Culloden Battlefield, Inverness
- Client
National Trust for Scotland
- User
Client and Public
- Budget
£9.4 million
- Completion Date
December 2007
- Build Time
17 months
- Building use
Visitor centre

Following a competition The National Trust commissioned Gareth Hoskins Architects to design the new 2400m² visitor centre. Three times the size of the existing facilities it replaces, it is designed for up to 250,000 visitors a year, housing interpretation of the battle, educational and conference facilities, café, restaurant and staff facilities. Whilst the existing visitor centre was built on archaeologically sensitive ground the new centre is moved away from the battlefield lines, ensuring that graves or artifacts were not disturbed. The new building is anchored between an existing field wall and a new gently rising berm aligned to the rearmost government lines, screening visitor traffic from the battlefield and delivering visitors onto a planted roof terrace for a unique view of the site. The building and berm act as a portal to the site. When the centre is closed the site can be accessed via the portal formed by the bridge to the roof, passing the memorial wall which offers a visual interpretation of the historic site and its status of a war grave and burial ground.

The building is located within a conservation area containing a number of ancient monuments. The site is extremely sensitive and of national and international significance; therefore planning consultations involved Historic Scotland, Scottish National Heritage, Royal Fine Arts Commission as well as The Highland Council which set strict parameters for heights, views, and materials.

The building is constructed in steel frame with concrete floor slab and highly insulated timber walls and roofs. External walls are mainly clad with local untreated Scottish Larch, other areas are clad with local Caithness Stone and field stones salvaged from the site. Internal timber linings are made from untreated Scottish Larch with all other joinery made from oiled British Oak. There is a public viewing terrace covered with an intensive green roof system. The building is mostly naturally ventilated with under floor heating powered by a bio-fuel boiler fed from the estates of the local forestry commission.

Projects
P.78

Culloden Battlefield
Visitor Centre

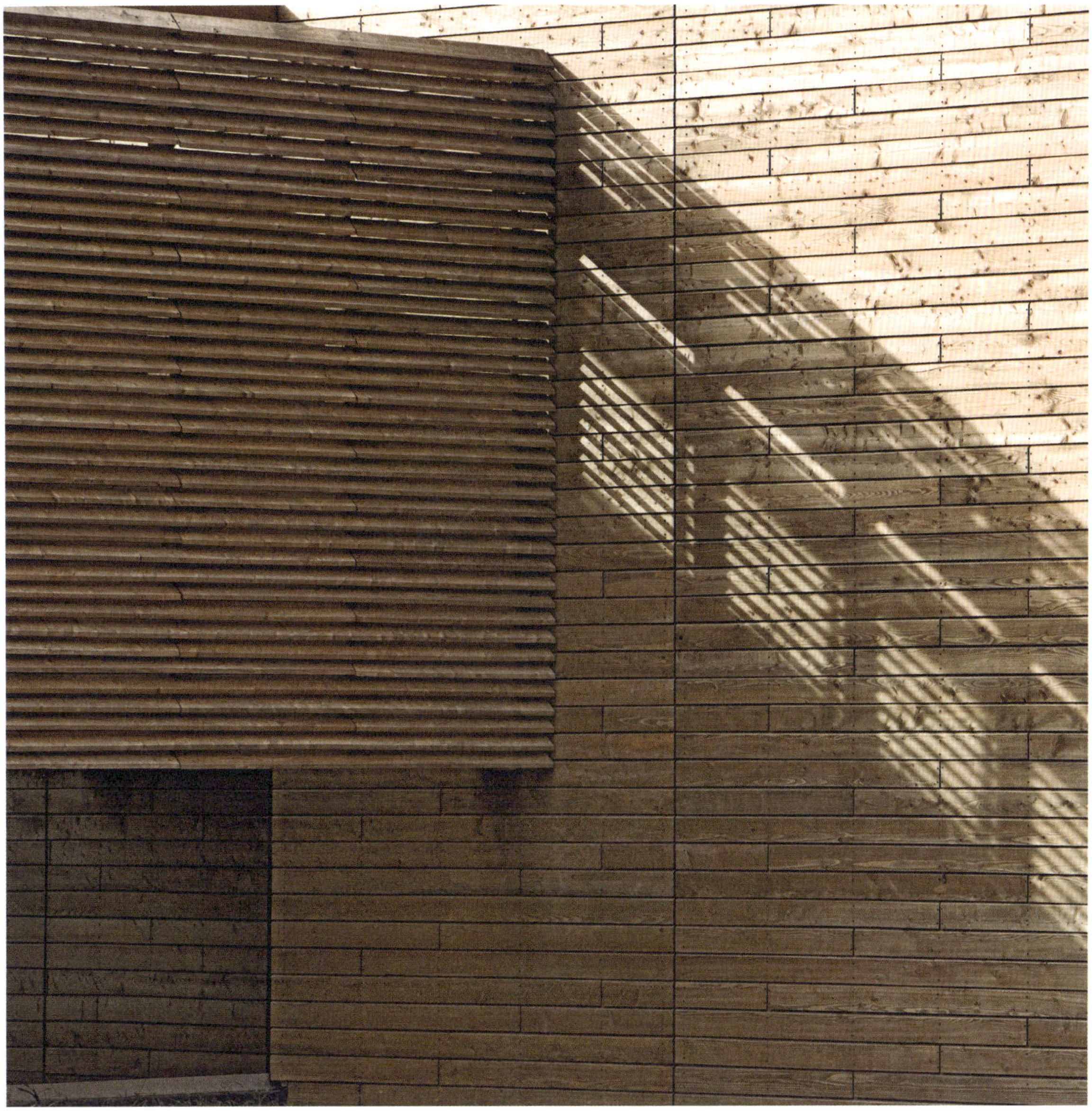

The Story
Gareth Hoskins Architects

Stumbling across the broken, sodden ground. Wind scythes the exposed moor. Long views across the Moray Firth atop the walls of the Culwhiniac enclosure to the Glens beyond. Lasting memories of a first visit to Drumossie Moor, site of the Battle of Culloden, the last battle fought on the British mainland.

A striking landscape that becomes all the more affecting with poignant knowledge of the bloody events that took place on this field – a mass war grave for the 2000 Jacobite and Government troops that lie buried beneath the moor – for some the end of the romanticised journey of Bonnie Prince Charlie's Jacobite uprising, for others, more tellingly the beginning of some of the most fundamental changes to Scottish society and culture and the stepping stone to the expansion of the British Empire overseas.

The affecting atmosphere of this landscape and its underlying memories, its exposure to the constantly changing weather and the found elements, the markings left by man on this moorland are the generators of the project.

Existing dry stane field lines come together with battle lines drawn from mappings of the events to create a point of arrival – a stepping onto the field.

Extending into the landscape, a larch groyne marks the impenetrable wall of the Government redcoats, the point of collision between the two armies – a marker seen from the Jacobite lines at the western edge of the field, defining scales and distance to those viewing the field today.

Internally, an environment of deliberate contrast between framed views across the landscape and the darker enclosure that twists through the building taking the visitors of today through the unfolding events of 1745.

A simple palette of tactile materials – Scottish larch set against field found stones – controlled to bring a sense of permanence, of reverence and of belonging within the landscape. Stacked, stratified Caithness slabs marking the route onto the battlefield and the remains of those that lie beneath.

Why choose these materials?
Materials which the visitor can touch and experience ground the building in its locale but also express its sustainability. Flat laid Caithness Stone which form the memorial wall to the fallen are from quarries only 40 miles away.

Where is it and why?
By eliminating the last internal threat to a unified British state, the battle of Culloden completed the process begun with the execution of Charles 1st over a century earlier and ushered the extraordinary transformation of Scotland into a nation and partner in the British empire. It also began both a systematic assault on elements of Highland culture and incorporation of others. The visitor's centre attempts to express these conflicts both in form and materials.

Projects
Culloden Battlefield Visitor Centre

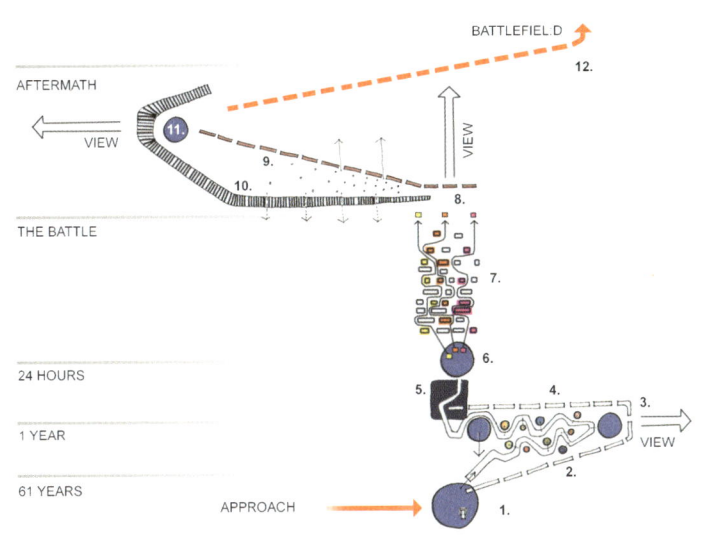

	BATTLEFIELD		
AFTERMATH	12.	1.	INTRODUCTION AND BACK-GROUND TO JACOBITE WARS
VIEW	11.	2.	JACOBITE ADVANCE TO DERBY
	9. 10. 8. VIEW	3.	THE TURNING POINT AND LONDON
THE BATTLE	7.	4.	THE JOURNEY HOME
		5.	NIGHT OF FRUSTRATION
	6.	6.	QUIET BEFORE THE BATTLE
	5. 4. 3.	7.	THE JACOBITE ATTACK
24 HOURS		8.	THE GOVERNMENT WALL
	VIEW	9.	THE AFTERMATH
1 YEAR	2.	10.	WALL OF REMEMBERANCE
		11.	THE LEGACY
61 YEARS	APPROACH → 1.	12.	THE BATTLEFIELD WALK

What were the influences?
The building is at the same time a memorial to the fallen and means of explaining their diverse stories. It is part of a narrative which extends across the bleak moor and beyond, from the Reformation to the present day. At points it dramatizes events. The visitor marches south with the Jacobites toward a distant view over the southern hills only to halt at the "Derby Council" landing and then retreat northward up an incline to their first glimpse of Culloden Moor and the impending battle. After reliving the battle, visitors follow the story out onto the Moor and thence via a long inclined berm to view the site in context from the centre's landscaped roof terrace. Each visitor follows a personality in their struggle and their history, through the day's events to its aftermath, a return down a gentle gradient alongside the stone memorial wall to review their experience in the centre's facilities.

Projects
P.82

Culloden Battlefield
Visitor Centre

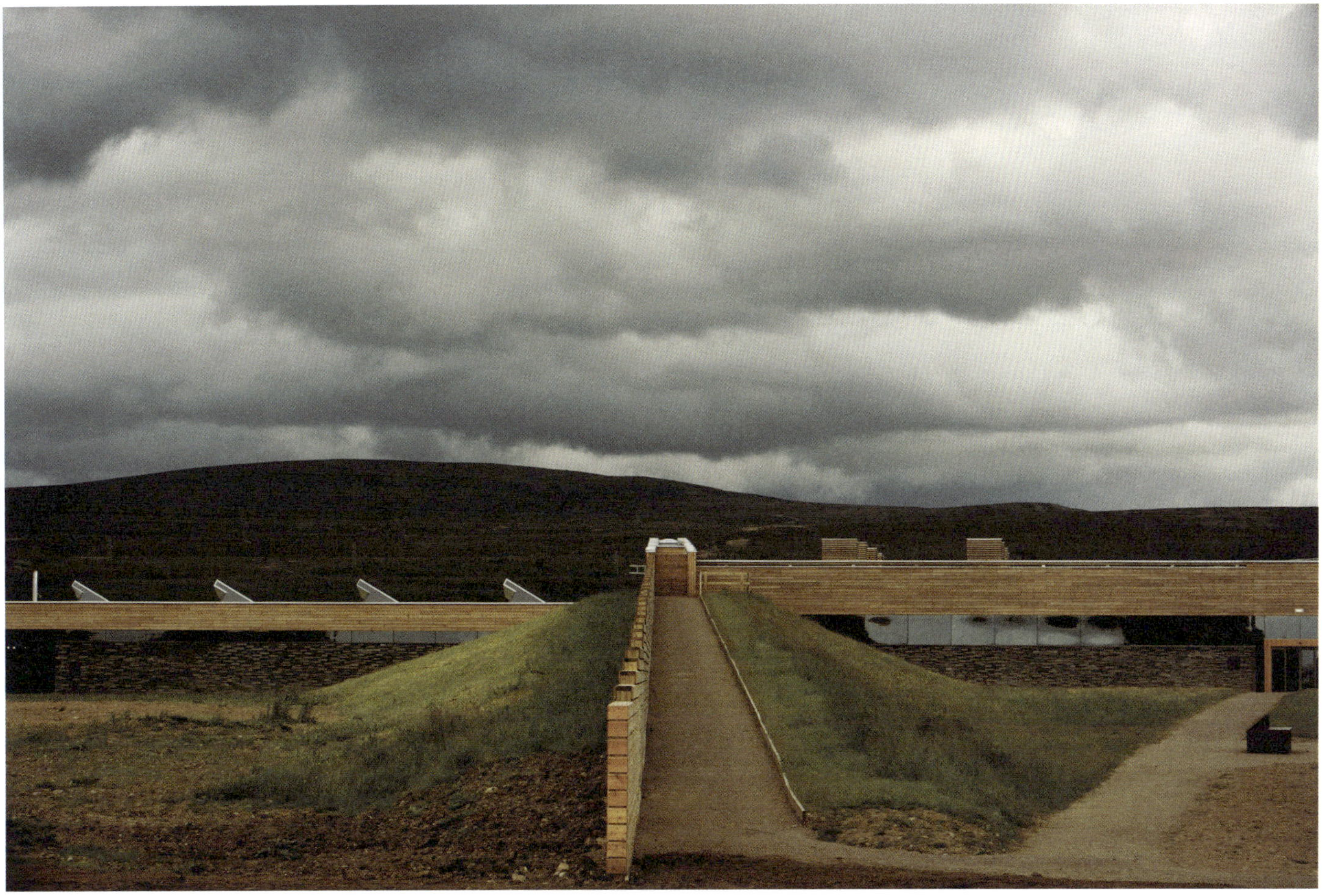

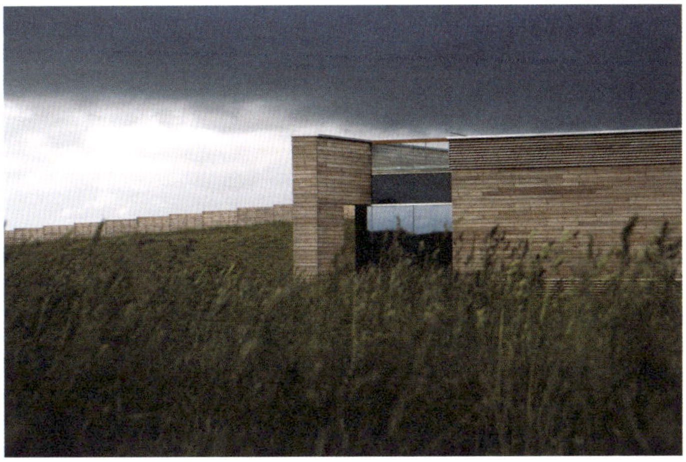

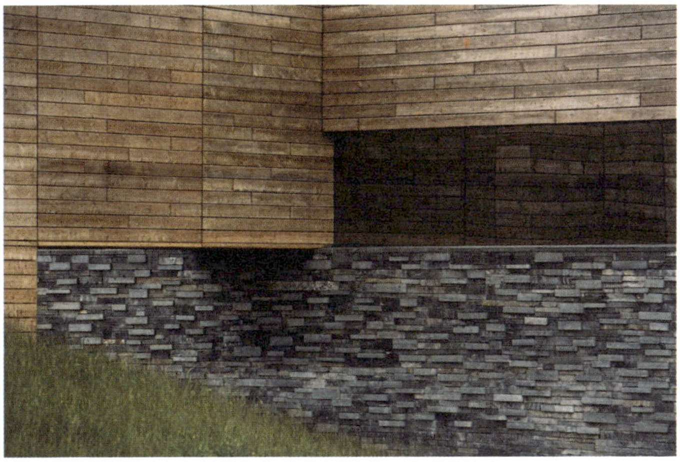

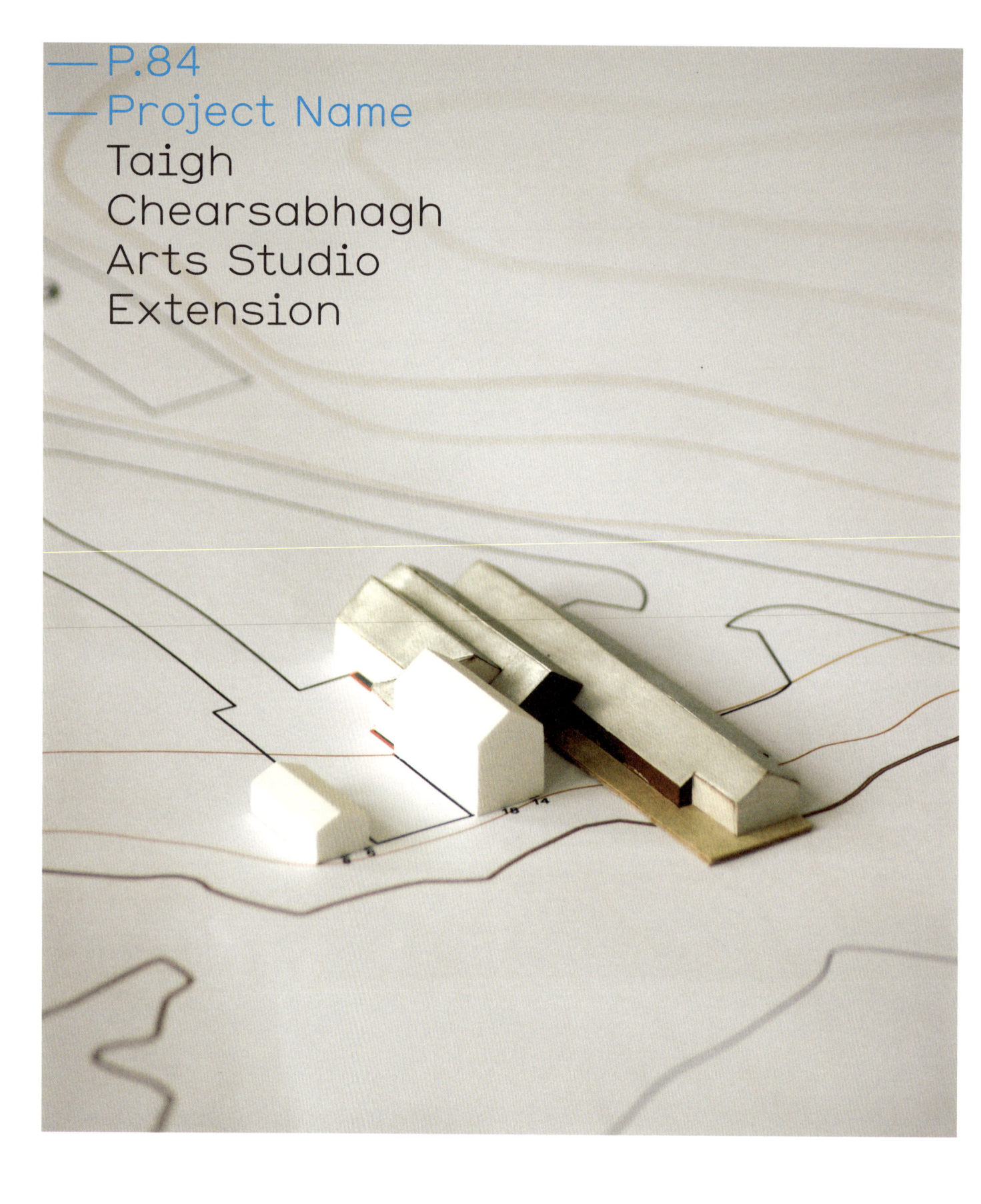

— P.84
— Project Name
Taigh Chearsabhagh Arts Studio Extension

- **Architect**
Locate Architects
- **Location**
Lochmaddy, North Uist
- **Client**
Taigh Chearsabhagh Museum and Arts Centre
- **User**
As above
- **Budget**
c.£250,000
- **Completion Date**
November 2007
- **Build Time**
6 months
- **Building use**
Artists' Studios

At the earliest stages, the Artists' Studios were conceived as a separate building. Adding them to the end of the existing building meant building onto the beach and moving the village sewer but the advantages more than outweigh this. Resource use and disruption were minimised and there are now three separate studios in a line which can be flexibly divided giving the Centre a variety of options. In addition, the building now dramatically extends over the high water mark and the adjacent deck allows wonderful vistas with water lapping and crashing directly beneath you.

This is the third extension to the original buildings at Taigh Chearsabhagh, making it important to maintain a consistency of approach so that the complex did not develop into an unholy mix of architectural forms and styles. The overall form and external materials of the building were very much set by the adjacent roof and walls, although the narrower third studio was developed a little differently as it protrudes over the original drop into the sea.

The internal spaces were kept faithful to the rest of the building in overall feel and details, although the steel frame is a new strategy for the buildings. This made sense in terms of giving the spaces a much higher degree of flexibility. High levels of natural light were considered whist at the same time controlling glare.

Extending the existing building kept resource use and disruption to a minimum. The main focus was on reducing energy use through good levels of insulation and airtightness. Several elements were reused including the large square window which was in the original building gable before extension. Natural paints and linoleum were specified internally to reduce internal health risks and underfloor heating was chosen as the healthiest option.

Projects
P.86

Taigh Chearsabhagh

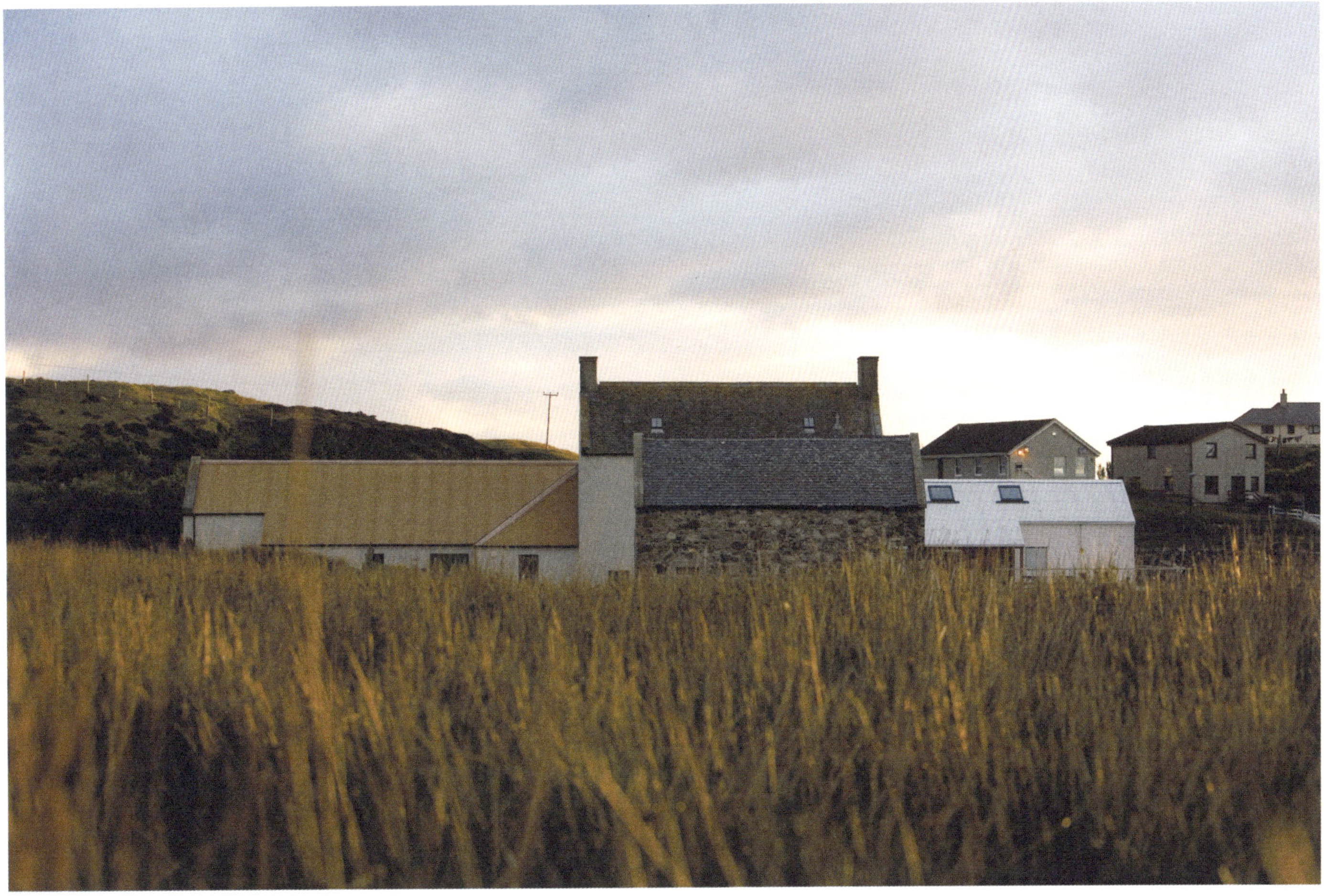

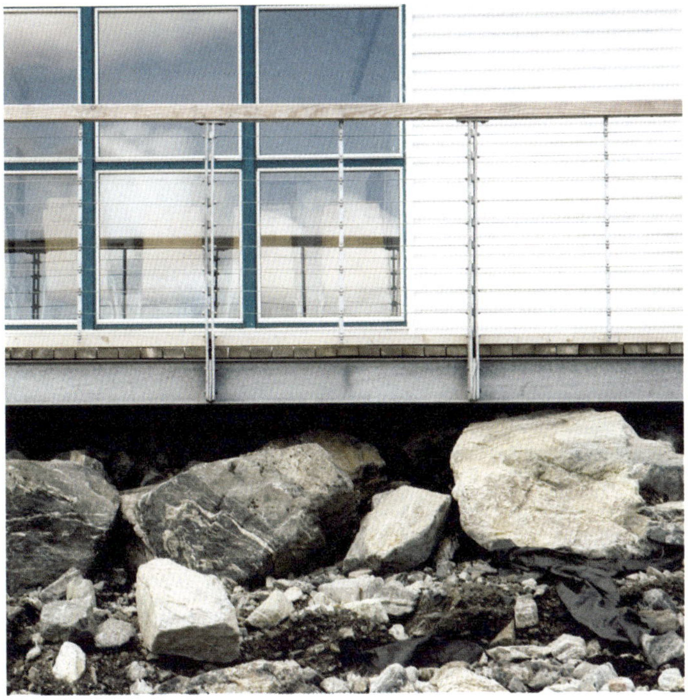

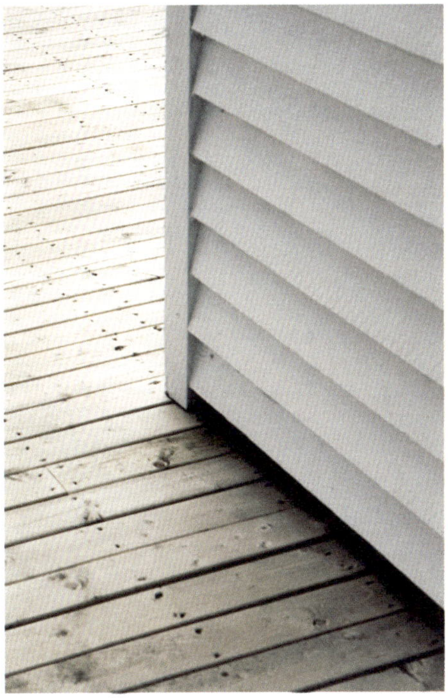

— The Story
Andy Mackinnon
(Arts Officer)

Our aim is to develop Taigh Chearsabhagh as a Centre of Excellence in Environmental Art and to present an accessible and integrated programme of interpreted exhibitions and related practical workshops. The unique landscape of the Uists provides the context within which we are able to offer a very special creative programme. This extension enables Taigh Chearsabhagh to make a significant contribution to arts provision both nationally and internationally. A programme of environmental art residencies and placements will be developed in conjunction with international agencies, positioning Taigh Chearsabhagh at the forefront of environmental art research and work.

Lead artist Ian Stephen said, "For me the walkway out from the

— **What were the influences?**
This is an image of the walls of the Centre for Development Studies in Kerala, India by Laurie Baker. Baker remains the person who has most impressed and influenced me. He produced literally hundreds of low cost, beautiful, comfortable, simple buildings, all of which were characterised by a creativity and willingness to adapt to local situations. My sense is that as architects we are being encouraged to produce 'star'. buildings but part of what makes places great tends to be the relatively high quality of ordinary buildings, not the presence of extraordinary buildings.

— **Where is it and why?**
The new extension we built is where it is because of the existing building. The Old Inn dates back to 1741 and adjoined the original landing place for the village, so this part of Lochmaddy has a long history and the beach and shoreline continues to be an inspiration for artwork at the Centre. The fish shown is on the motif for Taigh Chearsabhagh.

building to the tidal loch suggests a journey, much more far reaching than a hundred metres or so of shoreline. I see Lochmaddy as a confluence – it is a shelter reached from the Little Minch but also a staging point to await conditions for transit through the Sound of Harris to the open West. And it's a place where life ashore can't avoid looking out to the maritime world.

The architect's emphasis on possible re-use of materials and sensitivity as to their environmental impact has struck a chord with a developing pattern in my own work. For instance, I have been recycling artworks for many years now. Often an object, placed in a different context in an exhibition will be returned to its practical function afterwards. This is an extension of the creative use of materials you will find in any Island culture worldwide. If you have to wait three days to get a replacement part you tend to invent another solution.

For me, the artwork integrated into the Taigh Chearsabhagh studio extension should lead an audience out into the immediate environment. Then it should suggest infinite journeys, but from a starting point which gives initial guidelines."

What does it feel like?
One of my favourite quotes is by Michael Benedict in 'For an Architecture of Reality' in which he argues that "we count upon our buildings to form the stable matrix of our lives..." which we cannot do if they are busy 'saying' something. If our buildings instead simply get on with their job of fitting in and providing good quality accommodation, low energy, are healthy and enjoyable, then the occupants, the ones that matter, are left alone to experience their surroundings without interference.

— P.90
— Project Name
Talla Choinneachaidh

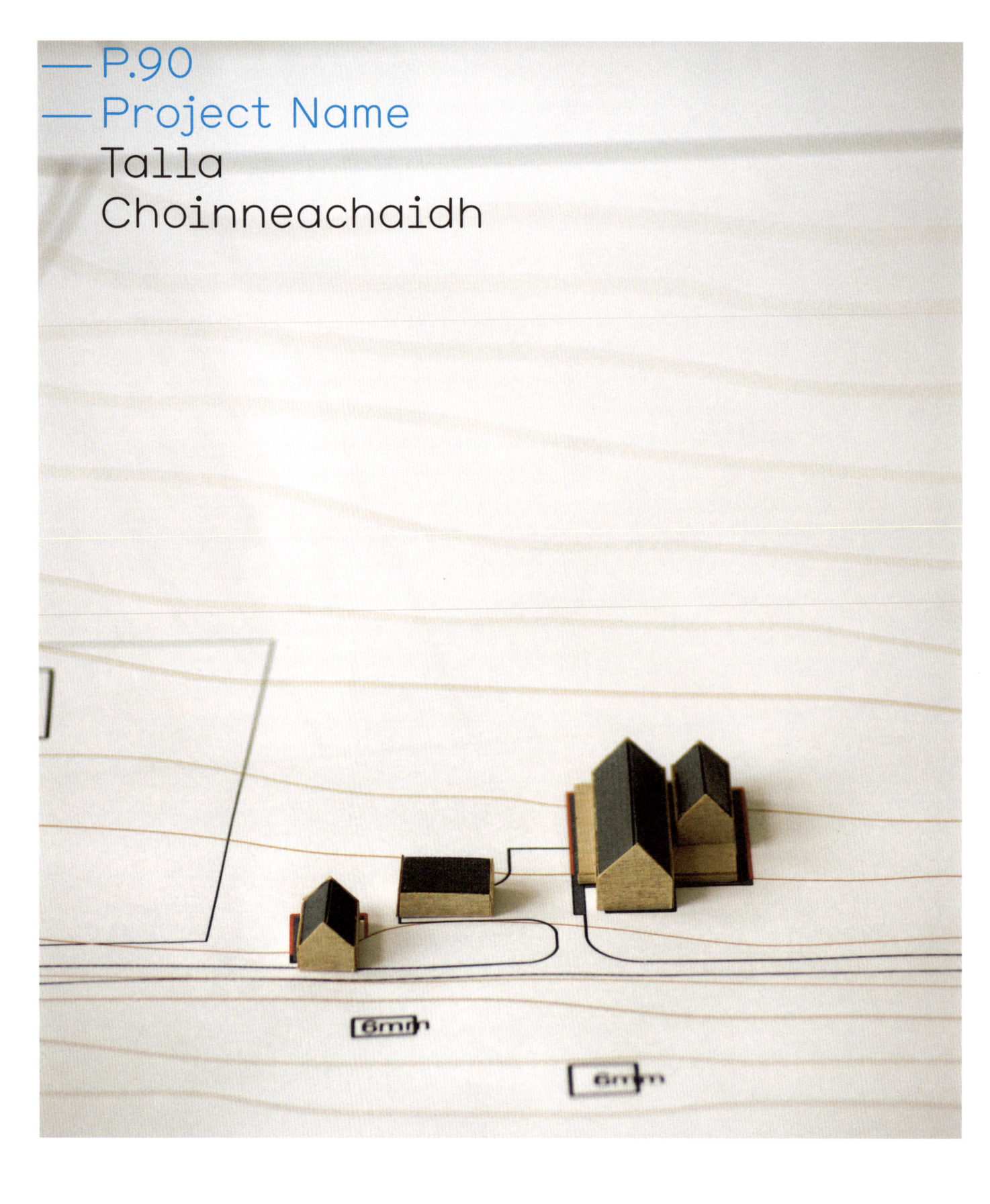

Architect
Dualchas Building Design

Location
Breanish, Uig,
Isle of Lewis

Client
Gordon and Jackie MacKay

User
As above

Budget
£360,000

Completion Date
April 2008

Build Time
12 months

Building use
holiday home

The traditional blackhouses of Lewis reflect a response to the topography and the weather – a rugged bleak landscape and ferocious winds. The clients wanted a building which showed a similar response but was also modern and comfortable.

The house is cut into the hillside, and is broken into two expressed structures keeping its appearance modest. The idea of the building becoming part of the landscape was strengthened further by the choice of external materials – a stone retaining wall and larch rain screen.

As the client couldn't be persuaded to go with a metal roof, grey slate were used to tie in with the large rocks that litter the landscape.

The house is highly insulated with a heat recovery system. A simple palette of material helps express the simple volumes of the interiors, and focus the eye to the distinctive landscape viewed from the large areas of glazing.

The house is used as a holiday home. It comprises a utility room, three bedrooms, two bathrooms, kitchen / dining, living room on the ground floor and a bathroom and bedroom on the upper floor. Two outbuildings are built to the same external detail as the house. One building is a garage, the other is a small 'mission hall', which contains some remnants from the old Presbyterian hall, which formerly stood on the site. A Gaelic bible on a lectern forms the centrepiece.

Projects
P.92

Talla Choinneachaidh

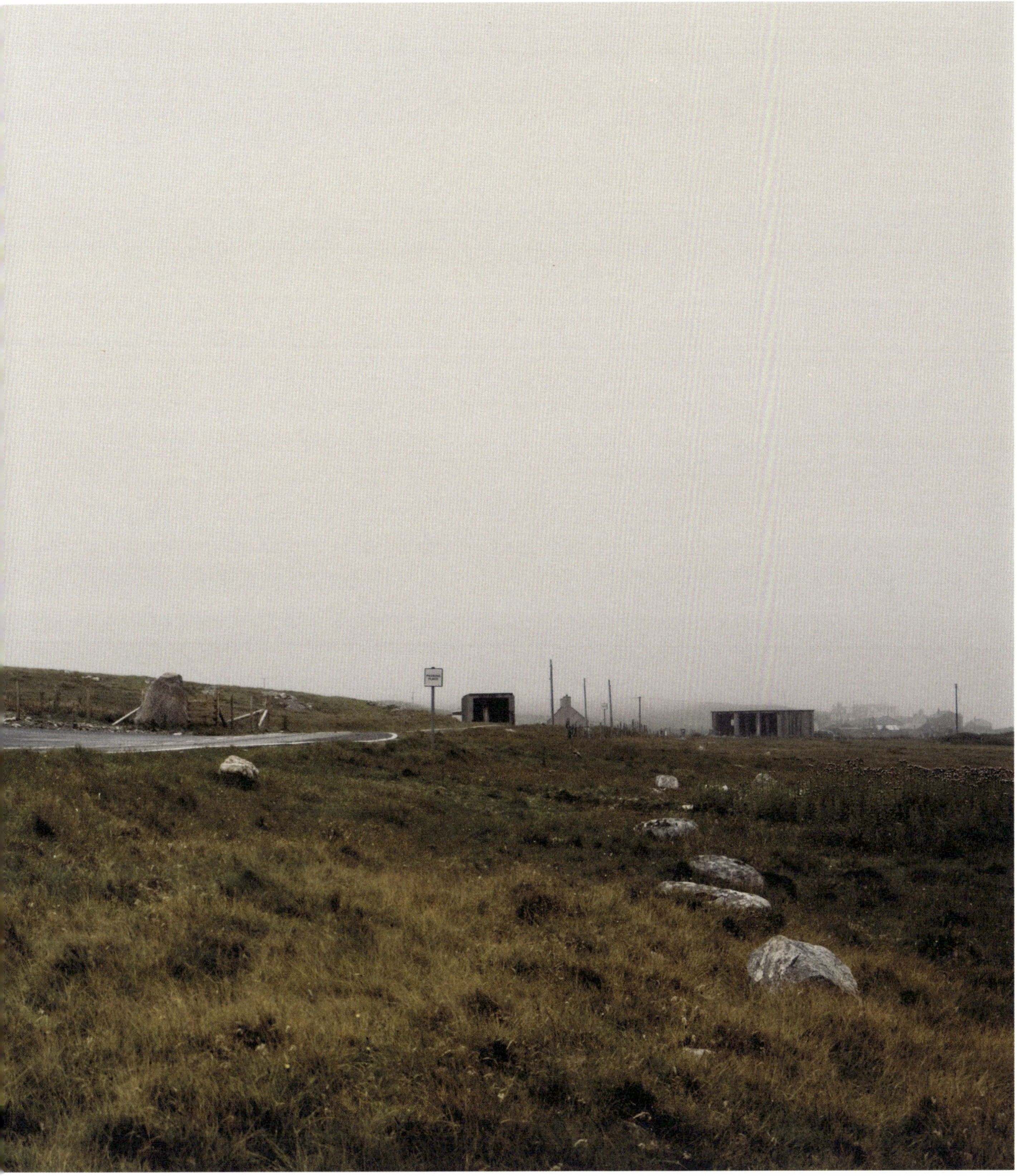

Projects
P.94

Talla Choinneachaidh

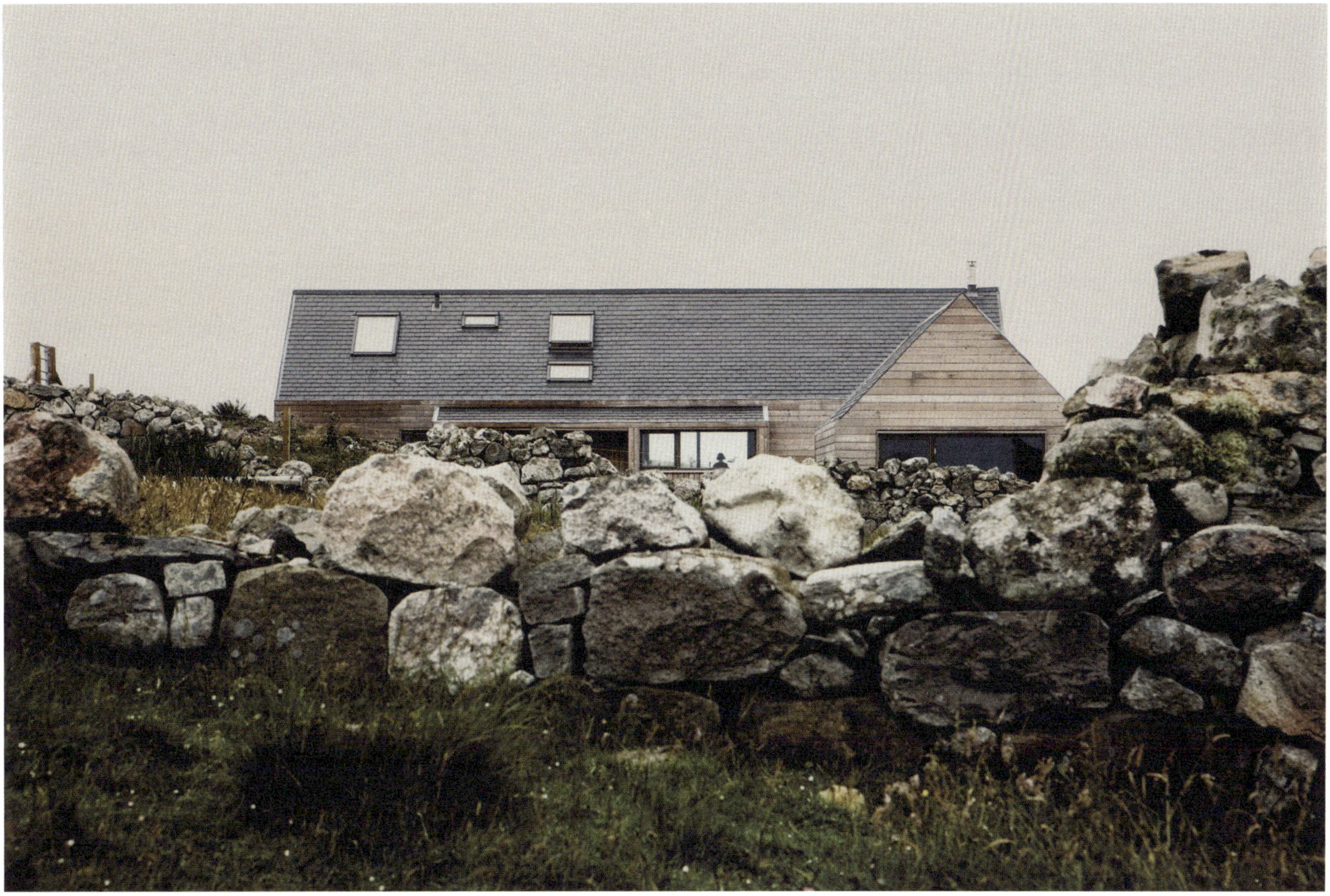

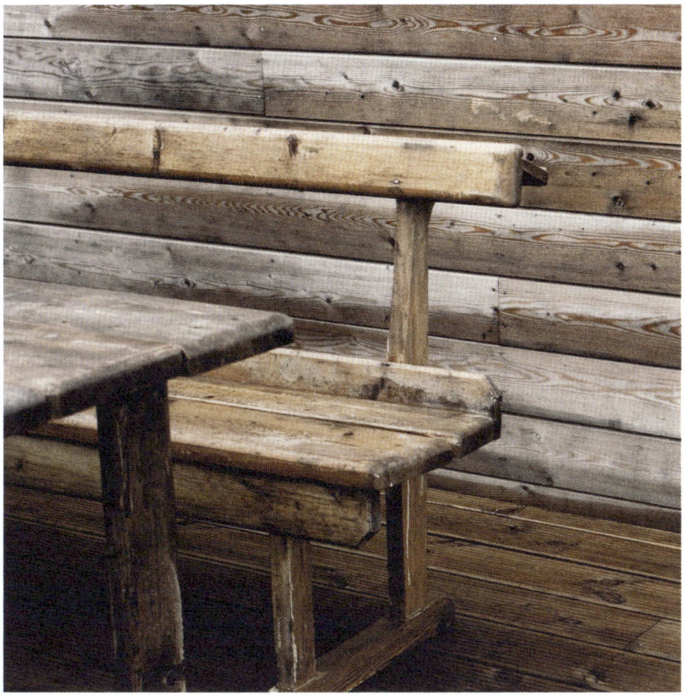

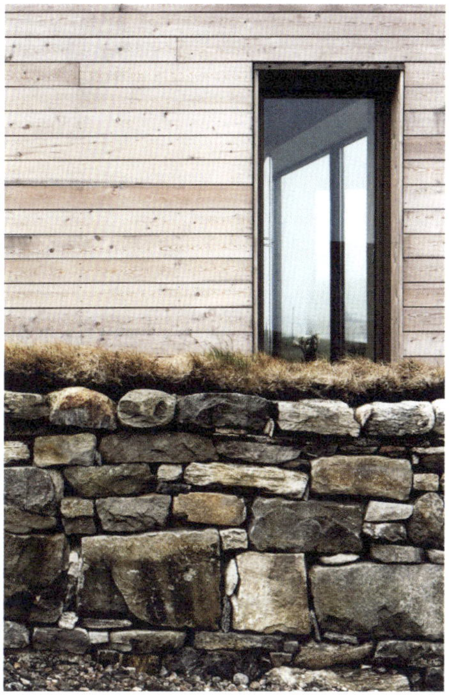

— **Why make it like this?**
Simple forms in dramatic landscapes.

— Projects
— P.96

Talla Choinneachaidh

The Story
Dualchas Building Design

The west coast of Lewis is characterised by swelling Atlantic seas, and expanses of white sand: a bare treeless landscape, where people, beasts and plants hunker down against the gales.

A mission hall stood on the site – grey, Presbyterian and functional. No one had worshipped there for years, but inside it was complete with alter, pews and open Gaelic bibles, as if abandoned mid-sermon.

The clients, the MacKays, are not from the area – they do not have Gaelic, or family in Breanish – this is a place they have found, where the intensity of the elements blows away stresses of city lives.

Others have come here too. An orange, Scandinavian log house stands tall to confound the wind, another has built a tower, alien forms in a remote township, strangers to tradition.

The MacKays wanted to lay low. So the house was cut into the hill to keep it within the topography. Stone, larch and galvanised metal, the materials of crofting, would let it blend in and hide itself amongst the rocks.

Two parallel structures followed the blackhouse form breaking it down to smaller components, making it less obtrusive. Yet beneath the skin are steel portals, and mass concrete founds, an engineer's response to fears of Hebridean hurricanes and lateral loads.

A small mission hall was built to replace the old, complete with salvaged alter, pew and bible. Where passers by can pop in for shelter, find peace or remember the past.

Years from now, the house may have suffered the same fate as the first mission hall, and an inscription, Talla Choinneachaidh, will be discovered on a boulder amongst the debris – a curious reminder of a culture that once filled halls with the sound of resounding psalms, and ended up a house name in a settlement of strangers.

What were the influences?
Weathered larch in faded grey.

Why choose these materials?
The materials of the local tradesmen, Murdo, Malky and Bob.

P.97

— The Projects
Europe

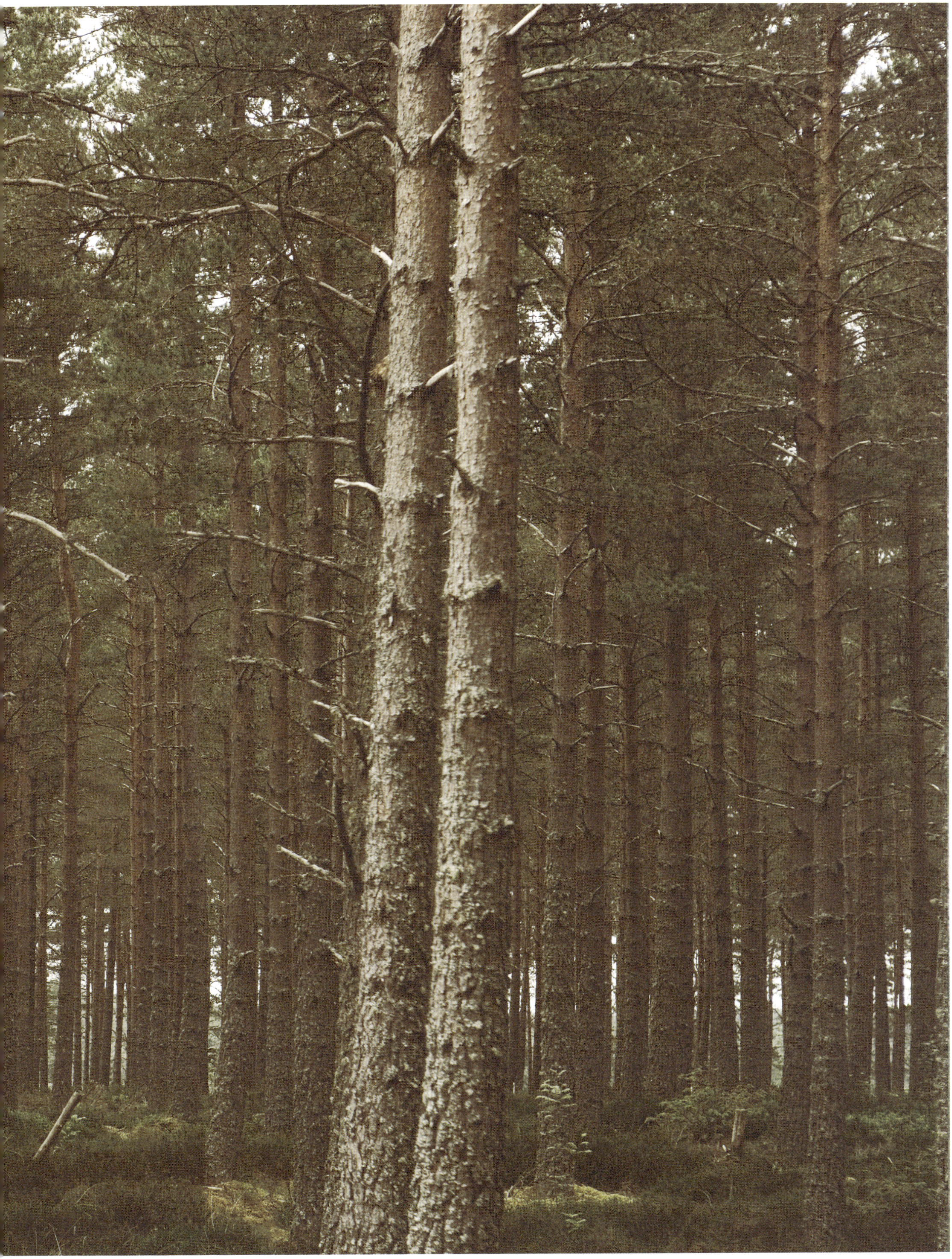

—P.100
—Project Name
Extension Winery Gantenbein, Switzerland

Projects
P.100

Extension Winery
Gantenbein

— **Architect**
Bearth & Deplazes
Architekten, Char/Zurich
Valentin Bearth
Andrea Deplazes
Daniel Ladner
Façade in collaboration
with Gramazio Kohler
Architekten, Zürich

— **Location**
Fläsch, Switzerland

— **Client**
Martha and Daniel
Gantenbein, Fläsch

— **User**
Martha and Daniel
Gantenbein, Fläsch

— **Budget**
N/a

— **Completion Date**
2008

— **Build Time**
1 Year

— **Building use**
Winery

Gantenbein wines have an excellent reputation world wide. They are produced following the growing and production principle of 'Terroir', which is also found in the organisation of the winery and in its architectural language.

The buildings are grouped around a courtyard, situated on the edge of a wine yard, where the vines are being picked. Below are basements rooms and the distributon facilities. The production line follows the principle of gravity, low tech and much experience are the basis for the maturing process of exclusive wines. Only three people: Daniel, Martha and father Gantenbein are running the wine yard, high efficiency is garanteed by optimised operating sequences.

Those are the preconditions the new building, both functional and representational object at the same time.

Typologically, the building resembles horse stables with facades of perforated brickwork. They have been laid by the robot and have been prefabricated into wall elements.

Central issues are room organisation and choice of materials, a controlled, natural room climate and natural ventilation. Every storey has its own operational logic. The brick construction provides thermal mass and is prefabricated, with few exemptions of distinct details.

The fermenting cellar is a hall level to the ground. Here, the vine harvest ferments in oak barrels. Underground, a columned cellar joins the existing to the new buildings, carried by eight mushroom shaped columns.

Above the winery is the lounge, an open but sheltered roof terrace, which offers views across the Ragaz Rhine valley.

The attraction of the facility lies in the contradiction between complexity and quality of the product, and the directness and reduced (nearly archaic) force of its production. The same is true for the architecture, which derives directly from the inner and outer context of the winery.

Projects
P.102

Extension Winery
Gantenbein

— The façade showing the robotically laid bricks.

The Cuverie (fermenting room) — a large room lit by light and shade as the sunlight plays with the gaps in the bricks of the façade — every day, every hour is different. The wine is fermented once a year in open oak casks — afterwards the room is idle for a year.

Projects
P.104

Extension Winery
Gantenbein

— The 'almost sacred atmosphere' of the underground pillared hall which joins the existing building to the new. The mushroom-shaped pillars are ceiling supports and water channels which evacuate water from the courtyard.

— The oval stairwell in the intense blue of the wine yard labels.

— Above the winery is the banqueting room (lounge and restaurant). Large sliding windows bring the vine landscape and the mountains on the horizon into the room, offering views are across the Ragaz Rhine Valley. A terrace among the vines in the summer, a tent in winter.

The Story
Köbi Gantenbein (GA) is Hochparterre's Chief Editor and brother of the winegrower.

At the vineyard, it's the robot-built facade that catches the eye. It tells you what characterises the wine growers, their business and the building: a curiosity for the technically avant-garde and respect for good craftsmanship.

Valentin Bearth, Andrea Deplazes and Daniel Ladner are three architects who have had a close partnership for a good 12 years as Bearth & Deplazes Architekten. The three work together because the principle that the whole is more than the sum of its parts is also true of architecture. Depending on the building brief and the client, one or other does more or less of the work. Daniel Gantenbein comments: "Which idea was whose I never knew." The masonry robot venture would have been unthinkable without Andrea Deplazes, and his enthusiasm and academic contacts. He sparked off the idea and found the solution with Gramazio & Köhler. Valentin Bearth, the second academic, provided intellectual impetus. "He asked intelligent questions and again and again opened our eyes to beauty through his knowledge" according to Daniel Gantenbein. "We worked closely and intensively with Daniel Ladner", Martha Gantenbein sums it up, "He made sure our ideas and improvisations with whichever architect was on site were put into

— The crane operator assembles the 72 wall sections into a façade.

Why make it like this?
The research team from Zurichs technical university, Gramazio and Kohler, developed robotics that can construct precision finished walls. The robot places one brick on top of another in the ETH factory: each at a slight angle to the next.

Projects P.106 — Extension Winery Gantenbein

practice very accurately. And he made sure that we didn't lose the fun and pleasure of the adventure. He explained, arbitrated, held the purse-strings and encouraged us." The Gantenbeins remember many a conversation that went like this: "Martha, we have to dare to do it. It will be worth it. Daniel, I know it will come out all right, even if I don't yet know how."

— **What were the influences?**
Small cottages in the Valle Maggia (CH) were an important influence.

— **Where is it and why?**
The starting point for the extension was the existing structure of the vineyard and the row upon row of Gantenbein vines stretching across six hectares of flat and sloping land around Fläsch.

—P.108
—Project Name
Terrihütte,
Switzerland

— **Architect**
Gion A. Caminada, Architect BSA/SIA

— **Location**
Highland 'Greina'
District of Sumvitg

— **Client**
SAC Piz Terri Quadras
(Swiss Alpine Club)

— **Budget**
1.2 Million sFr.

— **Completion Date**
Spring 2008

— **Build Time**
12 months

— **Building use**
Mountain hostel

The SAC chalet, which was built in 1925 and twice extended, has again been renovated. The difficult spatial arrangements in the entrance, the inconvenient access to the sleeping area and the sparseness of the chalet warden's accommodation were the critical factors leading to this project.

The aim was not primarily to increase capacity during peak periods, but rather to improve the quality of the hospitality, for longer stays as well.

SAC chalets have always been built in stone. This project goes back to that tradition and less to contemporary building, which in these locations is all too easily dictated by ease of transport. The main material is sourced on site. The intention is to produce a new homogeneous whole with the existing building. The differences between the periods of architectural expression are to be blurred rather than forgotten.

The somewhat erratic effect of the main structure meets the walker and leads him through the rocky mass to the protection of the chalet. It is there to protect the visitor not only from wind and weather but also to provide him symbolically with security.

This effect is to be achieved from afar, as well as through physical immediacy. There is no attempt to frame the landscape, on the contrary the metaphorical distance between the observer and the landscape is to be raised a notch.

The upper floors, extending the lounge and the kitchen, and chalet staff accommodation, are a composite construction of stone and timber. In contrast, the lower ground floor, which with its camping accommodation is an invitation to bivouac, is built only of stone.

The sleeping accommodation is much more varied. The new bivouac units can be opened to the outside so that you feel you are out in the open. You still cannot see the Greina plateau, but you will feel it:

"An almost painful silence, a joyful calm. The silence is white, pink, violet and black, it can call forth hate or bring peace. The Greina is as wide as the sea and like the sea has its storms and quiet times. In the silence we see the stars shining, our spirit beats and lives. Silent are the burgeoning flowers, silent is the coming of the pinky dawn. Silent is the rising of the sun, silently we sleep."

Katja De Mitcheli

Projects
P.110

Terrihütte

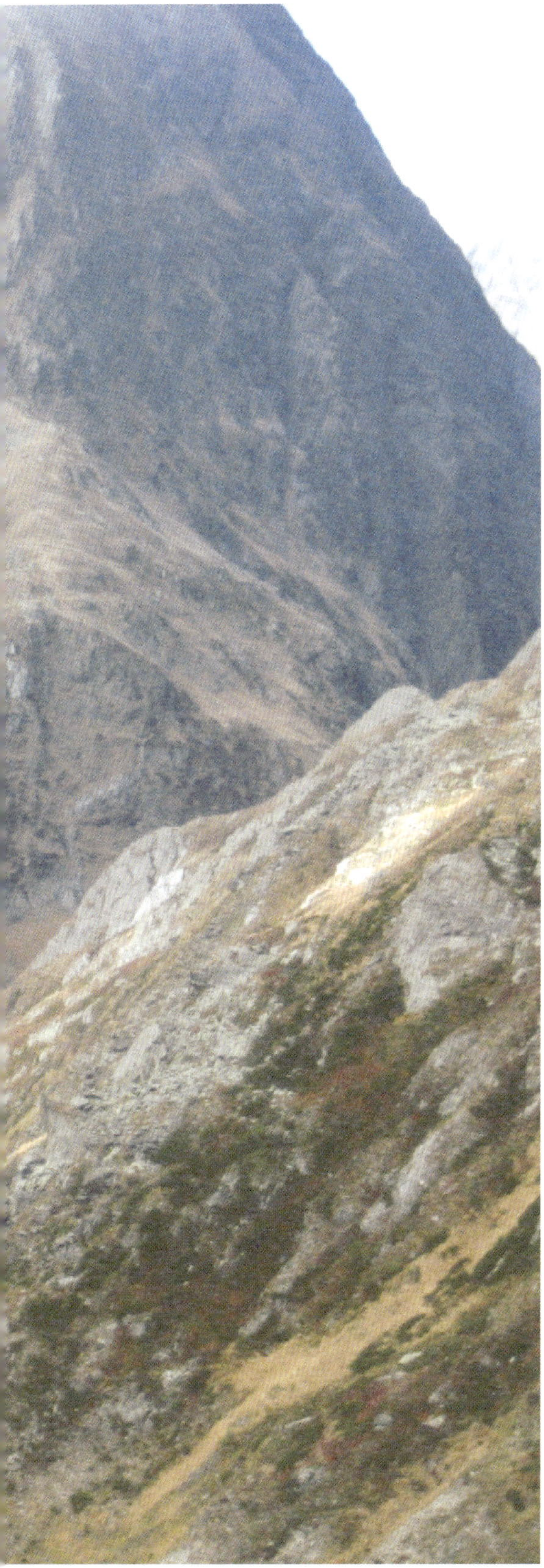

The Story
Gion A. Caminada

The right building for a powerful place Greina is a clearly delineated plateau that from time immemorial has been used intensively by the inhabitants of three valleys. It was a travel and trading route from Vrin to Milan, it was grazing for goats and horses (nowadays sheep and cows are to be found there in the summer), it was a hunting ground and in the war a natural border to be defended, and mountaineers climb the peaks all around it winter and summer.

In the 1980s a plan to build a dam was stopped. Attention was drawn to the beauty of the landscape through art and campaigning. Since then, the legend of the powerfully beautiful has resonated as a counterforce to the purely functional.

A former shepherd and author wrote his first book from Greina. It is the story of a shepherd who loves Greina and who perishes on the plateau. Resistance and reconciliation with the wild, protection from the elements and the helplessness of human nature faced in the face of solitude.

Excerpt:
Who is Giacumbert?
Who is Gaglinera?

You may perhaps find out because you feel it, and
not otherwise, in God's name.
But when you once come over the pass, then
your eye will see the bleakness of the ground and
the scantiness of the words, and perhaps then you will feel
the impalpable soul of that

— **Why make it like this?**
Craftsmanship is challenged anew again and again by timeless building methods — that is how tradition is created.

— **Why choose these materials?**
The chalets of the Swiss Alpine Club are always built in local material.

Terrihütte

man of flesh
I call Giacumbert.
If you feel it, then you yourself are Giacumbert
or Albertina, and your favourite colours are
red and white.
(Leo Tuor, Giacumbert Nau – Schafhirt auf der Greina, 1988, Octopus Verlag, Chur)

Nowadays many walkers cross the plateau and spend the night in one of the three Swiss Alpine Club chalets.

Each will have a very personal experience of the landscape.

But how can we show that something else was going on in front of us, that there are things in this place that cannot be understood by reason alone, how can we make people feel the fascinating yet irritating forces that you discover when you abandon yourself to this place?

How can a chalet meet everyday needs in a functional way and yet be a reference to something mysterious, something that cannot be deciphered, something much more far-reaching? One possibility is to use materials that are familiar, but put them together and build them in such a way that their impact is not aimed at our intellect but at those places within us that are still open to experience.

Plaun la Greina – eine Gebirgslandschaft der ungeteilten Wildheit, Rauhheit und Einsamkeit. Kaltnadel

— **What were the influences?**
Plaun la Greina, Kaltnadel, Bryan Cyril Thurston.
The stories and legends about the Greina plateau are closely connected with the stones, rocks and ledges of the landscape.
Art gives us the opportunity to look at nature differently.
Can we create living spaces that do the same?

Projects
P.114 Terrihütte

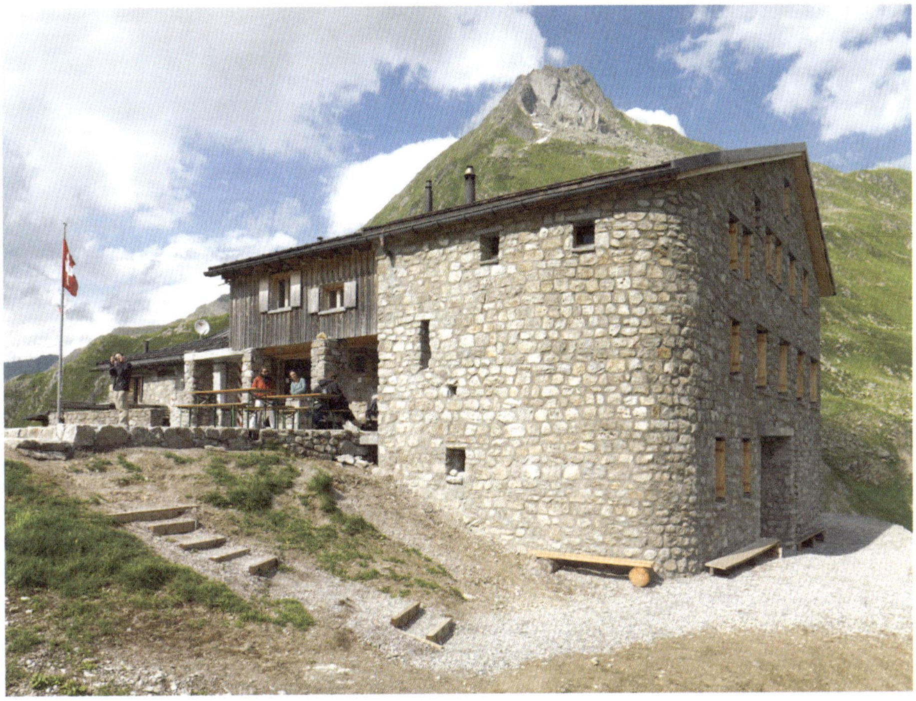

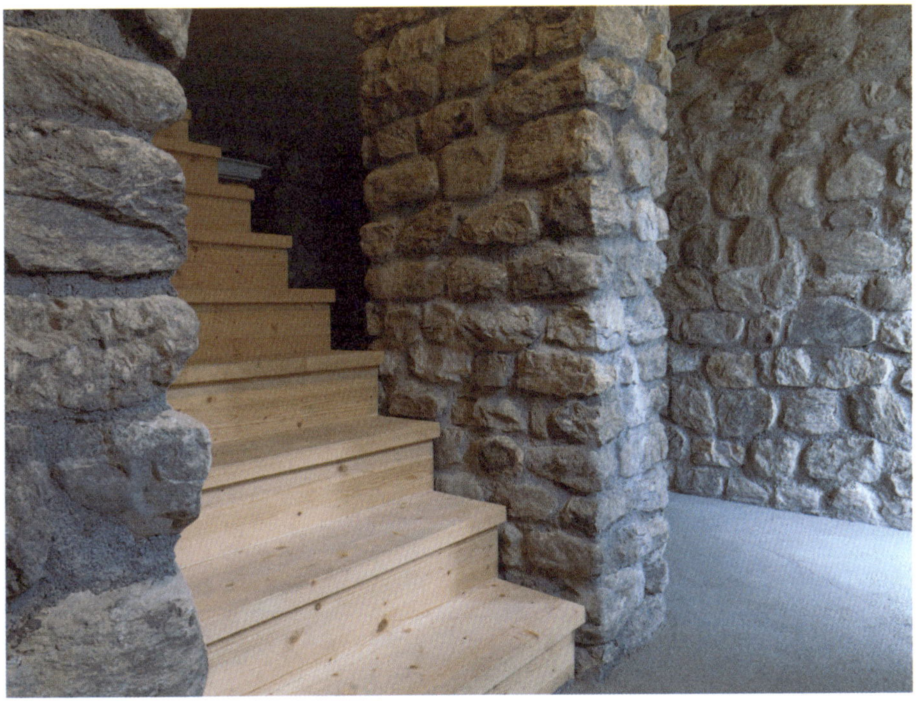

—P.116
—Project Name
Mountain Chapel, Austria

— **Architect**
Cukrowicz Nachbaur
Architekten zt Gmbh
— **Location**
Andelsbuch, Alpe
Vordere Niedere
— **Client**
Feurstein family
— **User**
Feurstein family
— **Budget**
£2.8 million
— **Completion Date**
October 2008
— **Build Time**
2 months (Estimated)
— **Building use**
Chapel

The chapel is built on the small hill between two footpaths. Enclosed by gently sloping grassland, it is situated in the changeover between cultivated and natural landscape.

The entrance is located at the upper path, which leads to the protecting room just like a traditional church path. Nearby is a steep fall. A wonderful view impresses from this safe place.

The chapel, which is built from local materials, is a building with a single room. The external and internal volume are identical. A plinth of natural stone forms the foundation. The building has a simple shape, which derived from the traditional buildings of the alpine area. The slightly steeper roof gives airiness to the building. The plinth awards safety. Internally, the building is both soaring and sheltering.

One single profile is the basis for this type of timber construction. The pre-profiled timbers are planed on three sides, and are assembled as a solid wall, roof and floor. The elements are working like braced frames, the junctions in between are 'knitted'. The external façade and floor are left unplaned, to be more resistant. The furniture is built from the same type of timber sections. All parts of the construction have untreated surfaces, which supports the archaic and vertical effect of the room. The external face of the roof is waterproofed, with a protective wooden screen above.

Entering the chapel means leaving the solid ground, and entering into a wooden volume. The space is enclosed and silent. It is composed of a single material. Its orientation is clear and refers to the sloping of the site. The altar wall appears to be independent from side walls and the roof, and is lit by a slot of layered glass. It is permanently connected to daylight and seasons. The block of layered glass is flush with the timber wall both internally and externally replacing two elements of timber. The bell is located above the entrance. A traditionally ornamented filter provides protection and opening for the noise. A cross in the back wall is emblematic both internally and externally.

Projects
Mountain Chapel

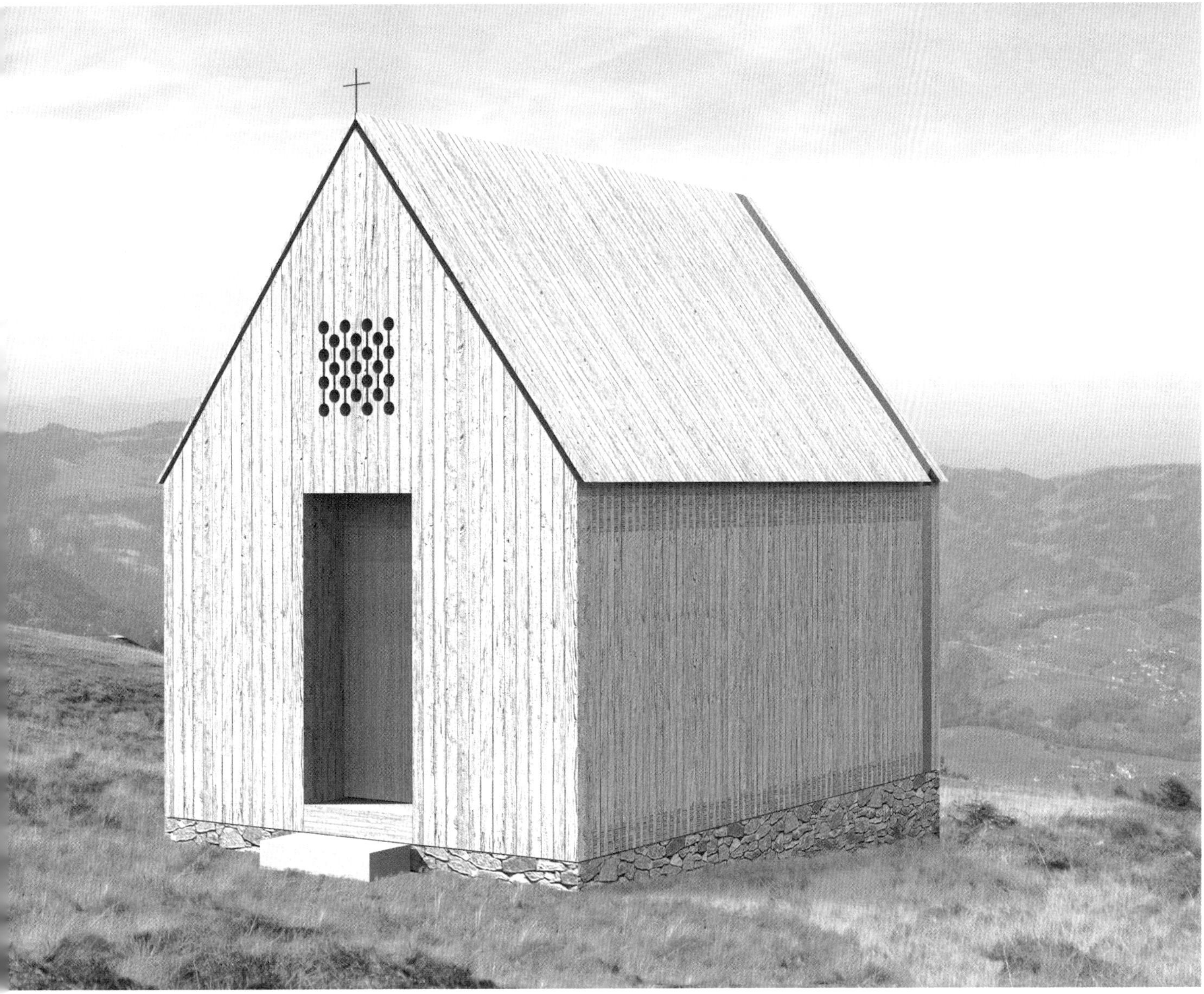

The Story
Cukrowicz Nachbaur

The building brief originated in a vow made by the clients some 20 years before. Their wish has been fulfilled, the vow has now been kept with the building of the chapel. The clients organised a competition between architects and designers, the prize was handmade cheese. The siting of the chapel was jointly determined on the spot. Theodulus, the patron saint of the chapel, is the patron saint of bells, weather, winemakers, and in Vorarlberg, cattle.

The building brief called for a material environment that would give the visitor protection and security. The walls are made of planed timber, the floor of rough sawn timber, which gives the material a bit more weight. The intention was that the space should give a feeling of lightness, strength and warmth. As visitors walk through and about the space, they practically float or glide across the room. The person becomes the focal point. The space becomes a receptacle. Visitors entering the room are met with a gentle fragrance. The space breathes through its untreated surfaces. Like the untreated skin of our bodies.

Why choose these materials?
The chapel was to be built with locally available materials. The materials are present, they give the place its characteristic features, they make it what it is; they give the place its unmistakable identity, its appearance, its being. The materials therefore exactly match what has been used here for building for centuries.

What does it feel like?
Anyone going into the chapel leaves solid ground behind and enters the timber shell. It is a self-contained space that offers repose. It is made of only one material. The space has both a soaring and sheltering effect, it conveys security and warmth. The space breathes and is fragrant.

Projects
Mountain Chapel

Why make it like this?
The classical Strickbau construction consists of horizontal timbers; when the sections are used vertically, they reinforce the soaring effect of the space and achieve a special and subtle symbolism because of the specific way in which this design departs from the traditional style.

P.121

— P.122
— Project Name
Frühling —
Spring,
Austria

— Architect
architekturwerk THE EDGE gmbh
— Location
Wolfurt, Austria
— Client
Errichtergemeinschaft Frühlingsstrasse —
7 families: Becker, Scheibler, Ritter, Salzgeber, Schlader, Lenz, Reis
— User
Clients
— Budget
€2300 m²
— Completion Date
July 2006 / September 2006
— Build Time
10 months
— Building use
Family housing

An intensive two-year preparation process preceded the "Wohnanlage Frühlingsstraße" (Spring Street Residential Complex) project. Five families grappled intensively with their personal housing needs, wishes and ideas and viewed all the relevant examples of residential building in the region. A list of desires were prepared and three designers invited to take part in a private architectural competition. After the second round, architekturwerk THE EDGE Christoph Kalb was chosen. Two more families, who matched the building design criteria were sought.

Appearing to be detached single-family dwellings above ground, the seven units below ground level are combined as a row of terraced houses. The East and West houses are partly or fully basemented. In the basement, the cellar runs like a centre line connecting all the houses with heating and services.

A top priority for the building cooperative was a protected, un-overlooked, highly usable garden. The big south-facing windows of each house look out onto its particular garden. In order to ensure the gardens would not be overlooked, the special recessed windows are alternately west or east-facing. On the ground floor, at viewing height, it is not possible to look over into the neighbour's garden. On the upper floor, wooden visual protection leaves project from the facade in order to ensure privacy. The large leased neighbouring plot of land to the west is presently used as a communal playground and meeting place.

A communal car park is located directly on the access road. Eleven parking places have been created, three held in reserve, on the basis that the possibility of adding them later had been demonstrated.

Community: The rounding of the edges of the opposing facades, which tracks the meandering arrangement of the structures, should be interpreted as a structural symbol of the links that exist between the houses underground and also between the families responsible for the building project.

The bringing together of individual and communal needs has been very consciously thematised. The residents want to be able to make contact with each other but not feel forced to do so.

Projects
P.124 Frühling — Spring

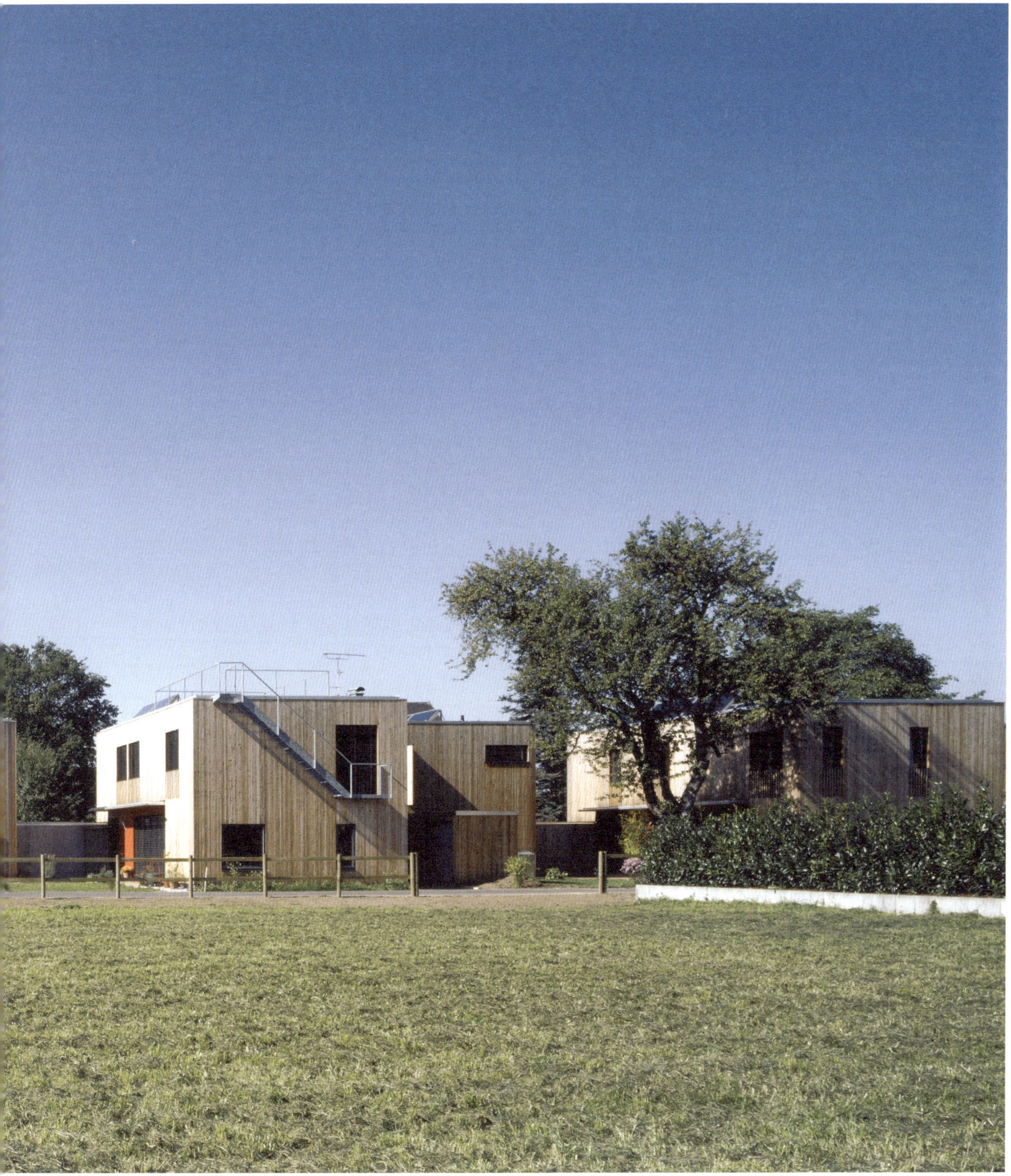

Projects
P.126

Frühling — Spring

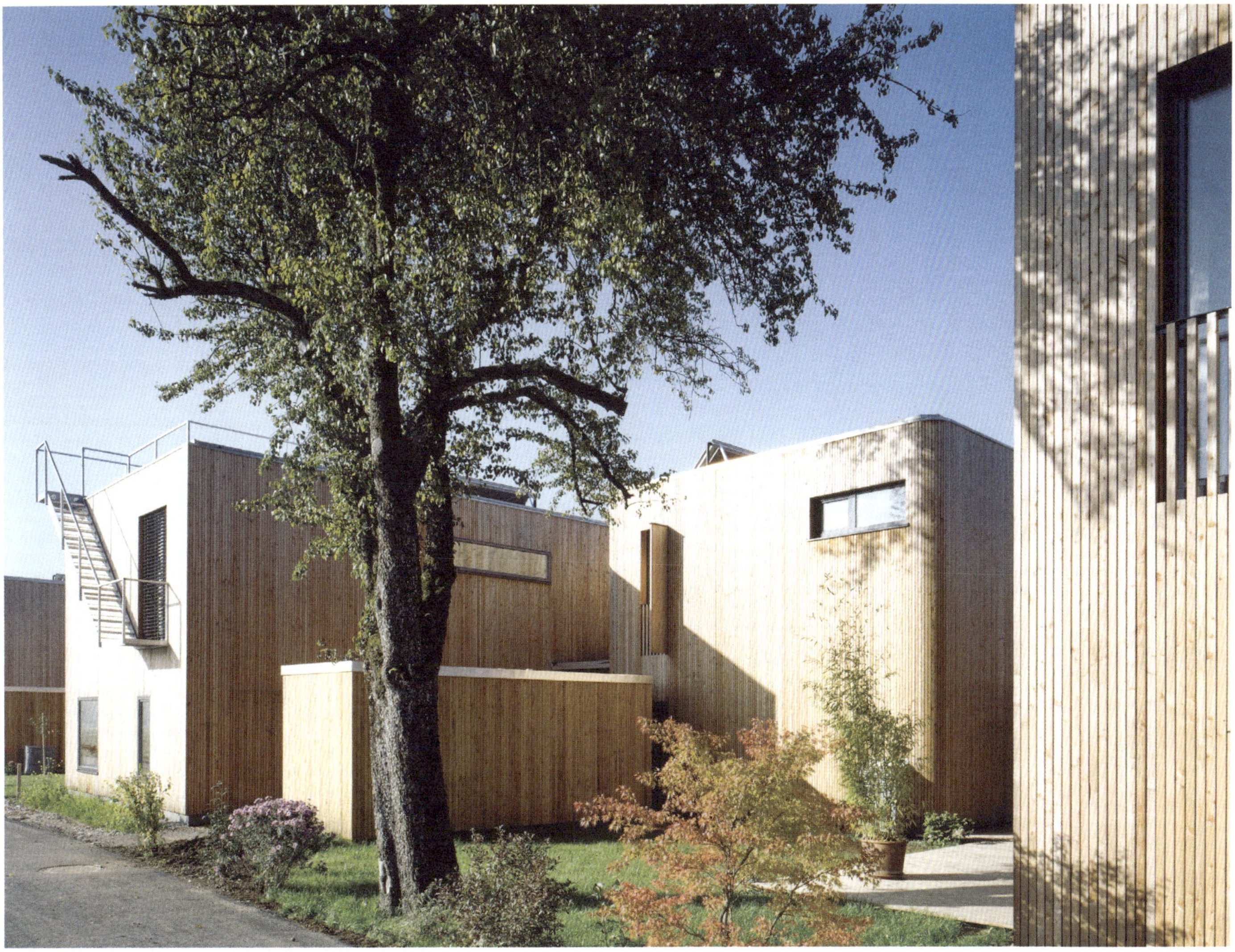

The Story
architekturwerk
THE EDGE gmbh

Low-energy house
Ecology and energy efficiency were the most important specifications of all seven clients. The extremely compact, cost-efficient, very low-energy houses have a pellet-fed central heating system, controlled ventilation and air extraction.

Timber is used systematically: prefabricated timber sections with larch cladding on the outside and glued laminated timber inside. Other materials respect organic building principles. Sheep's wool insulation, biological surface treatments, adhesives and loam are used. Extensive rooftop greening and rainwater use round off the picture of a responsible use of resources.

All the houses are the same – yet each is different.

Each one of the seven houses was tailored to individual housing needs. There are variations in the number of rooms, the configuration of the entrance, positioning of the stairs, size of the bathroom, choice of materials. The living rooms are mostly open design. A common feature is that in the east-facing houses all the recessed windows face east.

The centre of the house
In all the houses the kitchen opens onto the living accommodation. The variety of arrangements follows the variety of personalities of the residents. For example, in one kitchen there is a 'floating island', in another a functional range of kitchen units.

Community
The bringing together of individual needs and the communal was consciously thematised. For example, it was soon clear that the residents wanted actively to be together, wanted to leave their houses in order to meet the others, but did not want to be forced to. That is why there are no communal rooms or facilities. Only the jointly

Where is it and why?
The building plot is in a typical, slightly congested, built-up area of detached single-family dwellings in the Vorarlberg Rhine valley. In order to keep the footprint as small as possible, the design was based on as high a permitted development density as possible. This was approved because of the large number of environmental measures. Conclusion: environmentally friendly building leads to density – leads to quality – leads to space – leads to the Frühlingsstrasse project.

Projects
Frühling — Spring

leased garden constitutes a meeting point. Privacy was the leading principle.

Function

And how does it work? Wonderfully well! Common synergies are made use of. The baby intercom can be heard from the house next door, if there are issues an extra place is set at the neighbour's table and the mutual contact ensures a good outcome. Everyone's concerns are taken seriously, when compromises are reached, equilibrium is restored; above all there is an openness that allows everything to be talked about, which prevents misunderstandings.

— (Right) Two interiors showing different layouts.

— **Why make it like this?**
The tradition of timber construction and the strong craftsmanship in Vorarlberg; local firms were awarded the building work. All the companies are based within a radius of 30 km. Local value creation scored highly. In addition, availability, methods of transport and energy consumption during manufacture were taken into account for all the decisions about materials. The timber sections were made in the carpenter's workshop, erecting a house took 8 hours.

— **What were the influences?**
Helsinki – Käpylä workers' housing estate 1920-25, Arch. Martti Välikangas, Master plan by Birger Brunila and Otto Meurmann.

In Vorarlberg, collective building is a 40 year-old tradition. Collective housing developments attracting international attention have existed here since the time of Hans Purin's 'Halde' residential complex in Bludenz (1963-67) and the 'im Fang' housing estate by the Eberle-Koch-Juen-Mittersteiner Cooperative (1978).

Or international projects such as the 'Weissenhof' estate in Stuttgart, the 'Halen' estate in Berne or the self-build houses of Walter Segal in England.

The building cooperative's 'Frühlingsstrasse' project slots into that tradition with its own contemporary style.

— P.129

—P.130
—Project Name
Svartlamoen
Nursery,
Norway

— **Architect**
Brendeland & Kristoffersen arkitekter AS

— **Location**
Strandveien 33, 7042 Trondheim, Norway

— **Client**
Municipality of Trondheim

— **User**
Children

— **Budget**
N/a

— **Completion Date**
August 2007

— **Build Time**
8 months

— **Building use**
Nursery

Svartlamoen nursery is located in a former car dealership on a post-industrial site next to the harbour in Trondheim, Norway's third largest city.

The concept was to make a complex urbanity or a wooden landscape inside an existing glass pavillion of the old showroom from 1983.

The first choice was to reuse the existing steel and glass pavillion and to treat this as the site for the nursery. The second choice was to use solid wood panels to achieve a complex wooden geometry but still manage easy on-site assembly. More complexity, not more build time. All unique wooden parts for the nursery were prepared by CNC milling machines in the factory before arriving on site for assembly. This enabled a more intuitive process using a 1:20 physical model for testing the spatial sequences in detail before finalising the drawings.

The wood is a renewable local resource and brought other benefits as well: wood has a relatively warm surface to touch, it makes a good interior climate, it smells good. The use of wood also gave a homogenous and calm overall expression, but it still has an enormous variety on the micro level. Every wooden board has its own grain pattern, chips and cracks. Over time this will only get stronger. This is a micro landscape that kids can explore.

The most important factor is the users: the children and the employees of the nursery. Interiors and the exterior are not yet finished and never will be. Surfaces will get scars, the gardens will be planted, altered and developed through seasons and over time. Seasons have a large affect on the interior feeling. Light, and especially the lack of light in the short winter days, makes the glass facade reflective and the spaces more introvert.

The nursery is most of all a place of great contrast. Large, small, light, dark, sheltered exposed. Transparency and reflections. Uglyness and beauty.

— **The Story**
Brendeland & Kristoffersen
arkitekter AS

Svartlamoen nursery is the latest chapter in the ongoing development and regeneration of the old working class area Svartlamoen next to the docks in Trondheim.

Svartlamoen started life in the nineteenth century as an outlying working class neighbourhood. It had a reputation for being the roughest area of the city. It was an area with a strong identity, but also an area of deep social problems and poverty. In the 30's more than 3,000 people lived in this part of the city.

Because of its social standing the entire neighbourhood was re-zoned for industrial use in 1947. But the development of industry was slow and many of the houses were not demolished. Instead, Svartlamoen slowly degenerated until the late 1980s when young people from the city's alternative scene, gradually started to appropriate some of the forty or so remaining buildings.

This led to a long and bitter fight betwen the new residents and a large car dealership situated in the middle of the old neighbourhood. The city council and the car dealer were in favour of demolishing all the old houses. But they underestimated the power of the alternative community. Skillful political work, clever use of media and pure energy saved the area. The politicians changed their minds and finally the car dealership was given new premises. In 2001 all plans for industrial development in Svartlamoen were scrapped and it was re-zoned for residential use, this time with a new label: 'semi-autonomous urban ecological experimental area'. All city-owned property in the area was also transferred to a housing foundation run by the inhabitants of the area.

The car dealer was the old 'enemy' of all the people in the area. It was a real triumph when the new nursery opened. The cars were swapped for kids.

— **Why choose these materials?**
The use of wood gives a homogenous expression, but has a micro landscape that kids can explore. Over time this will only get stronger.

— Projects
P.132

Svartlamoen
Nursery

— **What were the influences?**
Visiting Iran in 2005 was important. It sparked the wish to work with complexity and multilayered spaces.

— **What affects it?**
Interiors and the exterior will never be finished. Surfaces will scar, the gardens will grow and change.

— An aerial image showing the
context of Trondheim.

Projects Svartlamoen
P.134 Nursery

Views of the interior spaces.

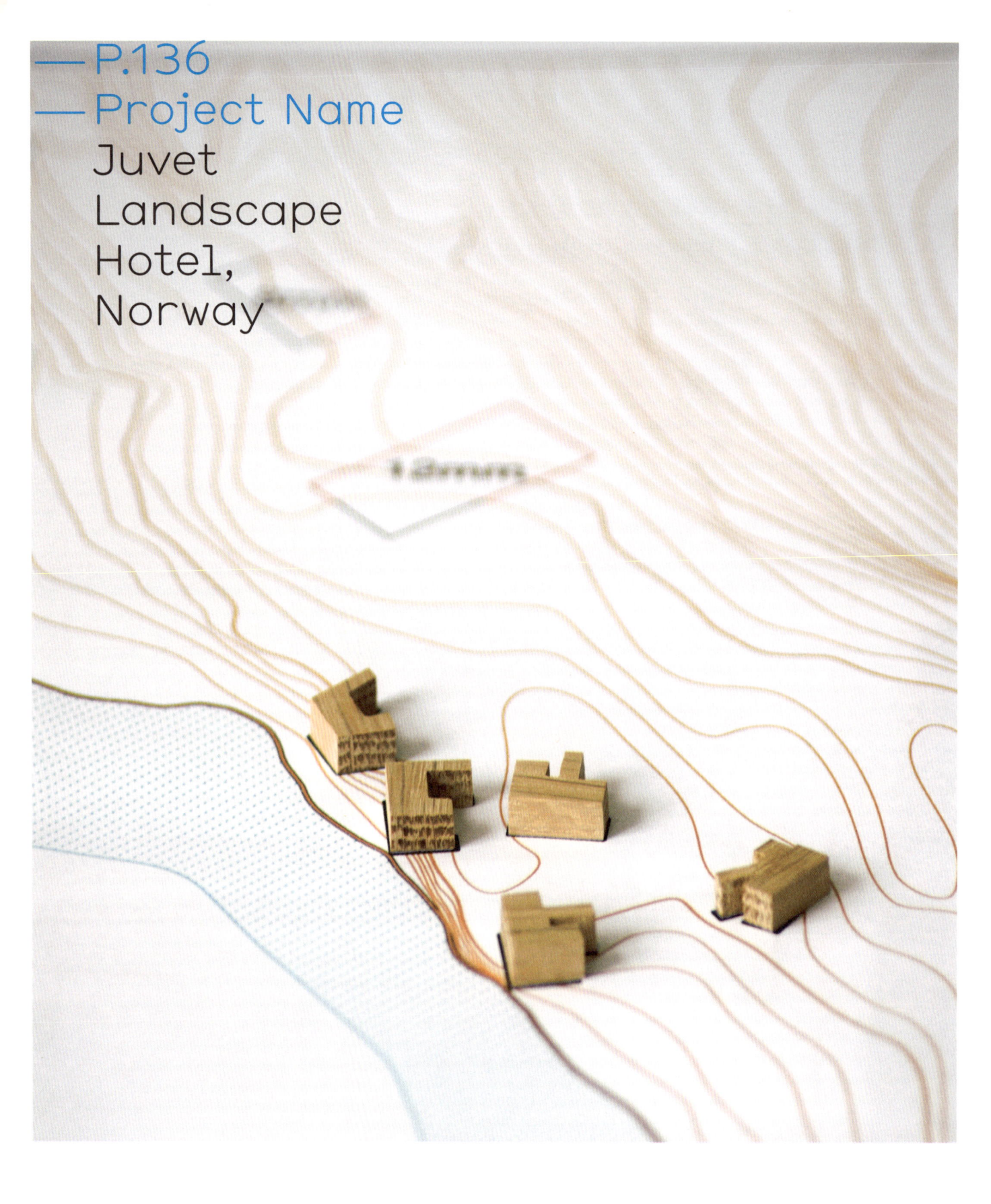

—P.136
—Project Name
Juvet
Landscape
Hotel,
Norway

- **Architect**
  Jensen & Skodvin Architects
- **Location**
  Burtigard, Gudbrandsjuvet, Norway
- **Client**
  Knut Slinning
- **User**
  Knut Slinning
- **Budget**
  €1 million
- **Completion Date**
  2008
- **Build Time**
  1 year
- **Building use**
  Landscape hotel, event holiday

The Juvet Landscape Hotel is located at Valldal, near the town of Åndalsnes in north-western Norway. Passing tourists are attracted by a spectacular waterfall in a deep gorge near the road, 'Gudbrandsjuvet'. The client, Knut Slinning, is a local resident. The idea emerged as an opportunity to exploit breathtaking scenery with minimal intervention, allowing locations which would otherwise be prohibited for reasons of conservation.

Instead of the conventional hotel, with guest rooms stacked together in one large building, the Landscape Hotel distributes the rooms throughout the terrain as small individual houses. Through careful orientation every room gets its own view of a piece of the landscape, always changing with the season, the weather, and the time of day. No room looks onto another.

The rooms are built in a massive wood construction with no exterior insulation, and are intended for summer use only. Each building rests on a set of 40mm massive steel rods drilled into the rock, existing topography and vegetation left almost untouched. The glass is set against slim frames of standard steel profiles, using stepped edges to extend the exterior layer of the main glass surfaces all the way to the corners.

Today's concern for sustainability in architecture focuses almost exclusively on reduced energy consumption in production and operation. We think that conservation of topography is another aspect of sustainability which deserves attention. Standard building procedure requires the general destruction of the site to accommodate foundations and infrastructure before building can commence. Conserving the site is a way to respect the fact that nature precedes and succeeds man. Also, dutiful observation of existing topography produces a reading where the geometry of the intervention highlights the irregularities of the natural site, thus giving both the intervention and its context more power. A sustainable connection is established between structure and site.

Projects
P.138

Juvet Landscape
Hotel

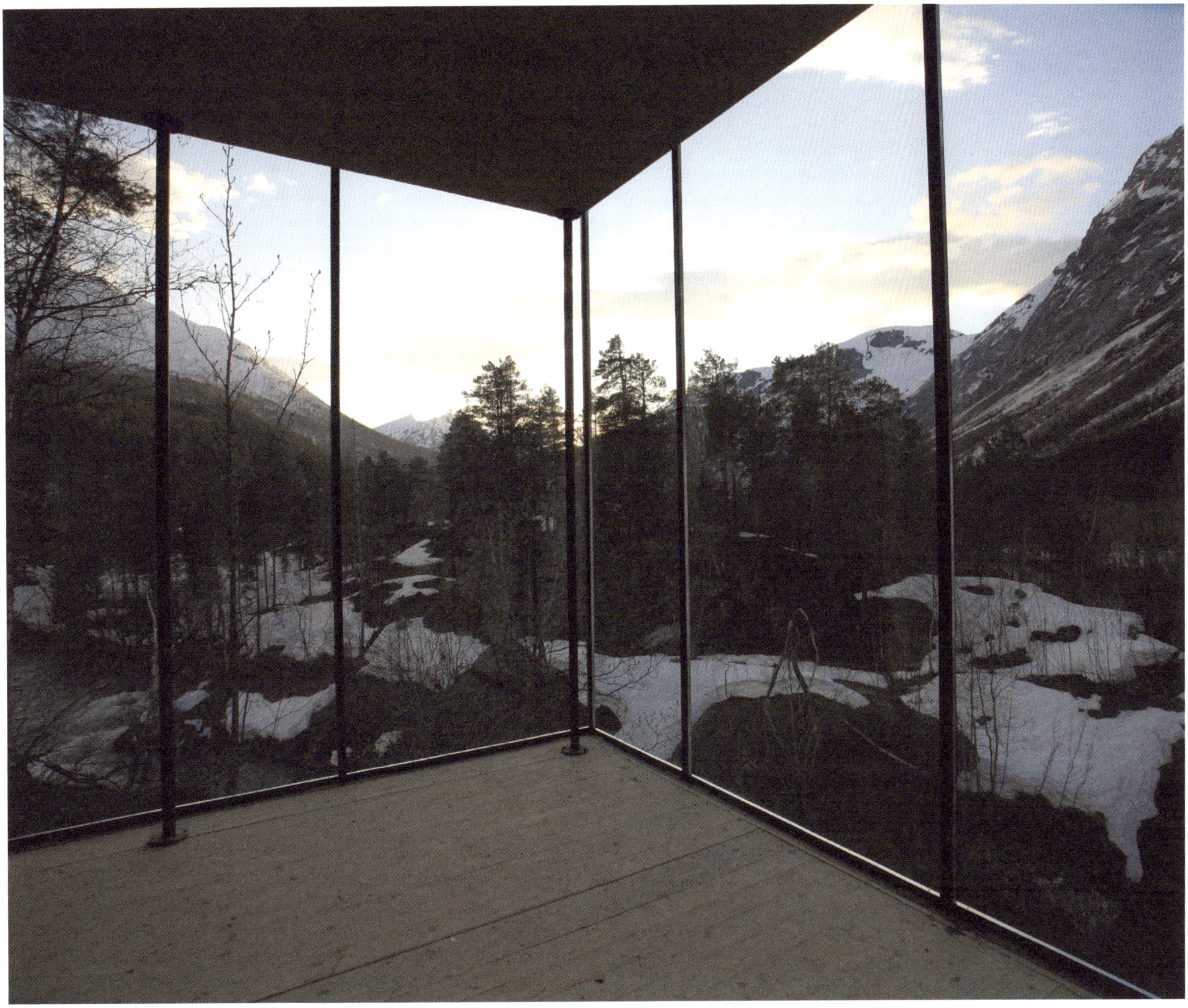

Projects
P.140

Juvet Landscape
Hotel

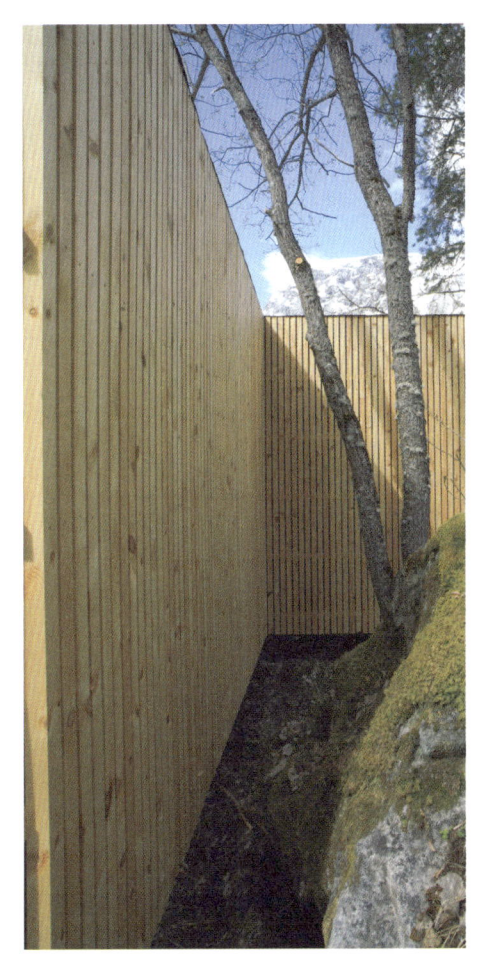

P.141

The Story
Jensen & Skodvin Architects

There is no doubt that architects differ in affinity; a personal predilection which is deeper than the current architectural vogue. We might call them our architectural darling children; ideas and projects which have been important to us and which have given rise to new insights and a platform to investigate other architectural topics.

Looking back, it is easy to point out the one project that has been most important to us. The Liasanden lay-by along the Sognefjell road represents an insight that has influenced most of our later projects in one way or another, and is the intellectual ancestor of a lot of our later work. In this project we understood that a complete architectural idea can be without a specific shape or configuration. The exact same architectural idea would produce different configurations and shapes when applied at different sites. Furthermore we saw a whole architectural landscape of possibilities opening up in related fields: of originals versus copies; of geometric uniqueness, of architecture that by definition could not be copied exactly, even if the identical instructions were to be repeated. Also there are interesting implications when it comes to realisation, for instance regarding tolerances.

Another insight is less remarkable, but no less true. We have come to deeply enjoy the process of making – of building. Knowledge about all parts of this process, how the machines operate, how the materials behave,

— The Liasanden lay-by.

— **Why choose these materials? Construction** – We wanted a building material that would allow for pre production of larger elements, as well as being light enough for easy transport, giving minimal damage to the site.

— Projects
P.142

Juvet Landscape Hotel

and what the craftsmen are capable of doing is of great advantage in our work. Architecturally, because it informs the architectural expression, but also because of the obvious authority knowledge provides. We have found it to be one of our fundamental sources of architectural grammar and we regard basic tectonic knowledge as a major part of the building architect's literacy. It is the language and the vocabulary that you need to tell a story.

—
Where is it and why?
Surroundings – The Landscape Hotel is located at Gudbrandsjuvet in Valldal, western Norway. The beautiful surroundings offer unique views in all directions.

—
What were the influences?
Camera Obscura – We wanted to make the room like a huge camera.

P.143

—re-Emerging Architecture
—Neil Gillespie

"There once was a small boy who lived in a place that seemed like a long way from everywhere.

Each morning he rose long before sunrise to begin his chores. At sunset he crept wearily back into his bed.

At sunrise he would gaze across the valley. In the distance he could see a house with golden windows. He promised himself that some day he would go there and see that wonderful place.

One morning his stern father was away at market. The boy knowing this was his chance stole out of the house and headed towards the house with the golden windows.

As he neared the house he realised that there was something very wrong. He saw no golden windows. Instead there was a place in need of repair surrounded by a broken fence. He knocked on the door, a boy close to his own age opened it.

He asked the boy if he had seen the house with the golden windows. The boy nodded and pointed back to where he had just come from. The setting sun had turned the windows on his house to gold."

Anonymous

I too imagine that better things must be happening elsewhere and in the case of architecture in Scotland this is undoubtedly true. However the story of the House with Golden Windows tells us that searching somewhere else for an answer to our issues is doomed to both superficiality and missing the value of our own voice. The development of an authentic and meaningful architecture can only come from within a culture. Architecture gains its authenticity from the well it springs from, not from imported visions, regardless how exotic and seductive they may appear; the beauty and craft of Scarpa's work stems from the opulence of his Venetian heritage, Lewerentz's intensity is born of a northern melancholy and Siza's poetry belongs in the brightness of a southern Atlantic coast.

The threat and challenge to all things local and distinct is globalisation, globalisation of form and ambition. Much celebrated contemporary architecture is marked by an obsession with formal gymnastics and manipulation supported and marketed by an increasingly agile computer aided industry. So-called iconic architecture is peddled by itinerant architectural celebrities who journey to foreign courts bearing sparkling wonders. The cult of the celebrity is endemic in our culture and spreading; their every move is documented and discussed at length. The fêted few are engaged in an exclusive and self-indulgent game where the startling image or extravagant visualisation wins. Architectural publications flow unabated, spreading the current crop of seductive images to insatiable consumers. I speak as a self-confessed monograph junkie, who in weaker moments can easily succumb to the enchanting narrative of the architectural sirens.

Juhani Pallasmaa writes in his seminal text The Eyes of the Skin[1],

"In western culture, sight has historically been regarded as the noblest of the senses, and thinking itself, thought of in terms of seeing. Already in classical Greek thought, certainty was based on vision and visibility.

The ocular bias has never been more apparent in the art of architecture than in the past 30 years, as a type of architecture, aimed at a striking and memorable visual image, it has predominated. Instead of an existentially grounded plastic and spatial experience, architecture has adopted the psychological strategy of advertising and instant persuasion; buildings have turned into image products detached from existential depth and sincerity."

The pre-eminence of the visual in our contemporary culture comes at the expense of ideas: ideas of how ordinary people actually live or might live. Concentration on the visual, the aesthetic, could be seen to reduce the work of the architect to that of a mere stylist only capable of making buildings either visually arresting, in the case for the iconic, or neighbourly, in the case for the contextual. We judge what is interesting and valuable by its visual impact, either by being striking or by being invisible. Designers may have always been prone to easy seduction but it is now a phrase that resonates through the halls of the planners and the drawing rooms of the amenity groups. How often have we lost a project because it had low wow factor? The search for the appropriate and subtle relies on an empowered and discerning client; they may be as illusive as a great architect.

The fixation with image is connected to the cult of the self, to a loss of the collective; it is concerned with the individual. It is concerned with personal self-gratification and gain. A simple series of aerial images of Edinburgh's urban form reveal a gradual loss of shared, social patterns in favour of the exclusive and the particular. This is seen as a breakdown in the balance of public and private space not to mention the quality of each.

Edinburgh, Old Town, 1500s – 1700s, a dense medieval street pattern within defined and defining city walls that produced, along with squalor, a vertical layering that was in part responsible for the Scottish Enlightenment. Aristocrat and pauper, intellectual and tradesman lived literally on top of one another. The High Street was the ultimate social condenser.

"Here I stand at what is called the cross of Edinburgh, and can, in a few minutes, take 50 men of genius and learning by the hand"[2]

Edinburgh, New Town, 1765 – 1850, a neo-classical plan for the affluent that imagined terraced houses masquerading as palaces fronting private, estate-like, shared gardens. Here the well off played out their aristocratic fantasy surrounded by mature planned landscapes and refined Georgian architecture. The price of this splendour and the resulting migration of the educated rich was the decline of the Old Town and with it the social stew that had proved so culturally fertile.

Edinburgh, Bruntsfield and Marchmont, 1850s, again shared terraces this time consisting of communal flats for the middle classes with private shared back gardens

— (Top) Edinburgh Old Town.
— (Bottom) Edinburgh New Town.

— Bruntsfield and Marchmont.

— P.147

and public parks close by. These tenement blocks are notable for their use of generous bay windows, a device that allow residents to observe the street scene and be seen in return.

Edinburgh, The Grange, 1860s, Victorian suburbs to the south of the city sees large individual houses within extensive private gardens. The villas are set back from the street and their neighbours. Already the idea of collective space is vanishing. There is no beginning and no end to the development pattern; all green space is private to the individual houses. The rich have removed themselves completely from the city.

Edinburgh Costorphine, 1930s, the Grange on a budget, the individual house and garden are smaller but the pattern is the same as the Grange. The speculative developer apportions all the land to the individual purchasers. There is no public space then to be concerned about in terms of ownership and maintenance; all is profit.

Edinburgh, Bughtlin, 1990s, suburbia at its most banal, the car and the individual have complete autonomy. The scene degenerates into a quagmire of houses and tarmac. Public space is reduced to turning space for cars, defined by the road engineer's radii and visibility splays. Green space is confined to edging the roads. Buildings appear like aggregate in a matrix of tarmac; there is no proposition for public and private, front or back; in short there is no architectural idea or collective responsibility.

Edinburgh Southfields, 1960s, Roland Wedgewood Architect. Immediately adjacent to the last scene is, at last, an architectural idea for social housing from a more enlightened generation. Terraced houses combine to form a continuous wall. Within the wall, the terraces are lined by private gardens that in turn open onto communal landscaped space. The inner green courts are extensive and secure. The individual contributes to an idea of shared space that benefits the community.

There is a growing sense that the primacy of the search for the iconic form is beginning to be questioned. Architects who place the human condition and common sense at the centre are beginning to find a voice. Concerns about the environment and the loss of local difference and character

— (Top) The Grange.
— (Bottom) Costorphine.

— (Top) Bughtlin.
— (Bottom) Southfields.

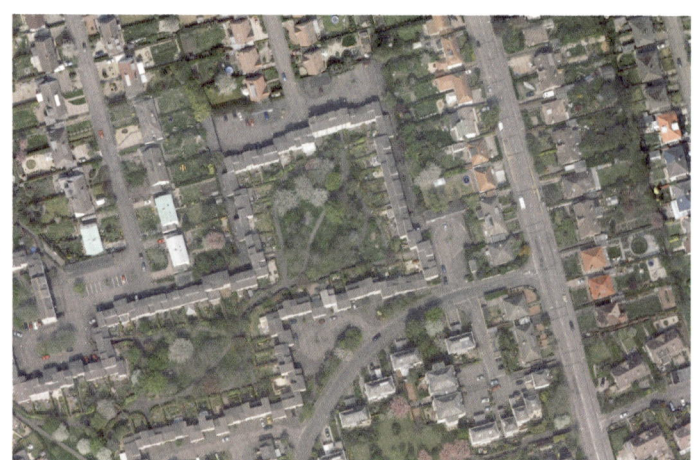

are becoming more newsworthy. The ordinary is slowly being seen to be of value as people turn from a prolonged period of decadence. Maybe sustainability concerns are the impetus we need to return to humanist practice.

The voices that inspire seem to all come from practice at the edge, either geographically or professionally. Dislocation and distance seems to help gain a critical perspective. Important work is being created in Scandinavia, Switzerland, Austria, Northern Italy, Portugal and Spain, away from the commercial centres. Iconoclast-in-chief Peter Zumthor, secreted away in a Swiss canton in monastic isolation with a group of close collaborators, has crafted a series of buildings that are marked by their exploration of the material and the sensual.

"Something new does not stand beside the old but grows out of it and is interwoven with the old."

Zumthor's work along with a select band of older architects, Luigi Snozzi, Alvaro Siza, Sverre Fehn, Jorn Utzon, the Smithsons et al have influenced a younger generation of architects who themselves now not only teach, they write and most importantly they build. They build sparingly at the moment but the rapacious commercial world is very quick to recognise talent and convert it into a product that sells. They must be on their guard.

Within the main centres, however, loose groupings of younger architects have also created their own territories and agendas in contrast to the prevailing commercial culture. In London architects such as Sergiston Bates and Caruso St John under the influence of elders Tony Fretton and Florian Biegel write eloquently and build poetically. Their architecture is directed at the London that exists beneath the synthetic surface of the City.

From amongst these refreshing voices I have chosen three, each of whom raises an issue that is critical to this debate.

Valerio Olgiati writes[3] about architecture as a continuing tradition:

"I tend to work with the same idea from project to project. I think of my work as a body of work that is something larger than each individual project. I do not plan change. Changes that appear from project to project are caused by the particularities of the task at hand, not by me changing my architecture for each project. It is possible that my architectural idea in my mind does not work at all for a given project. That is the moment when I have to invent something new. But that is how I approach it. I do not get up in the morning and strive to reinvent a new architecture."

Sou Fugimoto writes[4] about the primitive:

"To consider innovative architecture of the future is astonishingly equivalent to reflection on primitive architecture. That is because architecture transpires wherever people exist. Thus novel architecture must be a conception of a place for humanity that is fundamentally new."

Peter Markli writes about social responsibility:

"The question of the collective conception of architecture affects the political understanding of our work. I believe that the contemporary architectural debate is marked by a certain cynicism. Put in somewhat simplified terms: architecture is no longer a primary agent of social change – innovation almost always proceeds from the dynamic of an unfettered, globalised economy. Architects are latching onto the whole set of characteristics of this development – its speed, its absence of boundaries, its aggressive fragility – and pouring them, in a distinctive narrative furore, into absolute formalistic images."

I am not talking about architects as social workers, or artists, or developers. I am concerned about architects regaining the practice of architecture, of having the courage and skill to talk about architecture as a cultural responsibility. Architecture, we are told, will be lost to the engineer who is better placed to deal with sustainability just as it was claimed that architecture has been lost to the project manager or the surveyor in the recent past. Architecture can never be lost to anyone, architecture exists beyond any definition the professions, including the architecture profession, might give it.

Pallasmaa writes:

"The timeless task of architecture is to create embodied and lived existential metaphors that concretise and structure our being in the world. Architecture reflects, materialises and eternalises ideas and images of ideal life. Buildings and towns enable us to structure, understand and remember the shapeless flow of reality and, ultimately, to recognise and remember who we are."

There are two images that haunt me or rather console me; in a way both reveal an idyllic sense of harking back to simpler times when the greatest possession was a bag of sweets and the greatest danger was wasps. I suppose, like the boy in search for the House with the Golden Windows, they represent something that is actually unattainable. They do however place building as a central figure in the scene, a key reference point.

Familiar strangers are people we see in our everyday lives who connect us to a place; the business man we always pass at 8:15, the group of school kids we pass on the Mound; we do not know them intimately but we would miss them if they were not there. Familiar strangers offer a refuge from the unknown without the risk of becoming known. Buildings too ground us in a particular place. They bond you by being there, by their familiarity, by their reticence as opposed to the unknown faceless structures or strident iconic forms that assault the senses. For the most part architecture is about making the familiar building; houses, offices, shops and hospitals. These building types form the backdrop to our lives.

Maybe my images reveal naïve clues for a more sustainable future; windows that open, cycling, walking and simple construction. They probably reveal the hopeless sentimentalist in me. However they have a powerful and primitive sense of time and place. They pull us in; we are lost in a narrative we instinctively understand. We know what has happened and what is about to happen: in Flamatt a mother is preparing pasta, drinking a glass of wine and listening to the radio, she calls the kids from the balcony for their evening meal. In Glen Affric the sun is going down as these children wearily return to beans on toast and mugs of tea, sitting at a communal table, full of tales of their day's walk.

The scenes have a dignity and stillness that both lifts and calms the spirit. There is none of the exhausting wilfulness of much celebrated architectural design. There is no trace of the desperate search for that never seen before gesture. Sou Fujimoto's architecture has this quality, as does Valerio Olgiati's, as does Peter Markli's,

— Atelier 5, Terraced Houses, Flamatt, 1961.

a sense that space, people and experience are connected.

George MacKay Brown[6] writing in Northern Lights, Shetland: A Search for Symbols reveals how extra ordinary, ordinary life is:

"A blight on much modern art is an all pervading snobbery and elitism, and cult of personality – 'the famous poet'; ' the world-renowned sculptor'. We should think rather of art as being, in Thomas Mann's words, 'anonymous and communal' a whole community contributes to the making of a poem... to see the symbol in the common objects of daily life is to know a depth and enrichment."[6]

A new and emerging architecture in Scotland needs to regain architectural culture itself. It needs to make an ethical stance and create work that once more returns to placing people first through dignified and appropriate design. As a small nation on the edge of both Europe and the profession, I believe we are well placed to make a significant contribution to the developing debate.

Biography

Neil Gillespie is a Director of Reiach & Hall Architects and tutor at the Department of Architecture, Edinburgh College of Art.

Footnotes

[1] The Eyes of the Skin, Architecture and the Senses, Juhani Pallasmaa, Wiley-Academy 2005.

[2] Quote from a tourist in 1750 on Parliament Square from Edinburgh World Heritage Site publication.

[3] Valerio Olgiati, Conversation with Students, edited by Markus Breitschmid, Virginia Tech Architecture Publications, 2007.

[4] Primitive Future, Sou Fujimoto, INAX Publishing, 2008.

[5] Approximations, The Architecture of Peter Markli, Edited by Mohsen Mostafavi, AA Publications 2002.

[6] Northern Lights, George Mackay Brown, Polygon, 2007.

Glen Affric Youth Hostel, circa 1950s.

—Highlanders Have Long Travelled
—Mary Arnold-Forster

In the heart of Carradale village in Kintyre a sombre granite memorial records the excruciating loss of the men and boys in the trenches in France. Across the Hebrides cemeteries and memorials continue to describe communities decimated by remote wars. In a house on Islay the mother of a teenager seduced by a sense of adventure and a lack of employment into the Black Watch stares anxiously at a news report from Felluja.

A sense of displacement permeates the landscapes — abandoned villages, schools and churches converted into occasional homes.

If being a soldier is a job then it is just one of many that have taken men and women of the highlands and islands away from home but often to come back with new ideas and an open mind. A geologist from Muck working in Brazil, an engineer from Skye working in Nigeria, a merchant seaman from Ardnamurchan working in the Pacific, bring home to their culture a willingness to learn from others.

Whether people have returned or are settling for the first time in these landscapes they are likely to have lived and worked in some other part of the world. There is nothing conservative about their outlook and for the architects working with them it is a pleasure.

This tradition of exploration combined with an instinct to research fostered by television and the internet, a sense of optimism with the building of the Scottish Parliament creates an enlightened and engaged client base for private and community projects. This cannot be said to be true for many commercial, developer and institutional clients. Without engaging in a debate about aesthetics, some of the health centres, schools and suburban housing developments still being commissioned and approved are often simply not fit for purpose and lack an understanding of their context, both culturally and physically.

Often with the commissioning of new buildings comes a desire for some kind of sustainability. The definition of sustainability can be simultaneously abstract and precise: both a dream and a large gadget. There is no simple answer. Incredibly expensive sheep's wool insulation, like organic food, is really still only for the rich – like organic food. Thin foam insulations are extremely efficient but can be poisonous. Chinese and Indian slates are far more easily and cheaply available in Inverness showrooms than Caithness or Ballachulish slates. There is plenty of technology available that if inappropriately specified is expensive to buy and run. Sustainability can simply mean a well insulated, simply planned building that exploits the power and joy of the sun. Or it can mean building homes and communities that are built to last and that people enjoy living, gathering and working in.

In the last 10 years there has been a real change in the attitude of some individuals in the planning departments of such councils in The Highlands, Argyll & Bute and The Western Isles.

An enlightening study tour of timber buildings in Norway designed to teach some Northern Scots, the Faroese and the Icelandic participants – people of the so called 'Peripheral Nations' – about the use of spruce as a structural and cladding material was attended by planners, building control officers, wood scientist timber professionals, a councillor and two architects. It was clear that the slow grown spruce was not comparable to our home grown trees. What was really interesting to discover was the cultural divide. Norway has a culture of maintenance with every household owning its own scaffold and the tradition of painting wooden buildings every year preserving their pristine appearance. While the desire for maintenance free buildings is unchanged in this country, the dry dash render and upvc of the mid to late twentieth century has given way to an acceptance both by the users and the authorities of unfinished timber and corrugated cladding.

Occasionally a planning officer will miss the point, perhaps intentionally. A recently retired Highland Council planning officer could be reduced to a fury at the mention of agricultural buildings, sheds and byres, timber cladding or corrugated roofs. He went on holiday to Norway and came back saying timber cladding could be used but only if stained chocolate or marmalade in a woodland setting and painted white in the treeless areas of 'his patch'.

More importantly, however, the Norwegian study tour allowed for an exchange of ideas amongst the participants. Hopefully the next change of attitude will be a willingness to let the new architecture stand proud and stop always digging into the landscape. Afterall it is only appropriate in certain cases. Brian MacKay-Lyons says "I think you destroy the hill when you build half way up it".

More recently a change of attitude in the road engineers can be detected. To have a private house designed by a planning officer is regrettable but to have a community designed by a road engineer is unacceptable. There are no local precedents for cul-de-sac living in the Highlands, there is clear evidence that people like to live in high density villages with a door onto the street and there is no need to alienate neighbours by elevating the status of the car. With the impending publication of 'Designing Streets' it is hoped that communities can be designed for people and not for cars. A modern abstracted version of Inverary or Plockton is now a possibility.

These changing attitudes combined with an emergence of a generation of architects described by Richard Gibson in Shetland as 'on the edge' but clearly aware of developments in other peripheral, coast or mountainous regions of the world, is beginning to hint at an exciting future. There is often a desire expressed amongst this generation to meet to discuss their work and to analyse the work of such architects as Murcutt, MacKay-Lyons and Zumthor. So far there appears to be no evidence that this is happening and there is a hope that they are consciously and collectively inspired by such examples and in so doing are developing a specific 'Critical Regionalism'. Maybe this is contrived but there are clear emerging themes that unite their work.

Marlon Blackwell

"I live, practice, teach and build in northwest Arkansas, in the foothills of the Ozark Mountains. It's a place considered to be in the middle of nowhere, yet ironically, close to everywhere. It is an environment of real natural beauty and simultaneously, of real constructed ugliness. This land of disparate conditions is not just a setting for my work – it is part of the work. In these conditions I do not see a negative, but instead, a source of deep possibilities."

Neil Sutherland

"My inspiration comes less from the international heros of the architectural press and more from our landscape and time/place context, troubled as it is very often.

"With the increase in community buy outs and trusts it is possible to identify a new culturally enfranchised and confident patronage which has been responsible for some intelligent community masterplanning on Gigha, Comrie and Tiree some, site and community specific community buildings at Ardfern, Argyll and Abriachan, Invernesshire."

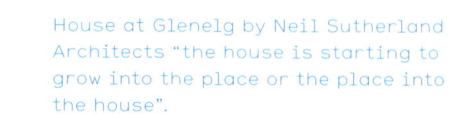

— Barnhouse by Marlon Blackwell.

— House at Glenelg by Neil Sutherland Architects "the house is starting to grow into the place or the place into the house".

Samuel Mockbee from
Rural Studio, Alabama
"I pay attention to my region; I keep my eyes open. Then I see how I can take that and reinterpret it, using modern technology. We don't try to be southern, we just end up that way because we try to be authentic. When you start to use historic references in a theatrical way, that's when I am out of here."

It is clearly evident that the works and words of two architects in particular have influenced a number of architects working in rural northwest Scotland; Brian MacKay-Lyons Canada and Glen Murcutt.

In writing about MacKay-Lyons, Murcutt clearly reveals much about his own work:

"Vernacular buildings inform us about how well various materials perform, and here Mackay-Lyons draws much of his knowledge through observation of the local building culture.

The traditional buildings, particularly those associated with fishing and lobster harvesting, are constructed with tight, crisp, timber-clad skins over simple, internal, exposed structures. This results in strong geometric forms that, over time, weather like the coast landscape to greys and silver greys. This regional construction method has influenced the thinking of MacKay-Lyons, rendering the work affordable, low-tech, tough and absolutely modern."

— Mason's Bend Community Center by Rural Studio "A work of avant-garde design perfectly at home in its rustic setting, a civic building created to 'act on a foundation of decency'."

— Marie Short House by Glen Murcutt Architects.

P.155

Brian MacKay-Lyons, building in the area of Nova Scotia he knows well, describes his work as 'landscape cameras... enhancing peoples understanding of the landscape... creating a body centred environment in which they feel this is their place in the world'.

Sean Godsell has a considered but unromantic attitude to sites. His principle is never to truck soil away from the site. However the Carter/Tucker House was cut into a sand dune, and the cut formed a continuation of the dune on the other side. His biographer described it as 'contained ruthlessness'.

Gareth Hoskins at Culloden by describing his visitors centre as part of a walk through the battlefield beds his building simultaneously into the landscape and counter to it both culturally and formally. Like Sutherland Hussey on Tiree, his response to the site is based on a rigourous study of its topography aspect and geology but with a sophisticated and powerful result.

If a Critical Regionalism exists in rural Scotland it is in its infancy and by its nature evolving. Kenneth Frampton defined it thus:

"The term 'Critical Regionalism' is not intended to denote the vernacular as this was once spontaneously produced by the combined interaction of climate, culture, myth and craft, but rather to identify those recent regional 'schools' whose primary aim has been to reflect and serve the limited constituencies in which they are grounded."

Malcolm Fraser
"For this new house we were concerned with making a contemporary Scottish architecture born out of respect for the work of our predecessors allied to an understanding that positive changes in the way we live in the world need to be reflected in our buildings. We understand tradition

— The Messenger House 11 by Mackay-Lyons Sweetapple Architects.

— Carter Tucker House by Sean Godsell.

to be an evolving thing, with the best elements of the past being altered by advances in building techniques allied to changes in social and cultural patterns. A living tradition would see established patterns of building altered by modern concerns such as: orientation towards landscape and view, blurring between internal and external spaces, more open-plan living and a consciousness of energy matters."

Alasdair Stephen
"The blackhouse is still a symbol of backwardness to many people in the Highlands and there is no point trying to romanticise it. But it was a vernacular response to the land, the climate and the poverty. People who hold it up as an example of the perfect eco design miss the point. The blackhouse represented their poverty, not eco living. A woman from the Earthship centre, an organisation that builds houses out of old tyres and mud contacted me once asking for insight into the relationship between the blackhouse and the earthship. She thought the idea of building out of turf, stone and thatch was wonderful. I took her to see Duncan Stalker who told her of the Boer war veteran in his village when he was a boy. When the men were fencing the clippings were collected and the old man spent his days twisting the wires together to make more fencing nails. But as soon as they could afford to buy fencing nails they did so and the old man had to find other ways to pass his time. I think she missed the point. Through the history of humanity people have been striving to make their own burden easier. New houses for the Highlands which are a development of some of the ideas of the blackhouse for the twenty first century have to be as modern as people can afford.

If there is movement in the Highlands and Islands as such it is at this stage coincidental. However, what is clear is that at the core of the best of contemporary architecture and design is a common concern to listen, to understand, to look and to produce thoroughly modern buildings inspired by the people, their ambitions, to capitalise on increasingly progressive authorities and to the specifics of some spectacular and humbling landscapes; buildings that both work and raise the spirits; buildings that make the ordinary better."

Biography
Mary Arnold-Forster is one of the Principals of Dualchas Building Design. She has worked there for ten years and has been instrumental in the development of the practice.

— Gareth Hoskins at Culloden.

—Designing a Future Forest
—Bernard Planterose

Parallel Histories

A group of Norwegian land use and rural planning professionals, visiting the Scottish Highlands recently on a study tour, took in the landscape, its patterns, its processes, its layers of human inhabitation, in the way that people involved in ecology of landscape do. Their reaction was one of shock, their collective response: "What has gone wrong here?". A Highlanders' historical perspective will respond with the well kent story of the Coming of the Sheep, of forced emigration, of the decline of a cattle grazing and shieling system: in short it will tell of the Clearances. Its emphasis will rather naturally be on the people and all that was lost of their ways of life, their culture.

But there is another story that the landscape tells, inextricably interwoven but extending both long before and after, much less often told, certainly much less understood. That story is the ecological one – one that tells how on a geologically 'new' landscape, only recently emerged from under the ice, there grew a varied and almost complete covering of forest in the space of three to four thousand years. And how, in a similar period of time, this forest was gradually fragmented, indeed all but decimated in most areas. By the time the great flocks of sheep came north (less than 250 years ago) clearly there was grazing enough to support them. The last two hundred years of ecological history could be described as only the nail in the coffin as far as soil and biological development is concerned – as native woodland was reduced to 2% of the land area and an explosion in the population of red deer (a tripling in the last 40 years) removed nature's powers of recovery and established its bleak regime.

As I move through the landscape of the Highlands and Uplands of the south of Scotland, but mostly the north west where I live, I see that forest wherever I go. Partly because of an obsession with hill running, maybe because I have read the history in the pollen analysis, but certainly because I have planted trees here for twenty five years, I see more of the ground beneath my feet and in more detail than many. And even though so often repeated, the shock of literally running into a 'field' of old pine stumps in the hills remains. That extraordinary contrast between the empty, barren landscape around and the forest that springs up in my imagination before me from the twisted, fleshless stumps, remains startling. There is a gut feeling: that same question hangs in the air, "What has gone wrong here?". As resonant for me in relation to the natural elements of the scene as the same question, no doubt, for the indigenous Highlander standing in the ruined crofting township.

I have also run through the southern Norwegian mountains, the low hills of Lapland, in Austria and just last week in the French Alps and all these landscapes with their intricately mixed forests and fields prompt me to think about that question. Not so much an answer to it – because that is well enough rehearsed from Fraser Darling[1] to Stevens and Carlisle[2] – but a way forward beyond that answer and into a strategy for recovery.

In these other mountainous countries of Europe and Scandinavia we see landscapes and land-use systems quite profoundly different in certain ecological ways that hold keys to our potential recovery. These landscapes have never been deforested in the nearly complete way in which ours has. To this day they retain a high percentage of forest cover – Sweden 75%, Norway 31%, Austria 47%. But it is the integration of this forest with inhabitation and agriculture that is important, it is the systems of management that tell the story to which we might listen.

So the story of Scottish rural life may be told in terms of social dislocation but it may also be told in terms of this one singular phenomenon – that of deforestation. A closer look at this context reveals impacts and meanings beyond the obvious. Indeed it could be argued that the ecological cul-de-sac of deforestation in Scotland has strong parallels with (and is inextricably bound to) the socio-political cul-de-sac of rural depopulation and the concentrated land ownership pattern with which the country struggles. Ecologists refer to such cul-de-sacs as 'plagio-climaxes' – in this case, where upland heath and blanket bog or grass-dominated communities have replaced the natural climax communities[3] of woodland. The significant point here is that the replacements are generally lower in productivity and biodiversity than the forest climax and in many cases considerably so.

Until we understand Scotland's history from the ecological perspective of deforestation, as well as from socio-political perspectives, we may never have the equipment to recover even a fraction of what we have lost. Acceptance of "the way things are" in terms of landscape and resource use is an obstacle to progress in Scotland. The bareness of the land is deep in the Scottish psyche. We have lost appreciation of the phenomenal power of natural regeneration as we have lost a large part of the varied seed sources to effect it. It represents a cultural loss or blindness – a century upon century destruction of a life force.

What I want to write about here is not a lament for what we have lost and certainly not an account of how it happened but to suggest how an understanding of this ecological history might inform a whole new land use approach – dare I say a revolution – and how this relates to bio-political strategies that are beginning to emerge in response to a perceived global ecological crisis. I will touch on (a) the link between the macro scale of global climate change and the micro scale of local habitat management – by which I mean to include both built and managed natural environments, (b) the link between Scottish and global deforestation and, (c) the way in

Scots pine roots dating from around 4000BP emerging from peat in an average Highland eroding peat hag. Advanced erosion of peat to reveal 4000 year old Scots pine roots can be seen throughout the Highlands from Tongue to Perth. Ironically such erosion reveals the glacial substrates that supported the first forest after the last Ice Age and which could once again support a future forest. A slight drying of the Highland climate could accelerate this process.

which a Regional (indeed a Bio-regional[4]) approach to resource use could lead to new or modified systems of land and water management designed to meet the ever increasing demands on natural resources that larger and more demanding Human populations are making.

This exploration, inevitably technical in places, suggests the need for a deeper and more fully rounded understanding of the 'place in which we live' than at any time in our previous history.

Biosphere Design

At the macro level, the first cornerstones of what we may call 'biosphere design' are being laid in the global approach to atmospheric composition that a number of relatively recent international initiatives and agreements signify.[5] The most tangible of these is the Kyoto Agreement and the subsequent Protocol whereby global targets are translated into meaningful national green house gas (GHG) emission targets.

The goal of this macro level approach is to design our way not merely through an immediate environmental crisis but beyond it into some new state of balance or harmony with the Planet, its natural resources and other species. This suggests an advanced level of design in all aspects of Human inhabitation, manufacturing and resource management joined up across many disciplines. It particularly suggests a creative collaboration of ecologists with agriculturalists and construction professionals in an avant-garde of Human endeavour where — as Kenneth Frampton has pointed out — architecture could play a central role if it chose[6].

The beginnings of that role are just developing as architects are asked to lead the way in designing very low and 'zero carbon' buildings. But other areas where architecture has barely started to fulfil its wider ecological potential are also apparent. The master-planning of towns and cities represents a shift in scale of influence and is extending rapidly as whole new towns are planned and designed in China and elsewhere. Even in the north of Scotland we have proposals such as Tornagrain to accommodate 10,000 people. Such projects are easily large enough to be linked to food production and energy systems supplying a good part of their own needs. A thorough integration of energy, water and waste systems with growing systems is the next creative step and there is much to be learned from a number of small scale eco-village initiatives including Findhorn on the Moray coast.

A further role for architects in wider 'biosphere design' is through material specification decisions. The straight-forward cause and effect this has on world resources has always been and will remain, of great significance. Larger or more influential architectural practices along with Local Authority procurement departments have a crucial role in respect of ensuring ecologically responsible sourcing. Setting an example at a higher level still, Central Government can also take matters into its own hands as in the brave and unequivocal policy recently enacted by the Norwegian Government which has banned the use of all Tropical timber in publicly funded projects.

Indeed governments across Europe and Scandinavia are at the forefront of emerging co-operative biosphere management and the beginnings of an appreciation of the need for a bigger scale of resource planning is clearly evident in emerging Scottish resource strategies that place 'Climate Change' at their core. Ironically in some respects, it could be said that the potential catastrophe of climate change is now driving the emerging field of ecosystem management faster than it would otherwise have evolved. The Scottish Climate Change Programme (SCCP) has formed the background to a clutch of land use and energy strategies and policies over the last two to three years including those for agriculture[7] biodiversity[8], forestry[9], biomass energy[10], deer[11] and building standards[12].

Each of them has called for policy integration of a higher and more considered level than before and several have explicitly identified a 'landscape' or 'ecosystem based' approach to resource management. The recent (Scottish Government multi-agency) draft deer strategy backs them both: "Responses to climate change are also likely to lead to more focus on ecosystem and landscape scale management of natural resources"[11]. This is a new and encouraging language but what does it really mean?

Reforestation as Paradigm

Despite the much-voiced need for integration of policy to achieve ambitious goals, it has often failed to recognise the relationship between the various problems of past and present land use. It might be said that it has failed to answer that fundamental question: "What has gone wrong here?" or at least failed to answer it from the informed ecological perspective of 4,000 years of Scottish (indeed British) deforestation. It is therefore not surprising that it has failed to identify the glaring synergy that exists between the recent climate change policy and a large number of objectives scattered throughout (and beyond) the list of strategies above.

To spell this out, the thread that links all of these — providing that elusive integration of their multiple objectives — lies in the most obvious of positive responses to our history of deforestation: that is a substantial reforestation of Scotland. This is not a new idea and has been 'in the air' in Scotland for some 25 years. Its roots can be traced back to Fraser Darling and on through Scottish ecological texts of the mid twentith century. But what may be called the 'reforestation movement' in Scotland is reasonably clearly defined by the formation of such grass roots initiatives as the Loch Garry Tree Group, Native Woods Campaign, Trees for Life and Reforesting Scotland all between 1986 and 1989.

It is interesting to note how the timing and steady consolidation of this movement corresponds rather precisely to the beginnings of an identifiable renewed interest in the use of Scottish timber in construction and it is no coincidence that key early members of Reforesting Scotland include Neil Sutherland and Howard Liddell (Gaia Architects) who are today at the forefront of 'ecologically informed' timber architecture in Scotland. And I preface timber with 'ecologically informed' to differentiate a strand that displays an understanding of the (often drastically) different consequences of using timber from Scotland and Scandinavia say than from Russia and Canada. The majority of Neil Sutherland's Highland houses utilise larch cladding and Douglas fir framing, sourced and milled within the region. Additionally, many of them incorporate floors and fittings with home grown hardwood. The Glencoe visitor centre by Gaia Architects took the same principles onto a slightly bigger scale, notably into ceilings lined with home-grown birch.

Returning though to Government initiatives, the notion of a reasonably large scale ongoing reforestation programme is quite explicit in the vision statement of the Scottish Forestry Strategy (SFS) but is also implicit in emerging biomass energy and carbon sequestration strategies. While the grass roots reforestation movement has paved the way for what may be called the social forestry aspects, the type and functioning of the State version of a future Scottish forest may be rather different from the ambitions of the now dozens of non-governmental and community based woodland groups in Scotland. Leaving this difference aside for the moment, the SFS suggests that Scotland should move from its current 17% forest cover to 25% by mid century, an increase in forest area equivalent to the size of the whole of Aberdeenshire, yet still leaving us well short of the average European forest cover of 36%.

Little or no flesh has been added to the concept of an 'ecosystem approach' in Scottish Government documents and perhaps the next stage could be to sharpen focus a little with language that helps to locate the subject in the realm of strategic level planning. I would offer 'Strategic ecological master-planning' as a possible label which strikes a chord with current approaches to integration of architecture and planning — albeit almost entirely in an urban context. The single overarching goal of reforestation has the potential to provide both a unifying objective and the scientific basis for this master-planning and would also have a strongly inspirational or motivational quality to many people.

Reforestation provides a large scale and coherent concept capable of delivering the Government's promise of 'ecosystem management'. It signifies the primacy of a proactive, design-led approach – as opposed to the customary, largely reactive 'managing what we have' approach. Essentially the task would be to reconcile the anticipated demands on the natural resources of Scotland with a genuine ecological remit to restore soil fertility, biological productivity and biodiversity at the nation level, and meet GHG and other targets at the global level. Reforestation has the potential to lead to this reconciliation – the pre-requisite of sustainable economic activity.

Scottish Timber Resources and Systems

One response to Peak Oil and the generally increasing costs of many material resources including their transportation is a move towards greater regional self-sufficiency and we are already seeing this in relation to energy. The Scottish Forestry Strategy signifies the start in terms of a regional prescription for cellulose production that will ensure the supplies we need this century and beyond. The limited resource availability is already becoming apparent as we move towards biomass energy generation and we can see an unhappy picture developing where demand for this use may increasingly compete with demand for construction material. Current, very limited supplies of home-grown hardwoods and the higher quality and more durable softwoods, already effectively limit building specifications but equally promote imports of foreign timber and timber products, a proportion of which come from ecologically and sometimes socially unsustainable sources.

Our response to an analysis of future demand should prescribe the establishment of extensive new areas of: (1) a variety of hardwoods – especially those with framing, flooring and cladding potential such as oak, ash, beech, (2) short rotation woody crops for energy biomass, (3) medium and long term broadleaved coppice for energy biomass on more fragile soils and for a variety of specialist timber products, and (4) the dismissively labelled 'minority conifers', ideal for external cladding as well as visible structural elements such as Larches and Douglas fir.

Our parallel objective of restoring soils, biological productivity and biodiversity will shape the establishment and subsequent forest management regimes along with the integration with other primary land use types. Of these, agriculture will be the most important along with a horticultural economy which could greatly expand in response to improved drainage, soils, fertilisation effects and shelter of major increases in surrounding woodland. The drastic reduction of deer numbers which will be an essential part, indeed pre-requisite, for forest establishment and for natural regeneration systems, will generally promote major expansion of forest food and other non-timber woodland produce systems – so many of which are currently out of the question without expensive deer protection measures. The opportunity cost of half a million stomachs grazing the land down to its bare bones in many places is yet to be fully appreciated.

Subjecting Scottish forestry to the same carbon budgeting analysis that we are now introducing for construction and other sectors of the economy will throw up some uncomfortable truths concerning the plantation systems we have worked hard to establish for over half a century. This 'cradle to grave' critique or analysis

— Lone rowan on a rock in denuded moorland. Emblematic of all that we have lost from the Scottish ecosystem. From refugia on cliffs and islands of many sorts, forest would return rapidly were it not for excessive deer populations.

would take proper account of the energy expenditure and emissions all the way from growing trees in nurseries, transporting them to site, mechanical ground preparation, to planting and fencing them. In a world of much higher energy costs and rigorous controls on carbon dioxide emissions, plantation systems of forestry will compare increasingly unfavourably with, and indeed may become completely uneconomic compared to, systems based on the more biologically and economically efficient processes of natural regeneration that our European and Scandinavian neighbours primarily enjoy.

Intergrating Construction and Forest Design

Timber could become Scotland's greatest construction resource as well as a major energy resource by the end of this century, if we choose. We have the physical space and the climate. In the drive for greater self sufficiency in all resources including building materials, this is a very plausible objective. Rising energy costs along with carbon policy backed by legislation may strongly endorse this strategy and promote more ambitious forest establishment rates than the SFS has suggested.

In this scenario, we currently stand at a threshold with regard to our land management systems and the landscape which they shape. A laissez-fair attitude at this time will, at best, waste an opportunity for improvements that could increase productivity across a broad front and establish sustainable long term production systems of increasing rather than declining biodiversity and fertility. At the worst, it will signal a major, further decline in ecosystem qualities, a long lasting deterioration of landscape and a deepening of the separation of Scottish systems from those of our neighbours.

Adopting reforestation as the central

— Symptomatic of the lack of integration in Scottish land use. Plantation forestry of just two species divided by a two metre fence from heavily grazed, natural pine forest remnant. The degenerate and the degenerating ? Neither represents sustainable ecosystem management.

— An intensively managed land use system with a close integration of forestry and building culture based on native tree species and meeting multiple objectives including construction, fuelwood, slope protection and field drainage.

theme of a considered integration of ecological restoration and resource management will do more than help to secure the resources of the future. It would help avert that possible decline as well as take critical pressure off threatened forests in other parts of the world (including the Siberian Taiga). Working with the ecological principles of Bio-regionalism involves understanding and respect for the climax communities[3] of that region which provide a basis for the design and management of production systems — agricultural, horticultural or forest based. Evidently, some crops and their management systems will represent major departures from the climax but elements of it should always be present. Forestry provides ready opportunities for relatively simple adaptations of natural systems where the climax is forest — as it is over most of Scotland. Forestry in what may be called the Boreal bio-region of Scotland (the larger part of the Highlands), for instance, would most logically be based around the native Scots. It is not difficult to see how such an approach to resource management tends towards 'an authenticity of landscape' — a relative trueness to nature and place. It follows that a building culture deriving its primary materials from such a bio-regionally organised landscape would reflect at least some local characteristics that essentially derive from vegetation, soil and climate.

As builders, architects, engineers, landscape architects, the timber we specify and choose — its species, quantity and even its quality — whether in constructions or their energy systems, has a direct impact on the forests that are planted and harvested around the world. If we only design timber frames and energy systems that require low quality softwood, we should not be surprised if the forests of the world are converted to produce predominantly this material. At a national level in Scotland we are perilously close to this situation already. Only a strategic master-planning approach of the type envisaged is likely to alter this course. In the scenario of a major expansion of demand for home-grown timber, in the construction and energy specification of buildings, it will be essential that these be linked in a reciprocal design process with the forest types that we require to meet the longer term and wider ecological objectives. To put one aspect simply, if we want a diverse forest, we must specify a diversity of timber types in our buildings. We specify the timber and we specify the forest — together.

In a visitor facility I have been helping Chris Morgan of Locate Architects design for Forestry Commission Scotland, we are taking this approach quite literally. The building has large internally expressed post and beam portal frames from Douglas fir while the hidden framing is Sitka spruce and Scots pine. The cladding and decking structure and boarding is larch. The flooring and ceiling is to be in a random mixture of hardwoods. We are hoping the mixture will include rowan, birch, ash, oak and sycamore amongst others. This spectrum of timber species will reflect the client's policies for a diverse Scottish forest and illustrate ways in which such a diversity can be easily specified by designers where the will exists, promoting the establishment and management of these species.

Conclusions

The complexity of future global resource management implies that design and specification by architects and other design professionals must rise to meet new degrees of sophistication in ecological understanding. Designers in Scotland should be encouraged to feed into the process of 'Designing a Future Forest' and strategic ecological master-planning at a bio-regional level. This will bring the necessary deeper understanding and consistency to decision making behind the material specification and energy design of buildings. It implies a new and creative coalition of designers of the built environment with strategic planners and managers of natural resources that will potentially lift architecture in its broadest application to a central place in the avant-garde of cultural progress.

The current emphasis within building standards on reducing carbon emissions in energy systems and the strategy for a low carbon future which the building industry is straining to implement is but a stage along the path to building and inhabiting the planet sustainably. The second major plank in reducing GHG emissions through the use of low embodied materials will grow rapidly in relative importance as very low carbon energy systems are reached. Timber is a growing part of low embodied energy specifications in Scotland but a limited forest resource is already constraining growth.

Good place making, good design must involve an understanding of place at many levels: in Kenneth Frampton's words: "the peculiarities of a particular space". It is important to an architecture of sensitivity and perhaps ultimately to a meaningful individuality that we understand a place ecologically as much as socio-politically. An appropriate modern response to such layer upon layer of complexity will need to be found in a new and similarly complex relationship between nature and culture in their broadest senses. A part of this new relationship we are seeking finds expression in the concepts of biosphere design which, at the risk of enormous hubris, challenge an alternative of lazy and irresponsible regard for Human actions across the planet.

In Scotland, due to a long and largely unacknowledged history of deforestation, understanding even of ecological basics – the 'way things are' – is generally as limited as understanding of the biological potential of the country – 'the way things could be'. A misunderstanding of the fundamental ecology of place will be a poor and ultimately hollow basis for its development whether in material or spiritual terms.

Biography
Bernard Planterose is an ecologist working in the field of timber design and construction. He was founder Director of the national charity Reforesting Scotland. He ran a native tree nursery and planting business in Sutherland for 10 years and now operates his timber building operation from a softwood plantation near Ullapool.

Footnotes & references

—1 Sir Frank Fraser Darling: pioneering ecologist and author of many books on land use and Scottish ecology including the West Highland Survey (1955) in which he first coined the term 'wet desert' to describe the state of much of the Highlands. The report on which he based this work was allegedly suppressed by his employer, the Department of Agriculture, and ensured that he would never hold a further government position.

—2 Steven H and Carlisle A: The Native Pinewoods of Scotland (1959)

—3 Climax community is an ecological term to describe the supposed natural group of organisms that would inhabit a particular place at a particular time if allowed to evolve 'naturally'. The term underlines the difficulty of accounting for Human influence and, indeed in defining the whole relationship between our species and all others.

—4 The term, Bio-regional in ecological science, refers to geographical zones of similar climax communities. Scotland is sometimes divided into two principal bio-regions. The southern or lowland part of the country where high broadleaf forest is the predominant climax may be referred to as Northern Temperate: the northern part of the country where Scots pine and birch form the predominant climax as part of the Boreal bio-region (extending across most of northern Scandinavia). An Atlantic (west coast) zone may be considered as a subset of both where high winds and rainfall restrict tree growth and limit species.

—5 Rudimentary or early initiatives would include CITES (Convention on International Trade in Endangered Species) and, more recently, the proliferation of timber certification schemes including FSC and PEFC which represent international collaboration in ecosystem management.

—6 Cultural sustainability – an interview with Kenneth Frampton, I.H. Almaas & E.B. Malmqist.

—7 A Forward Strategy for Scottish Agriculture: Next Steps – The Scottish Government, March 2006.

—8 Scotland's Biodiversity: It's in Your Hands. Scottish Executive, 2004.

—9 The Scottish Forestry Strategy. Forestry Commission Scotland, 2006.

—10 Biomass Action Plan for Scotland. The Scottish Government, 2007.

—11 Strategy for Wild Deer in Scotland: consultation draft, 2007. Deer Commission for Scotland.

—12 A Low Carbon Building Standards Strategy for Scotland. Scottish Building Standards Agency, 2007.

'Placelessness', 'displacement', 'replacement', 'misplacement', all have connotations of disturbance. When we 'place' an object we locate it in space, time and mind. If we move an object it risks being 'out-of-place'. In his Dictionary of Urbanism, Rob Cowan records place as, "A defined area; a distinct locality". He also records the suggestion of Yu Fu Tuan that "Space is transformed into place as it acquires definition and meaning". So what provokes and relieves this tension when designing new architecture in fragile parts of the Scottish landscape? Is the notion of place a precursor to design in the landscape, something that already exists physically or in the collective memory, a distinct place in a particular corner of Scotland familiar to certain people? Famous landscapes are well know places to many people: Fingal's cave on Staffa, Ben Nevis or The Trossacks, for example. But how does the status of place survive in more modest landscapes and those landscapes affected by new development. And what is the significance of place within the design process? What, if any, is the role of design in making new places?

We know that identities (through identity fraud, the re-branding of products, or marketing, for example of a particular beach as a golfing resort) can be stolen by design. However the notion of place suggests more rooted qualities, something that can be discovered, may be missed, but cannot be taken away. I will look at the architecture of three distinct Scottish landscapes, each with a 'sense of place' and each requiring a process of unearthing or exploration in its discovery.

Scara Brae in Orkney

The first time I visited Scara Brae, in the late 1970's, my father and I simply walked there over the grassy Machair to the sound of the sea coming at the shore, another trudge across the windy emptiness of Orkney, when we were suddenly interrupted by the extraordinary sense of revelation and discovery of the ground opened up into the rooms, passageways and furniture of Neolithic people. Forty centuries abandoned as if yesterday, thanks to the surrounding dunes that had protected the walls, doors, shelves and hearths before the seas of the bay of Skaill had exposed them in a storm in 1850. That sense of revelation does not quite survive the current identity of Scara Brae as a visitor attraction. The site has, through reverence, become divorced from its setting. It rests immaculately mown, discretely signed, with

— Scara Brae.

route marking paving distinguishing it from the nearby machair, pasture and beach.

But the walls of the houses at Scara Brae also demonstrate an extreme form of adaptation to local climate and resources. Earth banks insulate each house. The formation of walls, door and (most extraordinary) the furniture of beds, hearth and dresser are from local sandstone. In this sense the form places the building, the extreme type of climatic shelter, the use of sandstone and earth. If there is a sense of place at Scara Brae this derives both now in its sepulchral re-discovery and originally in its construction from a form that is inseparable from the landscape which it intersects. Despite the passage of identities and millennia the place remains.

One can imagine a time, perhaps not too far in the future, when the archaeological excavation of the site has been exhausted, when our reverence for its significance has been satisfied, the cultural cordon removed, and when Scara Brae could be abandoned once more to the tides and storms. Its schist-slab walls washed once more by the sea that once revealed them.

Visitor Centre at Oyne, Aberdeenshire

In the mid 1990s Ted Cullinan, Roddy Langmuir and I designed and realised a very modern building that is inseparable from the landscape that now wraps it, concealed like an archaeological site. The housing of an exhibition on archaeology, our brief, created a paradoxical relationship since the immediate landscape was, we discovered, already surrounded by significant Neolithic, Iron Age, and even Roman sites.

The building came after an office outing to Orkney, 30 architects taking a flight (to Inverness) and train (to Thurso) and a ferry (to Stromness, past the Old Man of Hoy). There was a strong sense of journey, distance, expectation and arrival. We saw the Stenness stones, the Ring of Brodgar, Maeshowe and Scara Brae, where we played football on the beach like the tourists we were. There was a powerful sense of departure and arrival in these journeys, of the experience of places very remarkable and distinct from each other, about the discovery of places that, despite being very ancient, maintain a powerful impact on the senses and landscape today. The stones standing high above the ground, their positioning aligned with distant hills, hidden chambers below the ground, set out to precise geometries.

The site in Oyne, Aberdeenshire struck us in a similar way. It is on an open hillside, part of a wide expanse of rolling pasture and staccato hills below the steep mass of Bennachie. Since this landscape condition meant openness and exposure of any building we became fascinated by journeys through and interactions with the landscape; above, below, across and through the ground, like a series of incisions into it and re-formations of it, as in a Neolithic earthwork. That interaction became the narrative that designed the building. The building became an instrument to tell the story of the landscape in detail. The local archaeology, as in Orkney, was bound up with high points, alignments, and intersections with the ground. The

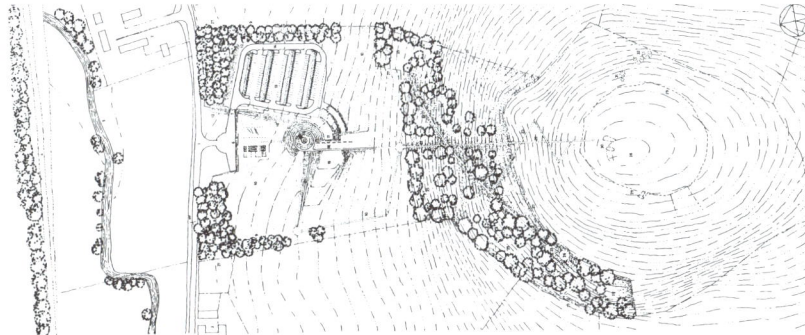

— Archaeolink, Oyne.

building charts the location of the nearby archaeological sites.

The geometries of the building derive from the mapping of topography, archaeology and the relationship between distinctive elements observed in the landscape. Materials relate to the limited palettes of grass covered earth and glass, the one used for the storage of heat and the other as a device for viewing through and collecting (sun) with. Both geometries and materials derive from the existing place. These qualities of place inherent in the local landscape have been sought out and revealed.

The building frames an unfolding experience of discovery and re-discovery of the surrounding archaeology and landscape. There is a sequence first seen from the road entrance that links the building (perceived as a grass hill) with the Iron Age hill fort above it and the Bennachie above that. Like the 18th century garden where the view/viewer relationship is manipulated, this first reveals then denies a view that is then revealed again on the rooftop when the axis is re-discovered and a footpath is aligned on the route to the summit of the hill fort. A second sequence makes reference to the experience of Neolithic sites such as Maeshowe. The entrance into the building is along a valley sliced into the hillside, the building an underground chamber that stores solar heat through glass walls. The exhibition is in a hidden vault which gradually re-reveals the landscape around it through port-hole like windows, one sighted on the battlefield of Mons Gropius. A third sequence relates a rooftop bridge and path, mounted on an embankment, with the hill fort of Dunnideer.

The convex walls of the interior cylindrical rooms refer views outside into the landscape. Banded paving inside extends into the landscape through the glass walls. The building subverts a sense of interior space, being more closely associated with the immediate and distant landscape beyond its glass walls. Ultimately the pasture of the surrounding fields has been designed to extend across the entire building, ½ m deep, such that it is absorbed into the rural landscape. Like hidden archaeology the reading of the landscape that the building encompasses can easily be missed.

In contrast to this narrative of place the identity of Archaeolink is better known, the name giving an identity linked with historical re-enactments, an exhibition and re-constructions that are the headline attraction for visitors. An audio-visual show, reconstruction exhibits and atmospheric chambers search after an experience of the myths and legends of pre-historic Scotland. These ephemeral experiences give a tangibly transitory identity to Archaeolink, which ties in directly with the way it is promoted and publicly advertised.

It is equally possible that the building could be re-branded with a new name, another exhibition. It could be re-invented as a gallery, a theatre or a nightclub. None of this would alter the narrative power of the landscape or the building's function as a device for recording that narrative.

The Highland Housing Fair, Balvonie

In September 2006 I visited a projected housing site on the slope 500ft above Inverness overlooking the Moray Firth, alongside Milton of Leys. This was the site for a housing Fair, to be designed to the Finnish model, a national exhibition and event. It was to be a showcase for imaginative architecture, construction innovation, micro-renewable energy technology, and an advert for forward thinking Inverness. Most interestingly, expanding to 100 houses, it would be occupied after the Fair and become a new village-scaled settlement. The Fair was intended by The Highland Council, The Forestry Commission, Scottish Government and other backers as a test-bed for new ideas.

But a sense of removal or departure from the landscape developed on the long, curving, disorientating roads as I drove again through nearby Milton of Leys, where new housing was being so rapidly built. The signage of national house-builders held my attention alongside the name 'Milton of Leys' itself a new identity. I could recognise the corporate success but I lost the place. I drove on, not knowing where to stop, despairing for the fair.

We were soon captivated by the under-layers of man-made landscape on the site at

Balvonie, where these layers could take us. We discovered that early patterns of Highland settlement were invariably precisely placed and could provide a point of reference or departure. There was potential, through masterplanning, to link current architectural thinking on energy efficiency, materiality, climatic control, modern lifestyle and urban design, with the notion of rootedness to a timeless landscape. Our job would be to provide the mapping of this landscape, establishing the routes, the qualities of spaces between buildings, the threads linking architecture with landscape. Through our brief for the individual architecture, an RIAS competition, we could also provoke explorations of a new Vernacular.

The site, with Milton of Leys to its west, forms part of a shelf of eighteenth century Improvement Parkland below Drummossie Moor. The many local burns running off the Moor have been diverted into linear ditches. A grid of trees planted for shelter on this high, northern, exposed land survives in tall, broken fragments. Old roads follow these orthogonal patterns, neatly negotiating the slope. Not mimicking the undulations but exposing the contour of the land by linear juxtaposition. This is a man-made landscape tackling high rainfall, strong winds and steep topography. Then the grid of trees and ditches suddenly transforms into deep curving gorges and native forest at the un-harnessed terrain downhill.

This threshold condition between man-made and natural conditions provoked a layout of hard built edges that then erode according to the pattern of the ditches turned burns, the tree belts turned forest, opening up to a discovered view. The experience of the threshold condition is another journey, as at Oyne, this time revealed along streets, amongst buildings and walking into the countryside. The

— (Above) Highland Housing Fair: A mapping of tree locations, waterways and roads affected by topography, Cadell2.
— (Left) Highland Housing Fair: Context Plan, Cadell2.

journey begins at a new wooden bridge, celebrating arrival, the first crossing of a series of waterways. A long view opens down a new tree-lined avenue, extending the eighteenth century alignment of trees. A close grain of new buildings is set with long terraces and low eaves against the wind and the public road-face to the south. Behind are workshops and studios, hard paved and yard-like, protected from the elements. This is hard rural in material and configuration, paving and buildings made from Caithness stone, granite and glass. Contemporary rural architecture. Progressing downhill the avenue accommodates different conditions as it goes: garden walls punctuated by gable ends, an opening up to one side for a small public space, a swale alongside the avenue to divert floodwaters.

Regular streets and building lines are eroded or diverted as they move down the slope. A whole street is swung across to reveal the discovered view, building fronts pulling back. Materials progress away from masonry to include larch clad houses, more glass and corrugated metal cladding, lightweight materials, materials that open up. Eventually individual houses are detached from their neighbors and the floodwaters are collected into two basins. The erosion of the man-made form is finally complete, the forest encroaches and the site reverts to nature.

However, presently under construction, the Highland Housing Fair can currently only be appreciated in terms of its marketing identity. The brand is there: 'a model of sustainable architecture' 'the first of its kind in the UK'; this is supported by a web site and a catalogue of well-known architects bringing strong images. The fair, well promoted, will have a public national identity and it will be a significant event for the new communities in the Highlands when its exhibitions and 55 houses open to the public. After a month the identity will change, exhibitions will close, the houses will be occupied and a new community will be formed. And only then will the new residents have the opportunity to get to know the place.

Addendum: Scotland's Future Place

So what, after all these detailed diversions, does a search for place mean for the currently much debated national planning process in Scotland and the drive towards place-making. Statutory Planning for new development tends to assess proposals in terms of impacts: drainage impact, traffic impact, economic impact, landscape impact and visual impact. These are blunt technical measures, testing the degree and type of change entailed, tending to be overly quantitative and incompletely qualitative. At Oyne and Balvonie the quantitative measures alone would fail entirely to capture the significance and quality of change to the landscape involved. Yet it is in listening to this narrative (or equally to those of town and cityscapes) where designers need the encouragement of planning authorities and local people. We need that help to celebrate the fragilities and relieve the tensions of placement.

The design work at Archaeolink and the Highland Housing Fair relates directly to

— (Above) Aerial perspective of The Avenue and Green, Cadell2.
— (top right) Home/work cluster at The Close, Brennan and Wilson Architects.
— (Right) Terraced Housing in Caithness Stone, NORD Architecture.

Essays
P.170

Narratives of Place in the Scottish Landscape

the presently active debates around sustainability, localisation and place-making in Scotland. This debate has yet to yield any significant change. For us the Fair came alongside several projects grown from an attitude towards place but most of this work remains to be built. The debate shines a spotlight on commercial housing development, mass-produced, that cuts across a broad spectrum of experience for all of us. Housing plays such a large part in recent debate simply because the rate of change to our landscapes is so fast and so out of step with the capacity of planning authorities to influence its quality. There has been so much wringing of hands about this amongst architects: Noddy houses, details from Buckinghamshire and Kent, half-timbering or ornamental barge-boards, whatever takes your un-fancy. But the detail of the architecture is only a small part of the effect. The cul-de-sac format and the lack of integration with surrounding neighbourhoods are equally as widespread factors in Scotland, equally un-Scottish. And in their configuration, in the spread of late twentieth and early twety first century suburbia, there is a widespread levelling-out of the contours of distinction between places.

In a recent lecture in Edinburgh an American theorist made the point that he had lectures on Mackintosh as a student and was impressed by his originality before discovering, years later, having visited Scotland, that much of the detail used by Mackintosh was already there in vernacular architecture. He was not aware of the narrative content of Mackintosh's works, seeing the vernacular instead as a badge of identity rather than an evolving revelation of the character of a place. If the vernacular is a function of place the genius of Mackintosh was not to copy vernacular architecture, as suggested in this lecture, but to be aware of the vernacular (qualities of indigenous place, time and architecture in Scotland) and having examined these to then invent a departure, much as Greek Thomson departed from another genre, a departure that was simultaneously in place.

On a more local note I met a group of women traveling from Elgol on Skye on a recent train journey south from Inverness. They wanted to know about the Housing Fair that had so much coverage in their local press. Having debated Highland characteristics with a number of people involved with the Fair project I thought I would try a small but important idea on these members of an isolated community. I asked whether the rattle of a cattle grid and the sight of a deer fence, signals for arrival at Balvonie, said something to them about arriving at a village in the Highlands. I was pleasantly surprised that these experiences had, for these residents of one Highland community at least, a happy association with coming home.

Architecture in Scotland, as elsewhere, may be polarised between the commercial realist architects, the modernists and the historicists, each undergoing a revival, each intent on a global polemic. However the complex expressive potential of architecture always has the capacity to explore more localised new ground, to expose more about the distinctive nature of particular people, sites and landscapes. This capacity offers a Scottish vernacular architecture beyond stylistic differences, beyond fashionable identities.

— **Biography**
— Johnny Cadell is an architect, formerly a director of Edward Cullinan Architects, now working with partner Karen as Cadell2, specialising in masterplanning and urban regeneration.

— **Footnote**
— The Highland Housing Fair, based on the annual Finnish Housing Fairs, is an exhibition of 55 houses to be open to the public in 2010. The fair will demonstrate innovation in design for modern day living as well as innovationin construction, energy efficiency, the use of local materials and skills and the application of micro-renewable technology. Cadell2 were appointed as masterplanners for the fair in 2006.

Placing the Region: A New Highlands Architecture
Oliver Lowenstein

Up in the Northerly Highland rim of the country an under-reported scattering of small in number, admittedly, but definitely identifiable, youngish architectural practices, has over the last decade co-elesced into Scotland's own home grown regional architecture culture. These architects are producing examples of domestic homes, commercial and public buildings, using materials sourced from the region, both timber and stone within a varied and loose ecological aesthetic, while extending aspects of traditional, vernacular and regional architecture. Also, a significant strand is energised by the potential to use indigenous timber, in part the architectural and building wing of the reforestation community. Four of the practices caught up with this new regionalists wave are represented in Building Biographies, while another participant, Bernard Planterose, has contributed one of the essays. It's debatable whether this is a movement, although at least one of the practices, Isle of Skye based Dualchas Building Design's Alasdair Stephen, acknowledges the idea of a new highland architecture.

The prehistory is vague, but an immediate historic starting point could be Neil Sutherland's early nineties practice, when, with Andy McIvoy, they began pushing a manifesto-like strap-line of putting architecture and design 'back on the rural agenda'. Years later this is still being maintained despite the early internal split between Sutherland and McIvoy. Sutherland started his current practice, Organic Buildings, near Inverness, providing a whole system design and build service, complete with sawmill and wood products.

Also on the Isle of Skye is Rural Design, smaller than Dualchas but again involved in Highland and Island vernacular, even if some of the design is imported from the new world, with buildings based on Nova Scotian traditions. In Edinburgh, ex Gaia-Architects Chris Morgan is using his Locate Architects as one node in a network of collaborators and although based in the lowlands, often collaborates with Bernard Planterose. Planterose, a founder of the grassroots Reforesting Scotland Charity

— Neil Sutherland's woodland centre at Strathnairn.

and magazine, is currently running his timber design and build business, North Woods Construction, from the far north-west, near Ullapool. Across the other side of the country, at Aberdeen's Robert Gordon University, Gokay Deveci continues to produce a series of interesting buildings, including the Lotte Glob House far up north in Sutherland. He is less committed to the timber enthusiasms of Sutherland, Planterose and Morgan, arguing for a broader interpretation of sustainability, than their primary focus on wood. His award winning seven-storey zero heating block of flats in Rothesay, on the Isle of Bute, aptly expresses this philosophy. All of these practices are young, consisting of thirty and early forty somethings, and their emergence may well be related to the energies released by the spirit of a new quasi-independent Scotland.

As far as the renewed receptivity to using timber is concerned, there's a mix of viewpoints, although the weighting appears increasingly optimistic. Some are keenly enthusiastic, others are of the view that incremental though slower change is happening and yet others who are plain sceptical. "You can see the lights going on in a few politicians heads' as one observer put it. Other major projects further to the south are also impacting on the perception of the use of timber, including the large-scale green timber frame Page\Park recently completed for the Loch Lomond and Trossochs park authority HQ.

Gareth Hoskins Architects' use of local larch on one of the exhibitions featured buildings, the National Trust of Scotland's Culloden Visitor Centre, also highlights the potential for using a local material, though this time for a building with clear modernist intent, a thought provoking move for some across the highlands architectural community. Similarly the first significant massive wood building in Scotland, Acharacle school by Gaia Architects is stirring a good deal of talk, both for kick-starting this well known building material in Scotland, as well as distracting from what David Page describes as 'Scotland's nascent indigenous timber industry'. These issues, while not being at the heart of the highlands regionalist wave, overlap and seem to be influencing its emerging direction.

— The Loch Lomond and Trossoch's National Park Head Quarters, Balloch – the largest timber-frame in Scotland – in construction and complete designed by Page \ Park.

— Gareth Hoskins Architects have applied larch to good effect at their Culloden visitor centre.

This crossover is most clearly evident in contributor Bernard Planterose's radical vision of a future forestry joined at the hip to architecture and building culture. Unusually for the construction industry Planterose originally, trained as an ecologist, which brings with it a different and focused perspective. While his essay expands on this 'future forest design' in greater detail, Planterose believes that a Scottish wood culture with genuine vision needs to be looking to a future, that is, fifty to a hundred years hence. Such a 'future forest design', would focus on growing species which both provide material in oncoming decades for a range of required building and other material requirements, and work to support and strengthen ecosystems and biodiversity of the region. "From an ecological viewpoint it's good to design a woodland that meets biodiversity and soil restoration imperatives. But best of all", he adds, "for tackling the issues holistically and model a kind of optimal compromise future forest (on a regional basis), that might provide construction and energy needs at the same time as the ecological ones." Planterose suggests long term and ecologically joined-up design and planning which seems to be just about beginning to be considered on policy and strategy tables, although the starting point of incentives for planting and growing, i.e. grants, are currently in abeyance.

Neil Sutherland also suggests that such a future forest-design approach is beginning to catch on. The way Sutherland sees it, the future forests meme has been in the air for the past few years, with people pursuing similar lines independently, unaware of each other, although now that isolation has gone, a network is emerging which is just beginning to throw these ideas around. Some in this ad hoc network are also beginning to advise the Highland Forestry Agency, with Sutherland going as far as to call this 'the new forestry'. If the language of added value to forests and woodland products he uses contrasts with those of Planterose, the aim, he proposes, is the same. He says that there needs to be an acceptance regarding the species of 'what we've got,' i.e. exotic species as opposed to native, and to begin to manage with the long term in mind. He argues, like Planterose, that whatever changes in climate, such as higher winds and rainfall, the main species being used as construction timber must be 'pretty resilient'. If others are more sceptical or cautious in their language, Sutherland seems confident that change is underway. While visiting Sutherland (admittedly some time ago) he also talked about a new wave of re-ruralisation being underway, with families and individuals moving back from city and urban life into parts of the country. In this context his original manifesto of putting architecture and

— Bernard Planterose and Locate's Chris Morgan have collaborated on an entry for the Highland Housing Fair, still at this stage on the drawing board.

design back on the rural agenda, is underlined by his commitment to architecture being, as he puts it, "an expression of the aspirations of the people".

Sutherland's optimism comes from a personal commitment to and passion for rural futures, and to forests as the source of materials, which, he believes, are the building backbone of such futures, dating back to the early nineties, when he completed post-graduate research on the use of local timber in regional buildings. "Very little was known about it" he says of that time. In the intervening years the technical knowledge base has grown, with the likes of TRADA, CTE and others, gradually extending the range and reach of research along with its dissemination.

Sutherland's company, Organic Buildings, is organised around providing both timberbuild expertise in the form of post and beam frame construction, as well as owning a sawmill. This means they can supply their own woods although they also work with both the two main Scottish companies, James Jones and BSW. Sutherland points out the degree of economic deprivation across rural Scotland, 'the big issue' is about owning their own home. Given this, Organic Buildings provide a service to people who are self-building, assisting with the design and helping build a part of, though not necessarily all, the construction. They also provide various specialist timber parts for domestic and some larger projects.

The houses Organic Buildings are building, are both localist and regional, "a construction type of its time" Sutherland calls it. He is not alone in this belief that "a new regionalism is beginning to make" its presence felt. Out on the west coast's Isle of Skye, the young practice Dualchas, founded by brothers Neil and Alasdair Stephen in 1996, have established a reputation and presence for a contemporary regionalist aesthetic based on elements of Highland tradition. With a further office now in Glasgow, Dualchas, (Gaelic for cultural inheritance), are perhaps more closely connected to the Scottish nationalist tradition running through the sustainability movement, than the other practices. Practically, this has meant an architecture developed from the Highlands, and particularly the Gaelic west coasts indigenous architectural and cultural inheritance. As they said in a 2006 talk, "if we cherish the music and language of the Gaidhealtachd, why not the architecture?"[1] Their response to this

— One of Dualchas' other most recent houses, abstracting the longhouse vernacular, this in northerly Drumbeg.

question was to develop a modern longhouse based around the traditional highland 'Blackhouse' form. The first of these was built with a Rural Home Ownership Grant for £35,000 in 1997. The building was characterised by its simple form, narrow, but with high volumes and extensive window space. Although these first versions used white render and slate, a commitment to green technologies and designing in energy efficiency, has meant a move towards timber clad versions including an updated Hebridean Contemporary Homes kit building. Some of this work has been with rural housing associations to up the design values of their housing.

Alasdair Stephens readily acknowledges the increase in interest in using timber, "an encouraging phenomenon", some of which he attributes to a new found acceptance in planning departments for the material, though also pointing to Edinburgh's Parliamentary directive Planning Advice Notice 72, which emphasises timber as a credible sustainable building material, as having helped significantly. He also acknowledges that clients are becoming more interested in timber; although the contrast with Sutherland and Planterose is plain when he says that if Siberian larch, (for instance) were specified because of cost advantages, quality and availability, it isn't up to him to try and change this. That said, Dualchas are specifying significantly more native larch, most recently and ambitiously for their Raasay Islands community hall. The problem is that new stands of larch are not being planted. The real challenge, they feel, is to develop uses for Sitka Spruce, given there is so much growing. Generally, for Stephen, such use of local materials adds to his perception of a new Highland architecture; one where sustainability is a part of this identifiable regionalist sensibility.

Considerably askance from these other Highland architects, Gokay Deveci, who teaches at RGU and runs a practice out of Aberdeen, may nevertheless be seen as another element in the patchwork of emerging regionalist Highlands architecture. Again Deveci's starting point has been the Scottish vernacular, but without the arguable bias of timber advocacy, he is also interested in stone and brick houses. He believes that timber doesn't always age that well, while stone not only ages beautifully, but its thermal massing reduces insulation as an issue. Only ten years ago, Deveci points out, timber was hardly a popular material. He interprets sustainability differently again,

— The Lotte Glob house on the shore of Loch Erribol, 2004. Architect Gokay Deveci's first building project for the Danish ceramicist.

stating buildings have to encompass the cultural, economic and social dimensions along with narrower definitions. To add to this, with temperatures rising in Scotland, as elsewhere, timber and insulation on their own don't necessarily provide the adequate thermal mass required and is leading to well insulated houses overheating[2]. Within Deveci's sustainability terms social affordability is more central, one which he's addressed through developing a series of zero heating buildings – with his award winning, seven storey A' Chrannag block of flats in Rothesay on the Isle of Bute being the best known. Some of his critique is aimed at use of wood in urban contexts, where it occurs, he feels is primarily fashion inflected. For rural environments, Deveci is happy to use timber where it is in sympathy with context, making it an appropriate material.

The Lotte Glob House, for the Danish potter Glob, in Northern Sutherland is one instance of this, where Deveci felt timber fitted well with the particular remote Scottish landscape. Built for £75,000, the green oak cladding justified itself. A minimal impact and dismantable lightweight structure, Glob's house sits peaceably within the surrounding landscape.

Scotland's far north and north-west may not have received the attention of the larger, well placed architects producing timber buildings further south, and the more radical whole systems future forest thinking isn't part of the mainstream agenda just quite yet. Even so, this disparate band and their associates is compelling evidence that small as it is, a distinctive and new regional architecture and building culture can be identified across the Highlands and Islands.

Websites that may be of interest:
Arts And Design Scotland
www.ads.org.uk

Page\Park Architects
www.pagepark.co.uk

Dualchas Building Design
www.dualchas.com

Neil Sutherland Architects
www.organicbuildings.com

Bl@stArchitects
www.blastarc.co.uk

Northwood Design
www.northwoodsdesign.co.uk

LocateArchitects
www.locatearchitects.co.uk

Rural Design Architects
www.ruraldesign.co.uk

Gokay Deveci
www.rgu.ac.uk/sss/staff/page.cfm?pge=10993
Association of Scottish Hardwood Sawmills
www.ashs.co.uk

Scottish Ecological Design Organisation
www.seda2.org

Footnotes
[1] Lecture by Neil Stephen and Mary Arnold Foster at the Rural Housing Service Annual Conference, March 2006, Dunkeld (Gaidhealtachd is the Gaelic term for the cultural reach of Gaelic Scotland).

[2] I am grateful to Fionn Stevenson of Oxford Brookes University Architecture School for pointing this emerging issue out to me.

An earlier version of this piece, The New Highlands Regionalist Architecture was published in Building for a Future, Vol 16. No 4, Spring 2007.

—The Significance of Building Culture — Building as Discourse
—Robert Fabach

Why Vorarlberg Building Culture? Prologue

To write about Vorarlberg architecture is to work a rich and fertile field. An extensive heritage of anonymous building, but also famous characters from the era of the Vorarlberg baroque master builders, provide an exciting contrast to an impressive development from the late 1950s through to the present day, that in a very small area reflects cultural and social movements. At the same time, any description of this architectural biotope constitutes an imponderable risk, because on the one hand it has always been the aggregate output of single characters with enough room for contradiction and individuality, and on the other hand the continued further development constantly leads to reassessments between journalism and history writing.

Building culture not architectural superstars

In Vorarlberg, the concept of building culture is definitely different from individual, artisitic top performances. What we find here is a concern about society as a whole and an active engagement with the built environment. A distinctive system of patronage, a particular need for representation and an academic environment for an elitist, architectural high culture was largely absent when it came to building in Vorarlberg. Fortunately perhaps, because the continuity and durability of the last 30-40 years would have scarcely been possible otherwise. Building culture developed and settled in Vorarlberg as a collective achievement.

Wide circulation and popularisation

There is above average investment in the building and care of dwellings in Vorarlberg, thus confirming the subjective impression travelling through Austria's westernmost Federal State. Contemporary buildings have long been more than the odd exception; rather, they can be seen as coherent ensembles right in the heart of villages. In the last 10 years, the popularisation of a modern architecture has imposed its emotional formulas on almost every development area: flat roof, lattice facades and floor to ceiling glazing.

But this has also its downside. If external features are chiefly copied, there cannot but be trivialisation. The challenge for today's generation of ambitious designers is how to break away from formalisms and deliver adequate solutions to the new problems: the energy question, urban sprawl and suburbanisation, and finding forms of building and living for a increasingly heterogeneous society.

But let us start at the beginning.

Outline of 40 years of development

First generation – the pioneers

As early as the 1960s, a handful of individualistic designers with very different biographies had attracted attention by their pragmatic but stylistically confident handling of modernity. Hans Purin, Jakob Albrecht and later Gunter Wratzfeld, who had studied under Roland Rainer, translated their appreciation of the vernacular and closeness to the unpretentious Scandinavian modernism into intellectually precise timber structures that were astoundingly economic. The C4 Group (Max Fohn, Karl Sillaber, Karl Wengler and Helmut Pfanner) and Leopold Kaufmann had studied in Graz and produced comparably impressive housing and school projects. Rudolf Wäger, a qualified carpenter, designed innovative timber houses on minimal budgets, partly in cooperation with his brothers Siegfried and Heinz. The later brought by his design studies, under Max Bill and Otl Aicher at the Hochschule für Gestaltung in Ulm [Ulm Design School], important stimuli that were discussed and worked on together. Travels to Scandinavia and neighbouring Switzerland, but also reports in professional magazines were further inputs for them.

— A hunting hut by Leopold Kaufmann. One of his first, very controversial projects in the late 1960s in an extremly conservative cultural surrounding.

Second generation – The "Baukuenstler"

Barely 20 years later, a big push came in the shape of a generation of young architects who, influenced by the 1973 oil crisis, and following the burgeoning environmental movement and social upheavals, discovered participatory design, timber construction and intelligent ecology together with an also young generation of open-minded clients. Eager for practice, their first buildings were partly students work. Single-family homes and small housing complexes, but also sensitive and critical, independent renovations of historic rural houses were the basis for their practical experience and technical experimentation aimed at 'Simple Building'. Formally reduced and following the elemental typologies of Postmodernism and the 'Tendenza', the 'Tessiner Schule' a new way of building, was convincing because of its proximity to the client and the region and because of its craftsman-like pragmatism. Frequently, familial closeness to craftsmen or close cooperation with the designer generation of the 60s and 70s provided valuable support. From the collegial exchange of technical details through to joint projects and collective visits to building sites – they all happened in a spirit of openness and idealism that went back to the master classes of the Vienna Academy, to the conspiratorial atmosphere of the Technical University in Graz and especially to the sense of commonalty among regional craftsmen. This freedom, and the early independent work, was possible because of a peculiarity of the Vorarlberg building legislation. Vorarlberg is the only Austrian State which does not require an authorisation from the national Architektenkammer [Chamber of Architects] for building consent to be obtained, thus requiring long years spent gaining experience in other architectural offices.

The 'competency battle' in 1984, a legal conflict with the Austrian Chamber of Architects, precipitated the formation of the scene and a wave of solidarity unfurled far beyond the State borders. From this dispute there emerged not only a growing familiarity among a specialist public but also a solidarity among the public in Vorarlberg against the centralistic enemy, Vienna. Yet the new architecture did not only find allies among the customers and craftsmen. In addition to several officials in the State planning department, which was also the authority responsible for dealing with disputed planning consent applications, and a growing number of local authority officials, more and more people in political and administrative circles welcomed the New Building Wave. In Lustenau in 1985, a Vorarlberg architectural advisory board was established for the first time following the model adopted by Salzburg. Architects were called in to give professional advice to the local building officials and were able to provide augmentative training at grassroots level. That same year the Energy Institute, an architect initiative, was established, raising the environmental effort to an institutional level. For many years now, the examination of the strict

— Collective housing project "Im Fang" with a covered atrium between two residential buildings by the "cooperative".

— The concrete facade of the elementary school in Doren (A) by Cukrowicz Nachbaur comprising entrance, a lowered gym hall and the classroom windows.

— Essays
— P.180
The Significance of Building Culture

energy criteria for financial federal support and other State initiatives, have been managed through the Energy Institute.

Between 1985 and 1992, there was a bi-weekly television series in which the architect Roland Gnaiger reviewed positive and negative examples and was an important instrument in the broader understanding of architectonic concerns.

A variety of regional competitions brought forward high-quality community housing and further intensified discussion and acceptance. The public debate in the media was extremely controversial, but finally very well received especially outside Vorarlberg. In 1991 the 'Vorarlberg State International Art Prize' was awarded to Hans Purin, who accepted it only on behalf of the 'Vorarlberg building design artists' as a whole. The prize money was used to fund the first comprehensive documentation of the building scene, which resulted in 1993 in the 'Einfach Bauen' [Simple Building] exhibition and publication.

Third generation

In technical and artistic terms, building had taken giant steps towards professionalisation, when a third designer generation joined in during the 1990s, starting on the high level of craftsmanship and broadly-based appreciation of architecture among the population. The most important names in the group, who are now well-established, were Marte.Marte Architekten, Cukrowicz Nachbaur and Johannes Kaufmann, and his cousin Oskar Leo Kaufmann. From the beginning they had high formal aims and were competing with the experienced and formally developed offices of the second generation. The whole scene was soon characterised by an aesthetisation and a high degree of constructional perfection, successful in terms of quantity, as well as in their reputation. Of the pioneers, Baumschlager & Eberle, Hermann Kaufmann and Dietrich / Untertrifaller emerged as the most successful groupings with an international practice. Energy-efficient building systems and numerous constructional developments matured with them. Technical designers and craftsmen contributed to the dissemination of the new standards, which had been refined through the development work. During this period, new typologies were also developed. Contemporary and valid solutions were acknowledged, from the fire service to the farmhouse, via the compact multi-storey building.

Consensus and dissidents – a common self-image

None the less there was an appreciation and consensus around the basic issues across these generations of architects as a result of regional ties and a specific concept of their profession. It tended mainly towards the cooperative model of the craft guilds in contrast to the image of the creative artist. This led to a quite distinctive way of dealing with collective learning and cooperation with craftsmen and also to a mostly reluctant presentation of their own work.

Today

A class of international entrepreneurs and local authorities are increasingly discovering the effectiveness of spectacular branding through architecture. Names, or more rarely, promising no-names, are sought and found. The impressive buildings for SIE by Marte.Marte, for DGM and 'Montfort Werbung' by Oskar Leo Kaufmann or the recent conversion of the Bregenz Festival Hall by Dietrich| Untertrifaller again point to new possibilities and a wholly unsentimental and constant state of flux.

The summation of the whole movement in the major exhibition 'Constructive Provocation' with its accompanying book project, presented a broad sweep and convincingly exposed the various motivations. An initial wave of intense publicity in the professional media of this European-wide touring exhibition in three languages is now over with German architectural personnel now routine. Young offices are constantly emerging, often proving themselves in the tough competition with almost four generations of designers.

But all the fancy words embellishing the many essays about Vorarlberg architecture are questioned – as mentioned above – by a closer look. In the tourist resort of Montafon, hoteliers are trying to rebel against a State government that is too hand in glove with architecture; in the State capital, lists of signatures are circulating against 'concrete monsters'.

The Vorarlberg architectural development is entering a new stage facing not only practical and technical questions, but also the intellectual challenge of coping with images and clichés of their own work. A growing demand and an increasing popularisation are leading to off-the-peg buildings by property developers with no design ambitions, indistinguishable to the layperson. The collective idealism has clearly given way to distinctive cooperation and increasing competition.

The odd practice has been able to acquire an international reputation. Baumschlager & Eberle are building in Vienna, Zürich and Peking, Dietmar Eberle is dean of the faculty of ETH in Zürich, Hermann Kaufmann holds a professorship in Munich, Roland Gnaiger in Linz.

The following investigation of the causes and explanatory models highlights some of the qualities and motivations that have developed throughout and could help to understand the Vorarlberg Building Culture.

Approaches to a phenomena

Self-assesment between art and craftsmanship

Dietmar Eberle, in 'Architectura practica', Bregenz, 2006, writes: "In architectural creation there are two models, because after all the way work is organised also depends on the subjective perception of what architecture actually is. On the one hand there are those in favour of seeing architecture continue to be understood wholly in the sense of 'the art of building' as an autonomous act of creation on the part of the architect, thus putting individual performance to the fore. For others however, architecture is a cooperative endeavour in which the individual is part of a collective exchange and in which the focus is much more on the benefit to society."

In the 90s standards were developed, also accepted by craftsmen, which turned ambitious solutions into cost efficient details.

In 1996, Eberle's partner, Carlo Baumschlager, gave clear expression to something that until then had been regarded as a discrete difference in relation to the international architectural scene: "Not every detail that we design has to be sensational. Our belief is rather that well tried details can be used until something better and more reasonable is shown to exist. That is really the only argument for changing any detail. I do not have to reinvent the wheel every time."

This quotation again sums up a common identity and also describes one of the reasons for the rapid development of high technical and economic standards, which after a few years had already become international exports. Development does not come from the designing of a singular object, but with progressive optimisation over a series of projects, sometimes using smaller objects as fields of experimentation.

This way of developing by improving the same solutions happened not only in architects' offices, but was practised much more widely.

First this practice was done openly or in cooperation, later, because of the increasing spread of modern buildings, by the mere view or simply through the executing craftsmen suggesting improvements to the technical design. In general this practice is still accepted today among colleagues. Outside however, it has always caused irritation, criticised as mindless repetition and led to a series of mutual misunderstandings between building cultures.

The concept of region

With the concept of critical regionalism in his essay 'Towards a Critical Regionalism: Six Points for an Architectural Resistance' in 1983, Kenneth Frampton attempted to describe a richer context for modern architecture. In an interview 20 years later, he describes it as still being an important attitude in creative practice, but warns against misinterpreting it as a stylistic concept.

A feature essential to the Vorarlberg building culture came from the concept of region, the regional identity. Evoking regional specificities is a delicate undertaking, especially in the German cultural sphere. The distinctive feature can easily be self-referring, leading to stagnation and cultural narrowness. As a calculated tourist advantage it has mainly had even more devastating consequences,
if you think of the building culture in neighbouring Tyrol, still struggling with the economic calculation of an omni-present and stagey Heimatstil [Domestic Revival or Homely style].

It can be said — with all due caution — that Vorarlberg has succeeded in creating a positive identity for itself in architecture as well. During the social upheaval of the 1968 generation, which in Vorarlberg occurred very late and against massive resistance, something like a regionalistic reinterpretation of a politically problematic Vorarlberg-consciousness occurred, which was overlaid by postmodernist approaches and the environmental movement ideas of the early 1980s. In concrete terms, this produced self-built, single-family dwellings, in native wood with gabled roofs and postmodernist stylistic elements. At the same time, there was a struggle to retain old farmhouses and the regional identity, paradoxically defended by 'social revolutionaries'.

The Balance between innovation and tradition

Vorarlberg never had a tradition of isolation. Always historically on major traffic routes, it could not remain closed to the passage of goods and ideas. For almost 150 years, the Vorarlberg baroque master builders built churches and convents — exclusively outside their homeland — in their own version of the southern German Late Baroque style applying knowledge from northern Italian architectural treatises.

From the late eighteenth century the close and economically dominant Switzerland spurred the early industrialisation of Vorarlberg and the home production of laces for Swiss entrepreneurs brought significant changes to country life, that was always interspersed by unexpected details.

Regionalism in its ideal form also describes a productive relationship in the attention given to the local and the global. If you pay attention to foreign images and symbols, if you allow yourself to be captivated by transnational, competing worlds of consumption, you are lost for your own place. If on the contrary you simply close yourself to new sources of information or the foreign in general, you deprive yourself of many stimuli and much potential. From that point of view, globalisation does not necessarily have to be a threat. In regard to the disappearence of place, it is no longer a question of dispute over territory, but a matter of competition for attention as a good in short supply.

The Vorarlberg building culture exemplifies the extent to which the local and the universal can exist symbiotically, but also the extent to which one's own centre needs strength and appreciation. Vorarlberg is managing this balance by a traditional and deep-rooted mix of curiosity and scepticism.

It explains the striking coexistence of the traditional and the new and the moderate pace of change that makes it easier to cope with technical flashes in the pan and undesirable developments. In the current globalisation debate, this attitude stands as a paradigm with which to counter a transnational consumer culture.

The concept of craftsmanship

Another pillar of the Vorarlberg building culture that must be understood is a marked awareness of quality, and in this the mindset is very close to similarly Alemannic Switzerland. Not unconditionally, but frequently, when craftwork contracts are awarded, the best rather than the cheapest offer is usually preferred. The fact that quality is a selling point also guarantees the survivability of competent craftsmanship and also the feasibility of high standing building techniques. This is supported also by the joy for good work and for a well done object as a value in itself. Further, the close, social network in the Vorarlberg society easily persecutes anyone misusing the confidence that is put in craftmanship.

— The bar and ski hut "Schneggarei" by Philip Lutz. A sophisticated interference of clichees and authentic craftsmanship amidst a highly touristical environment.

— Hall for the two-weeks-exhibition "Handwerk und Form" 2003, built in only two days by craftsmen of the Bregenzerwald with piles of wood. The building is an interpretation of traditional, temporary workshops of carpenters and a comment on Peter Zumthors Swiss Expo Pavilion.

Essays P.184 — The Significance of Building Culture

Discourse of building

Discourse in architecture often appears to be limited to an intellectually theorising argument about the basic principles and concepts of building. As an academic vision or manifest, and couched in the form of theoretical considerations, it generally proves to have only slight sustainability and remains chronically distant from the actual act of construction. In Vorarlberg the discourse of architecture went its own way. In addition to media reports, a strong culture of cooperation with clients, building authorities and craftsmen was of primary importance to the design process. And there was another, quite special form of dialogue: building as such.

Architectural criticism

Professional reviews accompanied building in Vorarlberg to a far from negligible degree, and from the beginning had a direct link with Vorarlberg. Friedrich Achleitner, the central figure in Austrian architectural criticism had already paid regular visits to Vorarlberg in the 60s. Franz Bertel, initiator of the legendary 'Halde' estate of terraced houses in Bludenz by Hans Purin (1963-67), describes an early essay by Friedrich Achleitner in an Austrian newspaper about the danger of urban sprawl being one of the triggers for the communal residential project.

From this confirmatory and opinion-forming power in the press resulted an invaluable long-term effect on clients and decision-makers, with a peak of importance during the 1984 conflict of the Baukünstler with the chamber of architects, that set off a movement of solidarity with the new Vorarlberger Bauschule beyond Austria and triggerd the widespread professional and public prominence and acceptance.

Culture of cooperation

With the retention of local identities, a generally high degree of social responsibility and a pragmatic and constructive work ethic, a particular form of cooperative culture developed in the architectural field in Vorarlberg.

Dietmar Eberle (Baumschlager & Eberle) describes it like this: "The establishing of various forms of cooperation and close-knit networks and thus the methodology for integrating a diversity of know-how, together with the resulting formulation of a general strategy cannot be appreciated enough as a viable approach for the future. What distinguishes Vorarlberg is the possibility of being able to lock into a locally developed culture of communication with flat hierarchies. The quality of the collective learning and the mutual exchange, which was developed primarily by the architects among themselves during the 70s and 80s, has spread over the years to modern craftsmanship and to industry."

On the other hand craftsmanship became

— Japan meets Schrebergarten.
A private boat house with a weekend home on the top along a canal nearby the lake of Constance.
Architect: Marte/Marte

very familiar with the essential concerns of contemporary architecture. Initiatives like 'Handwerk und Form' [Craftmanship and Form] of the Bregenzerwaelder craftsmen are still fostering the idea of cross-fertilisation well aware of its advantages. A relationship of equals of this kind is the basis for a barrier-free discourse, in which the craftsman is taken seriously as a partner. So if there is a temptation to talk of a 'Vorarlberg phenomenon', it must be closely tied to the basic appreciation of the craftsman's work and with the fact that craftsmen and builders in Vorarlberg enjoy comparatively high status.

Eberle: "In Vorarlberg something happened that elsewhere remained a theoretical ideal talked about by the Modernists: the liberation of architecture from its academic milieu, the development of a modern culture for everyday life. Architecture here has become mainstream."

Building as discourse

A particular form of the discourse occurs when language and imagery are left behind and the built environment itself is taken as the medium. This 'discourse of the built environment' or 'discourse of building' transcends the purely technical optimisation process, if in doing so – as in this case – creative and typological questions are thought through in buildings or simply at the level of a detail. This leads to completely different contents and a completely different level in the argument thanks to collegial exchange under strict, but friendly circumstances. In public especially, real design and creation were hardly discussed. Designs were sketched out, mostly at top speed, functional arguments were mostly to the fore. But the built results were very closely examined and evaluated in detail by the colleagues.

Soon joint excursions were organised to just-completed projects, but also to building sites. Together they travelled in a minibus across the State and argued and debated about what they had seen. The intensity with which solutions were seized or worked on was and is a very tangible form of architectural criticism. Thesis, antithesis, synthesis or variation took an architectonic form. This tradition still exists today. Even now, the 'Zentralvereinigung der Architekten Vorarlbergs' [Central Association of Vorarlberg Architects] still invites its members twice a year to join group excursions over several days at home and abroad – opportunities that are intensively taken up.

Examples for the discourse of building

The lattice facade as an example

The focus on a functional structure and on the logic of form made surfaces more important. The visibility of raw materials like wood or concrete or their crafted treatment gave many buildings a highly sculptural quality. Their careful combination and transformation by weather and sun provide a visual density of structure and patina. These creative potentials from the poetry of surfaces require precise knowledge and experience in the use of these materials. Early projects referred to a vertical arrangement most appropriate to the material. During the 90s it developed to an open horizontal grid, visually lighter, sometimes like a translucent screen. A specific way of cutting and mounting the lattice was developed to provide its endurance.

Timber construction

Timber construction reached a high point right from the beginning. The need for precise design and intellectual rigour made timber construction with its visible structures a demanding discipline that seemingly matched regional mentality.

The structural visibility and severe demands on the craftsman became a question of character and well-nigh an ethical category because of its inherent need for order and honesty, in contrast to solid constructions where any inaccuracies were forgiven with a nice bit of render and a lick of paint. Already with the Halde estate (1963-65), the Kaufmann timber construction company in Bregenzerwald stood out because of their innovative wood glue binder. Laughed at as non-durable and pathetic, it was many years before timber construction achieved broader acceptance in the 90s. The building legislation was, and still is, a particularly significant area in which the building materials industries dispute the hegemony of their materials. Architects like Hermann Kaufmann, who from personal affinity and conviction have constantly pushed forward the possibilities of prefabrication and energy optimisation, were trailblazers in a development process driven largely by the concept of 'open source' — open knowledge to improve the technique in general. Today there is a whole series of hi-tech and intelligently cooperating carpentry workshops that unite top environmental standards and contemporary architectural language in bespoke and prefabricated building units.

The Monolith / The 'Einhof' farmhouse style

Practically the whole of the rural Vorarlberg housing stock is marked by the 'Einhof' style of building. This more than three-hundred-year-old building form has entered the collective subconscious of the State as an archetypal housing model. The concept of bringing all uses together in a single format and under one roof follows an economic rationale. But it also involves a spatial relationship, according to which the building is set as an object, a body, in an open landscape. Space is classified as surrounding space. Like a Greek temple, the model determines its position in relation to the landscape and in its distance to other buildings. And historically Vorarlberg has only very few areas specifically created as squares or streets.

It follows that this subconscious handicap still seems to be expressed today in the unbroken penchant for the detached single-family dwelling, but also in a latent unwillingness on the part of designers and local authorities to value the spaces between buildings and open squares.

The Monolith — as the contemporary design corresponding to the rural 'Einhof' is known — found its idealisation in the elemental building of the 90s, which is currently experiencing a renaissance of constantly new variations. Even several waves of criticism of the house as 'box' and demands for more variety and eloquence in the architectonic expression have hardly affected this particular theme of the discourse of the built environment at all.

Whilst the narrative of the 60s was often imbued with the aesthetic and all-inclusive idealism of the Modern, the statements of the second generation are essentially about economic questions, new typologies, timber construction, self-build and regional autonomy. Whilst the postmoderns in general positively surpassed themselves in the symbolicism of their architectures, architects here increasingly rejected formal debate. The linguistic exchange seemed to dry up completely with the creative fine-tuning of the 90s. Self-evidence, clarity and the power of material and form became the main technical terms used in the sparse self-commentaries and architecture concentrated on its intrinsic values, such as topology and space, proportion, weight and materiality.

The medium of discourse also determines its content. Frequently however linguistic arguments or the graphic representation of architecture reaches their inherent limits. In transformation of a Ludwig Wittgenstein postulate this paradox of architectural journalism could be practically solved:

"What you can't talk about, you have to build."

Biography
Robert Fabach works with Heike Schlauch in their architecture practice raumhochrosen, since 2001. He is the author for international publications on architecture in Vorarlberg.

Notes
The concept of 'Vorarlberg building design artists' as it appeared in connection with the so-called 'building design artist conflict' around 1984 is misleading here and has its roots in the then legal controversy over the term of 'Architekt [architect]', which in Austria is protected and energetically defended by the professional body.
Kenneth Frampton in: Hal Foster (Hrsg.) "The anti-aesthetic: Essays on postmodern Culture", New York 1993
Rassegna, No. 83, p. 9-19, Bologna 2006

—Authenticity Reconsidered: Recent Norwegian Architecture
—Morten Sjaastad

Authenticity is of long standing as an overriding value in Norwegian architecture. Earlier generations of modernist architects, culminating with Sverre Fehn, took sources readily validated in terms of authenticity — artistic integrity, nature, consistency of material and workmanship, forthright construction, freedom to imagine and form space — more or less for granted. Authenticity remains a fundamental value for most of the architects I discuss, yet not in any untroubled way. There is no escaping questions about its present relevance or about what the appropriate sources could be. Though by weight of historical investment alone, authenticity remains an issue.

You may ask how far the matter is peculiarly Norwegian. I should think that almost everywhere we look authenticity attracts enthusiasts, malcontents, and sceptics, as an insistent yet vexing notion in any bureaucratic or industrialised society. The best I can do is to offer up some fuller sense of what is involved, and to sketch a distinctive local role for the idea and a local expression of it.

Sources

If we seek to value a work for its authenticity, we want it to amount to evidence of those who made it, in the sense that no one else could have, not because others lack the requisite means, but because they could not have made it unless they became those authors. Where Wenche and Jens Selmer's own house displays their authentic detailing, every means available to them would have been available to other architects of their time except the Selmer's own abilities as evident in their style. Authenticity requires them to be indispensable to their own work.

Thus, an authentic architecture does not require an intention on the part of the architect to be authentic. Mere style is a mark of authenticity. A style may be collective — of its period, ethnic, or regional — or instead the style of a single architect, say, the unmistakeable style of Mies van der Rohe. As a mark of practical judgement, style is not simply a matter of realising an intention or of executing a decision. It is not only that you cannot just decide to sit down and design architecture in the style of Alvaro Siza or the Selmers: neither could Siza or the Selmers. A style needs to emerge. Though it may be influenced by intentions provoked by reflection, it cannot be banished by them or exchanged willy nilly for another style. A style is thrust upon an architect worthy of attention. At the same time, she is no style victim. Authenticity is to be interpretable not diagnosable. A work is to reveal its author in the difference she has made by her capacity for practical judgement, not by her pathologies.

Several leading architects such as Space Group and Ghilardi+Hellsten are unwilling to grant authenticity any remit beyond this general concern, often best tended by ignoring it. They are therefore able to respond without hesitation to contemporary social trends. By contrast, a quest for authenticity is likely to look to an astringent set of sources. Authenticity places unprecedented emphasis on the ability of the subject to lead a life peculiarly her own. This includes recognising the riches of inwardness, and one may expect that inwardness will favour certain sources as more immediately available, whether they are due to the environment or to the subject herself, and also that some sources will better lend themselves to reflection, or appeal more on reflection.

Hand in hand with the emphasis on inwardness goes a radical revaluation of the ordinary, since most of the material for inward reflection will be common everyday interests and experiences. Furthermore, once inwardness is understood as an capacity shared by all, there is is a strong tendency to egalitarianism. Individual style as noticeable in Art is only a special case of something at once more common, as a characteristic human possibility, and also quite particular, in that different cultures, societies, and individuals authenticate themselves by discovering and cherishing different sources available to them through the conduct of their daily lives.

Wenche and Jens Selmer's own house (Fig.1) is a case in point. Its forceful and imaginative articulation of sources central to Norwegian practice places it among the paramount postwar works. The wish to establish a place is clear in the negotiation between local topography and the trajectory of the sun, modernistically emphasising the latter. The interest in a house in touch with nature is of course widespread and of long standing, but is taken a step further in a very forthright relationship between interior and exterior. The equally direct linking of various sections of the house reflects a re-imagining of social relations with a bias to the natural. In the small scale and the lack of ceremonial transitions, Selmer's house articulates a frugal way of life shorn of traditional and conventional trappings, equally direct in engaging with nature, in the truck between family members, and in receiving visitors. The egalitarianism is apparent in the use of widely available woods, in the uncomplicated if exacting workmanship, and in reticent, inventive detailing. By foregoing the bourgeois pretensions of a villa and adopting the small scale and openness to nature of the

(Fig.1) Wenche Selmer's own house in Oslo, 1963. Interior view along the long axis of the house.

(Fig.2 Above) V-House, Nesøya, Asker, by Space Group, 2003. View across the terrace from the garden.

P.189

traditional holiday cottage, Selmer's small family house resonates with a national self image for a long time shared across classes. A Norwegian was best able to rehearse herself face to face with nature, a setting in which fellow citizens could be acknowledged unencumbered by the snobberies, conventions, and ceremonials of urban life.

Counter claims

Today, new holiday homes increasingly rival the steadily inflating programmes, volumes, and pomp and circumstance of single family villas. This has led to some amusing architectural kvetching in the press, confirming that the idealisation of a life frugally in touch with nature is a persistent if comical self-delusion. The unprecedented increase in wealth over the last fifty years, the vast sums released for investment in urban development, and the rise of an urban consumerist culture along continental lines have made a mockery of a national self image which many Norwegians nevertheless appear anxious to maintain, at some political cost. Once authenticity is awarded to individuals and to a wide range of social groups, whether subcultural, multicultural, or consumerist, as a prism by which to see their lives, the resulting pluralism puts paid to any consensus about sources of authenticity. Attempts to impose national sources, whether for holiday homes or for anything else, now appear crazily right wing, no less so when voiced by former leftists.

Related social changes put the very possibility of the earlier architecture in question. There is a renewed bourgeois interest in design. Sound workmanship in wood is no longer readily available. (It is no longer a luxury, but an eccentricity.) Consumerism and investment capitalism combine to commission packaged architectural projects at a scale which demands compositional strategies over attention to context (Fig.3).

The established sources have in any event long been conventionalised. Architects insisting on them run the risk of being, in Kierkegaard's phrase, 'town criers of inwardness'. Little could express this trivialisation better than official handbooks dedicated to developing the idea of 'place' as a goal of bureaucratic physical planning. The term has been adopted by a heritage lobby with political clout and by antiquarian authorities with the right to delay new projects by years – a right they abuse quite unconscionably. As a consequence, 'place' now honours any contextual gesture whatsoever, however meretricious.

Managerial attempts to develop made-to-measure places perhaps provide additional motivation for Space Group and Ghilardi+Hellsten to look elsewhere. They are freed to endorse consumer culture as long as it reciprocates by embracing design, and to pursue a logic of composition over received logics of place, thus to forge an architecture of the spectacular, not the ordinary. A forceful and imaginative piecemeal reshaping of the city is evident whether at the scale of a family house (Fig.2) or a motorway intersection and its hinterlands (Fig.3).

— (Fig.3 Above) Planning proposal and redevelopment project for Økern intersection, Oslo, by Ghilardi+Hellsten and Space Group, 2007.
— (Fig.4 Right) Kjøllesdal house, Lier, by Gerstlauer Molne Architects, 2003. Exterior.

The appeal of the above work, highly characteristic, yet with strong affinities to Dutch practices, may be acknowledged side by side with the very different strengths of work which recognises that continued engagement with authenticity requires (to be authentic) fresh materials and renewed practical judgement. Three sources are evident. There is an immersion in values handed down through the history of the practice and the history of building. Notably, modernist architecture has become a source of fascination, refinement, and reinvention. Secondly, there is a stubborn re-engagement with place. Thirdly, egalitarianism has found expression, not in a rhetoric whereby we are all equal before nature, but in a re-imagining of inherited building types and the structure of public and private space.

The inheritance of renewal

In Gerstlauer Molne's Kjøllesdal house (Fig.4), modernism is not accepted on its own terms as a break with the past, but placed on a historical continuum with buildings past and present. Ordinariness by mere stubborn insistence on it is transfigured in a remarkable purification of architectural means. The central column of the upstairs space leading to the bedrooms articulates not merely a logic of construction (Fig.5). In the shared yet intimate space it occupies, in the innards of the house, it is a symbol of insistent absorption in architecture and building as such.

The summer holiday cabin in Risør by Carl Viggo Hølmebakk (Fig.6) refines the frugality and small scale of the Selmer house. Enclosure is extended to the exterior. The small building is redistributed to articulate an environment. Approaches and departures within and without are subjected to feints and modifications. Directions are clouded. In what I take to be a tribute, the frugal forthrightness of Selmer's postwar house has become a bountiful discretion, a sophisticated murmuring.

Unsurprisingly, the two houses reveal that insistent historical reflection is a source of new architecture quite distinct from the old rationalist idea of autonomy. Authentic renewal can be no more autonomous than the history or the present on which it reflects.

Modesties of place

The widely disseminated theory of place due to Christian Norberg-Schulz is unabashedly normative. Some spots on the surface of the earth qualify as places, others do not. This has to be the point of departure for any theory of place. It makes no sense to talk about place except evaluatively, even if evaluations may be argued over, and even if a theory may be badly formulated or fallacious.

Many landscapes celebrated as places such as the terraced hillside fields of Italy, in the Rhineland, or in the Far East are built landscapes. The nineteenth century Italian writer and regionalist Carlo Cattaneo observed that a cultivated landscape is an immense "repository of labour". When we appreciate the distinctness of the landscape round

— (Fig.5) Kjøllesdal house, Gerstlauer Molne Architects, 2003. Upstairs interior.
— (Fig.6) Summer holiday cottage at Risør by Carl Viggo Hølmebakk, 1997. View of terrace.

Florence or along the Rhine, we are alive to the style of that labour. Likewise when we admire traditional settlements such as Bernkastel or Montaione as distinct places, we are alive to a local style of building expressive of a traditional way of life. The experience of place is of quotidian material, and belongs to the revaluation of everyday life typical of interest in authenticity.

However, a local tradition need not be entered into or understood in order to appreciate the style. Against the claims of the theory, it makes sense to understand experiences of place in terms of aesthetic evaluation, not quotidian practice. Experience of manmade places is akin to appreciation of Art, while experience of natural places is a species of appreciation of scenery. Thus the emphasis placed on a property like 'harmony'. which corresponds quite exactly to deeming something aesthetically 'appropriate'. Thus also the emphasis on the universal appeal of places, in direct parallel to Kant's understanding that aesthetic experiences speak to you as though they ought to speak in the same way to everyone. According to both Kant and the theory, Cathy's experience that the mountain is beautiful – an experience of place, if anything is – is compelling in the sense that part of the experience is that everyone ought to see it that way. Such an appeal is hardly characteristic of quotidian practices, about which we are prepared to take divergent evaluations and actions at face value. No one in their right mind would begin to discuss the choice between internet, supermarket, and local shopping on Kantian terms ("The internet just spoke to me…").

In experience of place, a pragmatically made object in everyday use is appreciated aesthetically. The style of the making and the traces left by use qualify the place as authentic. Yet there is no corresponding authenticity to the experience. Admiration of something authentic, whether of a work of Art, a place, or the conduct of a life, itself has no legitimate claim to authenticity. It reflects an interest in authentic objects, yet there is nothing authentic to the interest. The Kantian insight helps explain why. If a place appeals as if it ought to speak in the same way to everyone, its character cannot be attributed to the specific capabilities of the subject having the experience. All the same, authenticity is often mistakenly attributed to appreciation. In central instances of theory, in Heidegger and Norberg-Schulz, there is a strong tendency to assume that a critical experience of authenticity or of place, along with the arguments set around it, can be and will have to be as authentic as the materials they discuss. The result is a hubristic form of theory with an unwarranted lyrical swagger to its diction.

Usually, to experience a place in location is to take pleasure in it. Compare seeing a picture and wanting to visit. By virtue of style alone, the place appears to extend an illusory personal invitation, and experience of place tends to be sentimentalised as an authentic homecoming, however unlikely. The aesthetic appeal leads to a mistaken inference that the tradition by which a place has emerged

(Fig.7) Hotel Kirkenes by Sami Rintala, 2005. View from main road.

extends the invitation. The surliness of the natives is forgotten, their suffering glossed over, strangeness masked. Both the theoretical and the experiential misunderstanding underestimate the contentful yet at the same time pragmatic grounding of an authentic style in a particular form of everyday life. A place, just because it is a matter of style, needs to emerge, and the visibility of an appreciable style tends to underplay the rich grounding of the emergence in unique and different social traits.

If we value some spots as places, it seems sensible to go ahead and produce them, which no doubt is the rationale of the aforementioned handbooks. Yet this is more difficult than one may think, just because places need to emerge authentically. The fateful difference between the aesthetic appreciation of places and their pragmatic production means that one does not learn how to remake Mallaig somewhere else by wandering appreciatively along its quays, or even by drawing it up, whether in detail or diagrammatically, just as one does not learn how to 'do' Steve Reich by listening to Different Trains, however intently. Authenticity is firmly an attribute of the object, not of the experience or the documentation.

If places need to emerge, they cannot just be designed. Mallaig would not be experienced as the place it is if it were seen as the outcome of a single design, rather than incremental pragmatic decisions and stable everyday use. Some styles of architecture are therefore incompatible with place, in dispelling any sense of the quotidian. The prevalence of design features plays up to a sense of the spectacular, not the ordinary, to a sense of occasion, not the everyday.

Place therefore is a tricky source to handle and a rare achievement. Sami Rintala is a doubly displaced architect, having relocated from Finland to Norway, and having carried out a great deal of his work in the foreign realm of the Art world. His approach is invigorating in both settings. A spartan hotel for a festival in Kirkenes, to a brief and on a site of his choice between the main road and an inlet of the Barents Sea (Fig.7), testifies to a bolder idea of what it takes for a place to emerge, with affinities to conceptual Art. He trusts in fundamental precepts of place – the establishment of a horizon, a given concern for up and down and for orientation and direction – to emerge all the more strongly when forced to do their work in a new and precarious situation.

Jensen & Skodvin at the Liasanden layby execute a reverse archaeology of the site allowing a place to emerge (Fig.8). Every tree is preserved. The gravel is poured and a path for cars picked out according to a set of rules and a concept which would realise a different place somewhere else in another stand of trees. There is no design to follow. The drawings were done merely to calculate masses. The place is due to the style of the concept applied to a specific situation.

The supplementary power station at Pålsbu by Manthey Kula (Fig.9) in its meticulous fusing of site and programme articulates the dam as a place for the

— (Fig.8) Liasanden rest stop by Jensen & Skodvin, 1997. View along gravel path.

— (Fig.9) Supplementary power station at Pålsbu by Manthey Kula, 2007. Exterior view.

— P.193

retention and release of tremendous forces, and a focal point for a range of changeful tempi, seasonal, workaday, directed or in reserve, landscaped, cosmic, or engineered. Thus it is able to bring out a metaphysical attitude to place, not to come up with answers, but to raise questions about the way we experience time in a locality. Places tend to tell us that "everything you see will outlast you," as a reminder that others will succeed you in the same spot. The power station acutely expresses a tragic conception of life by chalking in the possibility of our collective absence.

To place a building in a landscape is in a sense to place a thought there. The style and strength of the thought is sometimes able to allow a place to emerge, or to articulate more forcefully a place already there. With the power station at Pålsbu, the thought evokes the possibility of its own absence.

Each of the three projects allows a place to emerge as a result of the architectural work by means of a modesty, even sparseness. Approaches reminiscent of conceptual Art allow ordinary objects to be presented without design flourishes. There is no need to follow the redundant lines of the architect's pencil. What is more, there is no sentimental welcome. Each project affords an experience of place without issuing any invitation beyond the brief sojourn required by the programme.

Social content re-imagined

The scope for authenticity has seemed narrow in and around the city. Accommodation to conventional or institutional values tends to be dismissed as inauthentic — whether a collective tradition or an individual will accommodates itself. The dismissal extends to inherited building types. What could be authentic about adopting the terrace house or the urban tenement as a model when no tradition demands them?

The bias is compounded by the Modernist insistence that artistic integrity presupposes a spatial imagination unfettered by property lines and, in particular, freed from the urban institution of private property organised along public streets. The freedom insisted on is of course paradoxical, since the architect is cut off from a range of imaginative possibilities central to social life. The attitude is by now itself an inherited professional convention, as a result of a strong but unreflective Modernist investment in authenticity.

Both the strong association between authenticity and nature and the refusal of inherited types in the name of untrammeled spatial imagination have reinforced attempts to remake the centre of cities in the image of nature. The reluctance or inability of many architects to acknowledge institutional requirements is painfully evident in Snøhettas well received, yet ill judged, Oslo Opera House. The sloping roof is announced as a public space, yet needs to be accompanied by warning notices, as though one really were traversing mountain scenery (Fig.10). Bureaucratic semantic juggling has permitted building regulations to be set aside to allow the architects to introduce unmotivated breaks

(Fig.10) Public notice about using the "public space" of Snøhetta's Oslo Opera House, 2008.

Vær varsom!
Caution!

Taket har mange avsatser, og kan være glatt. Bruk av sykkel eller skateboard er forbudt. Ferdsel på eget ansvar.

The roof has many steps, and may be slippery. Bicycles or skateboards not allowed. Use of the area is at your own risk.

and steps in the surface. It is an open question who is accountable for the inevitable injuries. Decency is sacrificed to slick imitation of landscape. The architectural imagination at work is unable to accommodate any reasonable concept of public space.

Some architects have by contrast placed inherited types and institutional urban space at the centre of their spatial imagination, whether the scale is small or large, and thereby found authentic sources of renewal. At the small scale, in the raised en suite step joining up the bedrooms along the glass window wall towards the garden in the Dysthe/Lyngstad villa (Fig.11), Knut Hjeltnes surgically articulates the conventional scheme. The innovative freedom and access afforded the children is achieved by emphasising just those partitions between rooms and between house and garden which are conventional and still in place, though changed. The social and spatial re-imagining operates on the convention. There is no need either to sweep it away or meekly to repeat it.

The street plays a pivotal role when we imagine cities. This by itself is enough to throw into doubt the authenticity of the quite different way architects tend to design them. In a series of competition entries beginning with Gjersrud-Stensrud, Jensen and Skodvin restore streets to their crucial function (Fig.12), thus re-imagining what could be a valid egalitarian urbanism. When the city is conceived as an explicit structure of public and private rights, the dimension by which equality is measured is reset as a matter of equal freedoms not similar outcomes. The choice of private conduct is not moulded according to a shared conception of the authentic, but ceded to the citizen to choose for herself, authentically or otherwise. While in the public street, everyone is in principle equally responsible to each other.

— (Fig. 11) Villa Dysthe/Lyngstad, Rykkin, by Knut Hjeltnes, 2004. Downstairs interior showing en suite connection between bedrooms.

— (Fig.12) Planning proposal for Gjersrud-Stensrud, Oslo, by Jensen & Skodvin, 2001. Perspective sketches of private facades on public streets.

— (Fig.13 Left) Svartlamoen student housing, Trondheim, by Brendeland & Kristoffersen, 2005. Exterior view.

— (Fig.15 Above) Restaurant Stim, Stavanger, by Helen & Hard, 2003. Interior view.

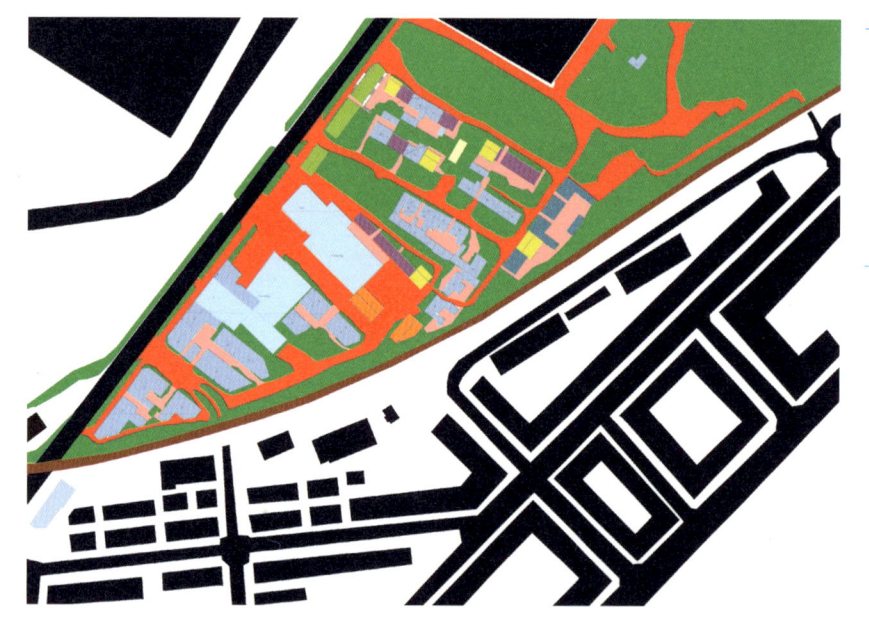

— (Fig.14) Analysis of building types at Svartlamoen in Trondheim by Brendeland & Kristoffersen, 2002.

Essays
P.196

Authenticity Reconsidered:
Recent Norwegian Architecture

Egalitarianism is removed from the realm of leisurely days in holiday cottages and transferred to the pragmatic realism of the everyday. No longer mythically absolute before nature, its basis is the right of citizens to be present and to participate in public space, and to present their private lives to a residential street with the discretion they choose.

In their work at Svartlamoen, a ramshackle area of Trondheim long scheduled for demolition and the location of a flourishing counterculture, Brendeland & Kristoffersen have embraced inherited building types responsive to local streets as an authentic source of new architecture (Fig.13). The competition was won by saying "If it ain't broke, don't fix it," to explain why the gravelled streets which have served the area well and lent it its charm would be left intact. The student housing (Fig.14) is a refreshing take on the traditional tenement, but now in wood, sufficiently fireproof with the advent of massive wood construction. The nursery is a playful version of the urban villa often converted to just this use. By contrast, say, to Helen & Hard's wonderfully playful work in Stavanger (Fig.15), the fun and games do not use a type merely as a straight man, but imagine and rearticulate it in its original function, whether it is the kitchen bench out of which children pour, the door framed by the skew-whiff section of wall, or the wall around the property recovering the kindergarten as a garden.

Singularities

The three sources I have named are interdependent. Public street space is a viable strategy for the emergence of place just because of its programmatic ordinariness and the authentic variability of the private properties addressing it. If I had not wanted to present one telling detail, Hjeltnes might perhaps have been better recognised in the section on historical reinterpretation. At the same time, by the way the Dysthe/Lyngstad villa folds into the landscape, the siting of the en suite shelf I have highlighted in front of the garden and landscape view might be said to create a micro-place. And so on and so forth. If we are able to accept the idea of a micro-place, it is a theme also in the Risør cabin.

But what unites these projects is the motivation of their differences. They persist with the idea of authenticity to uncover singular aspects of history, site, and social use of space. Not content to reiterate generalities, by working to reveal particulars, they demonstrate that authenticity, in the sense of a reflective practical engagement with especially valued local sources, remains relevant to architectural practice, however much it may appear to be under pressure from a complementary interest in global cultures and economies.

Biography
Morten Sjaastad was educated at the AA and at the Oslo School of Architecture and Design, where he has taught. He lives in Brighton and Oslo.

—The Contexts of Graubunden
—Steven Spier

— Splügen, high up in the Alps near the Splügen Pass to Italy.

— Traditional Strickbau.

The quickening pace of globalisation in the last 20 years has indeed induced increasing economic competition and a further homogenisation of cultures. But it has also surprisingly induced, less surprisingly in hindsight, a growing awareness and pride in regional differences. Europe, it could be argued, is struggling to find the balance between the global, the supranational, the national and increasingly the regional. This development could be viewed wryly from Switzerland. It is a wealthy, stable country in spite of four official languages, both Catholic and Protestant populations, a highly decentralised political system, and a position straddling northern and southern Europe geographically and culturally. Geography, history, culture and architecture are closely linked in Switzerland, a country where the regional defines the national. We will be looking at Graubunden's identity within the exceptionalism of Switzerland, and at a time when the concept of Switzerland is much in question.

Let's start with some geography. Graubunden is the largest and most easterly canton of Switzerland, bordering Italy to the south and Austria to the east. It is entirely mountainous. From its mountains stems the Rhine, one of the most important industrial waterways in the world. Its various Alp ranges are separated by valleys, which are amongst the highest in Europe. These valleys principally lie north-south. Communities in neighbouring valleys developed largely independently from each other, even linguistically.

And immediately we come to history and culture. It is true that Graubunden consisted of isolated, poor, mountain villages. But already in Roman times its north-south valleys and mountain passes were important transit and trading routes between northern and southern Europe. Indeed, it was the loss of Roman control over those passes that allowed the barbarians to enter Italy. So alongside the expected isolation of rural mountain communities there was also a mixture of northern and southern cultures; in short, cosmopolitanism. We can readily see the effects of this in language, food and architecture. Half of the population, particularly around Chur where various valleys converge and so has long been a trading hub, speaks German. In the southern valleys bordering Ticino and Italy resides the sixth of the population that speaks Italian. And around one third of the population speaks Romansh, a group of languages very close to Latin that have survived thanks to mountain isolation and indeed are quite different in different valleys. In food, a good example of this mix of cultures is Pizzoccheri, a short pasta but one made not from durum wheat but the far heartier buckwheat. In architecture there are two principal typologies that likewise reflect Graubunden as a crossroads. The traditional building materials are stone or timber, and the choice of one or the other is largely culturally determined. In short, in German-speaking villages the predominant material and construction technique is timber; in Romansh speaking villages it is stone. In timber an interesting hybrid building technique has developed called Strickbau (woven construction). Here massive pieces of milled timber are stacked on top of each other and joined by overlapping the corners. Walls support each other structurally and create a series of linked, rectangular rooms spatially. A typological feature in Romansh-speaking areas however is small timber buildings sitting on stone foundations that are separated by use but that over time might become joined.

There are then strong local identities within the region of Graubunden and they are still important. (We'll get back to why that's the case.) The architect Gion Caminada is one of the 280 residents of Vrin, actually just outside of Vrin, near the end of the high, Romansh-speaking valley of Lumnezia. His buildings in the village are based in traditional timber construction — Strickbau, and traditional programmes, but are by no means traditionalist. A very contemporary single-family house, for instance, uses Strickbau even though the building is four storeys tall: it adopts the typology of separate warm and cold buildings, though in this case separated by a stair. Reflecting again the perhaps surprising reality of Graubunden as a cross roads, Valentin Bearth is a professor at the Accademia di architettura in Ticino, on the southern side of the Alps, while his business partner Andrea Deplazes is at the ETH in Zurich. Both are equally far or near to the capital Chur. The founding of the Accademia in 1996 was not only important for Italian-speaking Switzerland but also for the south-facing traditions and culture of Graubunden.

That the manifestation of strong cultural identities in the built environment are still recognised as important can also be seen in the footbridges the engineer Jürg Conzett designed for the Viamala Ecomuseum, for which he gives primacy to the culture of materials in spite of their engineering challenges. The Viamala was the most direct route through the Alps between Milan and Lake Constance and had therefore been an important passage between southern and northern Europe since Roman times. It was only made fully passable again in 1996 thanks to the founding of the Ecomuseum. The footbridge in the northern, German-speaking part of the gorge, a parabolic, stepped suspension bridge is timber. That for the southern part of the gorge is stone, a decision at odds with the engineering requirements of spanning 40 metres and a 4-metre height difference between banks. The result is a stress-ribbon system, with the stone walkway pre-stressed to act like a monolithic slab. The two bridges are at most three hours apart by foot. They are both incongruous and contextual, wearing their cultural significance lightly. They are in no way a rustic-romantic, Heidi-like park architecture. Perhaps not incidentally Conzett is from Graubunden and worked in Zumthor's office for six years in the mid-1980s before setting up his own office, which is in Chur.

But how have such regional traditions in an age of DHL and the Internet remained relevant in Graubunden? And so we come back to history. Switzerland's founding

— Traditional timber details, Vals.

— (Top) Second Traversina Bridge, Viamala, Jürg Conzett 2005.
— (Above) Surasuns Footbridge, Viamala, Jürg Conzett 1999.

— Essays
— P.200

The Contexts of Graubunden

myth begins in the Middle Ages in the German-speaking Alps. The importance of the passes through the Alps was recognised by the Holy Roman Empire, which in the early thirteen century gave the inhabitants of the area around the St. Gotthard Pass the privilege of responsibility to the emperor alone. On the first of August 1291, fearing the local feudal powers after the death of Emperor Rudolf von Habsburg (1218-1291), the people from the three Waldstätten – Schwyz, Uri and Unterwalden, swore an eternal union against any attack on them. They did not, however, establish their own state. By the time of the Reformation this self-defense alliance comprised 13 cantons – both rural and urban, as well as affiliated areas and cities. (Switzerland's history, given its reputation for isolation and neutrality, is perhaps surprisingly bloody. It adapted armed neutrality as a policy only in the late seventeenth century.) It was a rather loose confederation whose aim was to be left alone against ever-changing threats from the larger neighbours north, south, east, and west. Switzerland's current configuration and recognisable nationhood is first enshrined in its 1848 constitution. Graubunden followed a similar history. In the Middle Ages it was largely ruled from the Episcopal See of Chur, the bishop of which was a prince of the Holy Roman Empire. Various groups formed against the prince's power – the Gotteshausbund (1367), the Grauerbund (the Grey League, named after the rustic grey clothes worn by commoners and that subsequently became the name of the canton) (1395), and the Zehngerihtenbund (1436). Communes eventually allied with the Swiss Confederation to win their practical independence from the Habsburgs at the end of the fifteenth century. Graubunden entered the Swiss Confederation in 1803.

There are several things about this history, in both myth and reality, that help define Swissness – and combined with geography help explain a few things about architecture in Graubunden. The first is the myth of a largely rural population in a harsh environment, which in itself tends to produce both self-reliance and a strong sense of community. More precisely about Graubunden: "The shift from self-sufficiency to the speciality of alpine cattle farming (in the fifteenth century) resulted in a sophisticated cooperative organisation of work and commercialisation… The way in which alpine communities emerged also led to the development of political entities in the modern age, which were quite unusual in Europe. The first of these were the village communes of Valais and Graubunden, which had so many autonomous rights that with time they became de facto sovereign ministates operating locally." (Diener et al, p. 366)

More peculiar still is the long history of Switzerland as a loose confederation, finally dragged to proper nationhood by Napoleon and then the revolts of 1848. One should consider what skills are necessary to make such a confederation – rural and urban, Catholic and Protestant, and four languages at the geographic, and, for centuries, geopolitical centre of

— The Thermal Baths in Vals in the context of post-war development.

Europe, function; namely, compromise and consensus. Switzerland is constitutionally still a confederation, which means it is highly decentralised. Most political power is at the municipal level – where you were born remains your administrative home, followed by the cantonal and finally the federal. The local level might also have its own dialect and the area its own architectural details. It will thus have a strong sense of pride and identity. The long tradition of direct democracy, with regular referenda, including all significant capital projects, at all levels of governance, has had a direct impact on architecture. It can of course lead to provincialism but seems instead to lead to communities taking responsibility and a demonstrable pride. Until the recent economic opening due to globalisation that even the Swiss couldn't resist, the extensive competitions system often favoured regional practices, which included practices of architects who were born there but might now reside and work elsewhere. In a small country of many regions this gave many young or less-known offices a good chance at the commission for a public building; or conversely, a village a building by a well-known architect. The now world famous thermal baths by Peter Zumthor are in a fairly remote valley with a once struggling tourist trade. He described the potential within such villages to me in an interview (Architecural Research Quarterly, 2001): "The client happens to be the village... (and) There's a lot of autonomy in these villages, not just formally... They decide on planning processes and so on. And they paid for the baths, so it was necessary every once in a while, at different phases and stages of the project, to go to a communal meeting and have the project approved. This is one thing, we talked to them. The other thing is that there were these two or three guys from the village who wanted to do something special, not something usual, a bath like everybody has, and they got excited as they found out slowly what we as architects were trying to do. We became this team, where they were open enough and cultivated, culturally minded enough, to get into my world, to participate critically but participate really and then take on the responsibility of doing a lot of things in another way; to say, but we want to do this. This has a lot to do with the sense of independence you can still find sometimes in certain people in these villages, in these places. You can feel this old sense of independence there."

Bearth & Deplazes's schools are likewise the result of local communities

Village School in Paspels, Valerio Oligaiti, 1998.

Essays
P.202   The Contexts of Graubunden

who demanded excellent architecture for their communities. A school or a community centre in these villages is often the major public building and can have a tremendous effect negative or positive. Inhabitants of such villages understand this. Furthermore clients have respect for the architect as a professional. Valerio Olgiati's school in the tiny village of Paspels is a 'beton brut solitaire' and a phenomenological investigation of space on the inside. Such buildings in Graubunden are, from a British perspective, impossibly rigorous and modern. But what they also reflect is a rural culture where extravagance was unaffordable, a harsh environment where survival alone was hard enough. Often only the church or town hall could have a plastered façade.

The faux chalet developments and sprawl around Klosters, Davos and Arosa confirm that not all is well architecturally. The major industry in Graubunden in the nineteenth century was already tourism, the Alps as we know them having been created by the British. To support this industry the Swiss developed a major railway network, spas, sanatoria (Thomas Mann's The Magic Mountain is set in Switzerland) and resorts. Switzerland has been a wealthy country only relatively recently and industrialised late. Unusually it industrialised not primarily in big cities, such as in Great Britain, but in towns too. Thus industrialisation, which even then meant globalisation, penetrated the countryside, again challenging rural stereotypes. Mass tourism only arrived after the Second World War.

The respect of the architect as a professional and the untroubled inheritance of modernism are largely the result of two educational developments. Architecture was taught first at the ETH in Zurich, which was founded in 1855 as Switzerland's only federal higher education institution and with a clear polytechnic direction and remit: to build a modern Switzerland. (It now ranks amongst the top five technical universities in the world.) There has never been architecture at art schools, academies, royal courts or universities. The later development of a more pragmatically oriented education at the cantonal Fachhochschulen (equivalent to the old British polytechnics) did not change the emphasis at the ETH at all. Instead, they produced the vast majority of architects who were extremely well trained in construction and building. At the centre of both educations stands an unquestioned belief that the role of the architect is to build and so building in its physical and

— Mass tourism infrastructure along the valley, Thusis.

— An early competition win for Gigon Guyer; The Kirchener Museum, Davos, 1992.

material manifestation is central to the education. It is noteworthy that there have never been manifestoes coming out of Switzerland, even now, while in The Netherlands it is de rigueur. One can bemoan this stance as fitting in with an anti-intellectualism that is indeed also part of Swiss culture. But there is a general feeling in Switzerland that the profession in the US, Great Britain and The Netherlands has almost been destroyed, and that the profession in Switzerland might be heading the same way. But for now one can build and build well. In any case the consequences for architecture are many and positive as one can see in the work of the last 20 years, which has essentially been examining the architectural consequences of how we now build.

The second educational development evolves from and supports the clear mission of the founding of the ETH. For the building of a modern country is fundamentally a modernist project but modernism in a pragmatic sense. Switzerland was never seduced by high modernism's heroics even while accepting much of its agenda. From as early as the 1930s Switzerland transformed modernism in to Swiss Modernism. This can be seen in the design of Helvetica typeface, its pioneering graphic design, Max Bill's 'good form', and of course architecture. The history and theory department at the ETH, which is of an international quality and outlook, has also been steadily publishing monographs on Swiss modernist architects who are hardly known outside of Switzerland, and have thereby helped to establish a canon. The compact monographs have such subtitles as 'The Other Modernism' and 'Pragmatic Modernism'. Unlike Great Britain with its century-long fraught relationship to modernism, the Swiss modernist tradition is accepted as a legacy and the architectural tradition within which one works. This has allowed for a continuous architectural development that is the opposite of continual and heroic new beginnings.

Such a pragmatic approach to architecture is only possible because the building industry can still build well and budgets are comparatively generous. (And as one architect told me, the companies tend to be Swiss and so also share a desire for quality.) Until recently it was common for the architect to be in charge of the entire process, with sub-contractors and craftsmen working under him or her directly. This allowed the development of methods and details with knowledgeable craftsmen and builders. Furthermore the polytechnic tradition and the rich history of extraordinary civil engineering that continues to this day produces architects with an understanding and respect for engineers, who are good collaborators.

The relationship between practice and academia goes further yet. The best architects are hired by the ETH in Zurich,

— House in Fläsch set amongst the vineyards, Bearth & Deplazes, 2001.

and since its founding in 1953, also at the EPF in Lausanne, in French-speaking Switzerland. Established architects become professors in a system that supports their development as well as the education of future architects. The recent set of booklets, Switzerland: An Urban Portrait, for example, which seeks to define the country through a new spatial taxonomy, is written by four of the best-known Swiss architects as part of their research as ETH professors, not as a vanity project from their offices. The reciprocity of practice and academia is also helped by the smallness of Switzerland. And so we come back to geography, and to culture. Andrea Deplazes, as professor at the ETH in Zurich, observed the latest developments in computer-assisted brick laying in its laboratories, which he then applied to the winery in the small village of Fläsch featured in this book. Previously they had built a house in the village using an innovative massive concrete with the insulation as part of the aggregate. His office, Bearth & Deplazes, is in the capital of Graubunden, only a half hour from the village they built in, both principals are from such villages, and the ETH is only 90 minutes away. Zumthor lives and works in a tiny village outside of the provincial city of Chur, which has not hindered him working all over Europe.

Much of what I have proposed as the exceptionalism of Graubunden can be seen clearly in the admittedly extreme example of Gion Caminada. His family has lived in the same valley for generations, remote even by Swiss standards. The village wanted to resist losing its centuries-old way of life through alpine farming and the fate that befell most of Ticino by becoming a village for tourists or weekend homes. So it developed a strategy that added value to its agricultural production, which meant building new barns and a slaughterhouse on the edge of the village, and added amenities in the centre like a community hall. The construction method and typology respect local traditions without mimicking them. That architecture could help sustain the community is taken up too by the trusses of the community hall, which are cleverly designed (by Jörg Conzett) from small laths so that they could be built from local timber and constructed by local craftsmen. And to return to the reciprocity between practice and academia, Caminada is now a professor at the ETH, looking at rural regeneration strategies and the role of architecture.

One can't easily unravel what is going on in Graubunden from Switzerland, and Switzerland from the world. It is though an exceptional region within an exceptional country, the result of its specific geography, history and culture with lessons nevertheless for how a region or small country can build excellent architecture.

Biography
Steven Spier is visiting professor in the department of architecture at Strathclyde University and Principal of the new HafenCity University Hamburg. He is an Advisory Board Member of A&DS as well as an honorary fellow of the RIAS. This article is based on his just completed AHRC research grant, "Constructing an Architecture of Excellence: The Case of Switzerland." He is the author of Swiss Made (2003) and of numerous articles on Swiss architecture.

References
Allensprach, Christoph, Architecture in Switzerland. Building in the 19th and 20th Centuries. (Zurich: Pro Helvetia, 1999).

Diener, Roger, Jacques Herzog, Marcel Meili, Pierre de Meuron, Christian Schmid. Switzerland: An Urban Portrait. (Basel: Birkhäuser) 2006.

Messeure Anna, Martin Tschanz und Wilfried Wang, Architektur im 20. Jahrhundert: Schweiz. (Munich: Prestel-Verlag, 1998).

Spier, Steven with Martin Tschanz, Swiss Made. New Architecture from Switzerland. (London: Thames & Hudson, 2003).

— Caminada Community hall, Vals, Gion Caminda architect, Jürg Conzett engineer, 1995.

—Credits

— **Exhibition Co-curator and book Co-editor**
Morag Bain
The Lighthouse

— **Exhibition Co-curator and book Co-editor**
Oliver Lowenstein
Fourth Door Research

— **Project Assistant**
Helen Nisbet

— **Book and Exhibition Graphics**
ISO

— **Exhibition Design**
Collective Architecture

— **Specially commissioned Photography**
Armando Ferrari

— **Exhibition and Book Funded by**
The Scottish Government

— **Photography**
The publishers would like to thank the following individuals and institutions for giving permission to reproduce photography. We have made every effort to receive copyright and acknowledgement for all images. We wish to thank in advance anyone we have inadvertently omitted.

P.04 Armando Ferrari

— **An Architecture of Elsewhere – Oliver Lowenstein**
P.10 (Left) © Luke Hayes/VIEW
P.10 (Right) Ernst Hiesmayr from Eine Moderne Tradition
P.13 (Left) Computer screen grab
P.13 (Right) Dalziel+Scullion
P.14 Alvar Aalto Foundation Aalto museum
P.15 (Left) Oliver Lowenstein, Fourth Door Research
P.15 (Right) Oliver Lowenstein, Fourth Door Research
P.16 (Left) Armando Ferrari
P.16 (Right) Oliver Lowenstein, Fourth Door Research
P.18 Co Evolution Quarterly, 1982, San Francisco
P.20 Jensen & Skodvin
P.22 Oliver Lowenstein, Fourth Door Research
P.23 Oliver Lowenstein, Fourth Door Research
P.24 (Left) Lorne Gill, Scottish Natural Heritage Image Library
P.24 (Right) Oliver Lowenstein, Fourth Door Research

— **The Buildings – An Overview – Oliver Lowenstein**
P.27 (Left middle) Armando Ferrari
P.27 (Right) Neil Sutherland Architects
P.28 (Left) Lotte Glob
P.28 (Middle) Angus Bremner
P.28 (Right) Keith Hunter
P.29 (Left) Nigel Rigden
P.29 (Right) Gavin Fraser
P.31 (Left) Jensen & Skodvin
P.32 (Middle) Bruno Klomfar
P.32 (Right) David Grandorge
P.32 (Left) Cukrowicz Nachbaur
P.32 (Middle) Lucia Degonda
P.32 (Right) © Ralph Feiner

P.34 Armando Ferrari

— **Lotte Glob Studio**
P.36 ISO
P.38 Lotte Glob
P.40 (Top) Armando Ferrari
P.40 (Bottom left) Armando Ferrari
P.40 (Bottom right) Lotte Glob
P.41 Armando Ferrari
P.42 Lotte Glob
P.43 (Top) Lotte Glob
P.43 (Bottom left) Lotte Glob
P.43 (Bottom right) Gokay Devici

— **Telford Drive**
P.44 ISO
P.46/7 Keith Hunter
P.49 (Top) Murray Dunlop Architects
P.49 (Bottom left) www.jamd.com
P.49 (Bottom right) Roberto Shezen
P.50/1 Armando Ferrari

— **Swinton**
P.52 ISO
P.54 Angus Bremner
P.56 Source unknown
P.57 (Top) Armando Ferrari
P.57 (Bottom left) Armando Ferrari
P.57 (Bottom right) Oliver Chapman Architects
P.58/9 Armando Ferrari

— **Strathnairn Community Forest Shelter**
P.60 ISO
P.62 Armando Ferrari
P.64/5 Armando Ferrari
P.66 (Bottom keft) Neil Sutherland Architects
P.66 (Top) Armando Ferrari
P.66 (Bottom right) Armando Ferrari
P.67 Neil Sutherland Architects

— **The Pier Arts Centre**
P.68 ISO
P.70 Gavin Fraser
P.72 Reiach & Hall Architects
P.73 (Top left) Armando Ferrari
P.73 (Top right) Ioana Marinescu
P.73 (Left) © Reiach & Hall Architects
P.73 (Right) © Gavin Fraser
P.74/5 Ioana Marinescu

— **Culloden Battlefield Visitors Centre**
P.76 ISO
P.78/9 Armando Ferrari
P.80 (Left) Gareth Hoskins Architects
P.80 (Right) © The Trustees of the National Museums Scotland
P.81 (Top) Gareth Hoskins Architects
P.81 (Bottom) Armando Ferrari
P.82 Nigel Rigden
P.83 All images Armando Ferrari

— **Taigh Chearsabhagh Arts Studio**
P.84 ISO
P.86 (Top) Armando Ferrari
P.86 (Bottom) Chris Morgan
P.87 All images Armando Ferrari
P.88 (Left) © Seema KK
P.88 (Right) Chris Morgan
P.89 Chris Morgan

— **Talla Choinneachaidh**
P.90 ISO
P.92 Armando Ferrari
P.94 Neil Stephen
P.95 All images Armando Ferrari
P.96 (Top left + right) Armando Ferrari

P.96	(Bottom) Mary Arnold-Forster	P.143	(Left) Jensen & Skodvin		—	The Significance of Building Culture – Buildings as Discourse – Robert Fabach
P.97	Mary Arnold-Forster	P.143	(Top right) Jensen & Skodvin			
P.34	Armando Ferrari	P.142	(Bottom right) unknown		P.179	Leopold Kaufmann
		P.144	Armando Ferrari		P.180	Melanie Büchel
—	Extension Winery Gantenbein, Graubunden				P.181	Hanspeter Schiess
P.100	ISO	—	Essays		P.184	(Left + middle) Architect Philip Lutz
P.102	© Ralph Feiner	—	re-Emerging Architecture – Neil Gillespie		P.184	(Right) Frank Broger
P.103	© Ralph Feiner				P.185	Robert Fabach
P.104	© Ralph Feiner	P.147/8	Bluesky-World			
P.105	© Ralph Feiner	P.150	Yukio Futagawa in Global Architecture No 23, Ateler 5. First published in Japan 1973, A.D.A. Edita, Tokyo Co. Ltd.		—	Authenticity Reconsidered: Recent Norwegian Architecture – Morten Sjaastad
P.106	All images © Gramazio & Kohler, ETH Zurich				P.189	(Top) Per Berntsen
P.107	(Left) © Bearth & Deplazes Architekten				P.189	(Bottom) Jeroen Musch
P.107	(Top right) © Ralph Feiner	P.151	Source unknown		P.190	(Left) Courtesy of Ghilardi+Hellsten
P.107	(Bottom right) © Ralph Feiner	—	Highlanders Have Long Travelled – Mary Arnold-Forster		P.190	(Right) Dagfinn Sagen
—	Terrihutte, Graubunden				p.191	(Left) Ivan Brodey
P.108	ISO	P.154	(Left) Richard Johnson		P.191	(Right) Carl Viggo Hølmebakk
P.110	Timon Reichle	P.154	(Right) Andrew Lee		P.192	Sven Erik Svendsen
P.112	(Left) Timon Reichle	P.155	(Top) Timothy Hursley		P.193	(Left) Jensen & Skodvin
P.112	(Right) Jules Geiger, Flims	P.155	(Bottom) Anthony Browell		P.193	(Right) Per Berntsen
P.113	Plaun la Greina, Kaltnadel, Bryan Cyril Thurston From: Greina – Wildes Bergland, 1986, Desertina Verlag Disentis	P.156	(Left) Jamie Steeves		p.194	Morten Sjaastad
		P.156	(Right) Earl Carter		P.195	(Left) Knut Hjeltnes
		P.157	Armando Ferrari		P.195	(Right) Jensen & Skodvin
		—	Designing A future Forest – Bernard Planterose		p 196	(Top left) David Grandorge
P.114	Lucia Degonda				P.196	(Bottom left) Brendeland & Kristoffersen
—	Mountain Chapel, Vorarlberg	P.159	Bernard Planterose			
P.116	ISO	P.162	Bernard Planterose		P.196	(Right) Emil Ashly Studio
P.118	Cukrowicz Nachbaur	P.163	(Left) Patricia MacDonald		—	The Context of Graubunden – Steven Spier
P.120	Ernst Hiesmayr from Eine Moderne Tradition	P.163	(Right) Bernard Planterose			
		—	Narratives of Place in The Scottish Landscape – Johnny Cadell			All images Steven Spier
P.121	(Left) Ernst Hiesmayr from Eine Moderne Tradition					
P.121	(Right) Cukrowicz Nachbaur	P.166	Johnny Cadell			
—	Fruhling – Spring, Vorarlberg	P.167	(Left) David Churchhill			
P.122	ISO	P.167	(Right) Edward Cullinan Architects			
P.124	Bruno Klomfar					
P.126	Bruno Klomfar	P.169	Cadell[2]			
P.128	Bruno Klomfar	P.170	(Left) Cadell[2]			
P.129	(Top + middle) Philipp Salzgeber	P.170	(Top right) Brennan and Wilson Architects			
P.129	(Left) Philipp Salzgeber					
P.129	(Bottom left) Christoph Kalb	P.170	(Bottom right) NORD Architects			
—	Svartlamoen Nursery, Norway	—	Placing the Region: in a New Highlands – Oliver Lowenstein			
P.130	ISO					
P.132/3	Geir Brendeland	P.172	Neil Sutherland Architects			
P.134	Municipality of Trondheim	P.173	(Left) Carpenter Oak & Woodland Co			
P.135	David Grandorge					
—	Juvet Landscape Hotel, Norway	P.173	(Top right) Page \ Park			
P.136	ISO	P.173	(Bottom right) Armando Ferrari			
P.138/9	Jensen & Skodvin	P.174	Northwoods Construction / Locate Architects			
P.140/1	Jensen & Skodvin					
P.142	(Left) Jensen & Skodvin	P.175	Oliver Lowenstein, Fourth Door Research			
P.142	(Top right) Jensen & Skodvin					
P.142	(Bottom right) www.nssdc.gsfc.nasa.gov/imgcat	P.176	Gokay Deveci			

Scottish Projects

Lotte Glob Studio
Gokay Deveci

Telford Drive
Gordon Murray and Alan Dunlop Architects
www.murraydunloparchitects.com

Swinton
Oliver Chapman Architects
www.oliverchapmanarchitects.com

Strathnairn Community Forest Shelter
Neil Sutherland Architects
www.neilsutherlandarchitects.com

The Pier Arts Centre
Reiach & Hall Architects
www.reiachandhall.co.uk

Culloden Battlefield Visitors Centre
Gareth Hoskins Architects
www.garethhoskinsarchitects.co.uk

Taigh Chearsabhagh Arts Studio
Locate Architects
www.locatearchitects.co.uk

Talla Choinneachaidh
Dualchas Building Design
www.dualchas.com

European Projects

Extension Winery Gantenbein, Graubunden
Bearth & Deplaze
www.bearth-deplazes.ch

Terrihutte, Graubunden
Caminada

Mountain Chapel, Vorarlberg
Cukrowicz Nachbaur
www.cn-arch.at

Fruhling – Spring
architekturwerk THE EDGE
www.architekturwerk.at

Svartlamoen Nursery, Norway
Brendeland & Kristoffersen
www.bkark.no

Juvet Landscape Hotel, Norway
Jensen & Skodvin
www.jsa.no

The Lighthouse
10 October 2008 – 11 January 2009

Touring nationally and internationally from January 2009

ACCESS to Architecture
Architecture in Scotland 2006—2008: Building Biographies is part of ACCESS to Architecture, a national campaign informed by key aims and aspirations of the Scottish Government's Policy on Architecture. One of the most focused and far reaching programmes on architecture ever aimed at a public audience, since its launch in 2001 it has brought to fruition a diverse range of initiatives, all of which have been driven by the commitment to increase interest in architecture and to enable wider accessibility to built environment issues in Scotland.

ACCESS to Architecture seeks to promote excellence; to raise aspirations; to make connections and encourage collaboration between the profession and the public at all levels; to challenge ideas and to stimulate debate; to research and develop current and future issues.

The Lighthouse
As Scotland's national centre for architecture, design and the city, The Lighthouse plays a central role in celebrating and debating architecture in Scotland. It is situated in the centre of Glasgow in a building designed by Charles Rennie Mackintosh in 1898, and with a major extension added by Page\Park in 1999. With five floors of exhibition spaces, The Lighthouse displays the work of architects from all over the world. Recent major exhibitions include Gillespie, Kidd & Coia: Architecture 1956–1987 and Marcel Breuer – Design and Architecture, as well as the highly acclaimed Six Cities Design Festival in 2007. Forthcoming projects include Gareth Hoskins, the first in the new The Lighthouse Architecture Series of monographic exhibitions; and a major retrospective of the work of Californian architect John Lautner with Between Earth and Heaven: The Architecture of John Lautner.

All rights reserved
No part of this publication may be reproduced or transmitted in any form or by any means, electronic or mechanical, including photocopying, recording or any other information storage and retrieval system, without prior permission in writing from Morag Bain at The Lighthouse.

Published by
The Lighthouse
56 Mitchell Street
Glasgow G1 3LX

The Lighthouse, Glasgow
ISBN 978-1-9-905061-18-1
Copyright for text – the authors
Copyright for images – the listed bodies and photographers
Copyright for publication – the publishers

Copyright 2008

Part of the ACCESS to Architecture programme supported by the Scottish Government.
www.thelighthouse.co.uk
www.scottisharchitecture.com